UNSANCTIONED VOICE

BOOKS BY GARET GARRETT:

Where the Money Grows, 1911
The Blue Wound, 1921
The Driver, 1922
The Cinder Buggy, 1923
Satan's Bushel, 1924
Ouroboros, Or the Mechanical Extension
    of Mankind, 1926
Harangue, 1927
The American Omen, 1928
Other People's Money, 1931 (pamphlet)
A Bubble That Broke the World, 1932
A Time is Born, 1944
The Wild Wheel, 1952
The People's Pottage, 1953, consisting of:
    "The Revolution Was" (1944)
    "Ex America" (1951)
    "Rise of Empire" (1952)
The American Story, 1955
Salvos Against the New Deal, 2001
Defend America First, 2003
Insatiable Government, 2008

Unsanctioned Voice

GARET GARRETT, JOURNALIST OF THE OLD RIGHT

BY BRUCE RAMSEY

CAXTON PRESS

2008

ISBN 978- 0-87004-465-6

Cover Photo: Garrett's passport photo, 1925. Used by permission
of the Houghton Library, Harvard University, bMS AM 1481 (68).

Library of Congress Cataloging-in-Publication Data

Ramsey, Bruce.
Unsanctioned Voice: Garet Garrett, Journalist of the Old Right /
by Bruce Ramsey.
        p. cm.
    Includes bibliographical references and index.
    ISBN 978-0-87004-465-6 (pbk.)
    1. Garrett, Garet, 1878-1954. 2. Authors, American--20th centu-
ry--Biography. 3. Journalists--United States--Biography. 4.
Conservatism--United States--History--20th century. I. Title.

    PS3513.A717Z87 2008
    818'.5209--dc22
    [B]

                                        2008008539

Contents

Writer's Note

This book was conceived as kind of a biography about an underappreciated journalist and political commentator, and kind-of is what it is. A fully fleshed-out biography needs raw material: diaries, letters, writings, news clips, interviews with the subject and the people who knew him. For Garet Garrett, there is not enough of it. He wrote about other people, but he did not make the task easy for people to write about him.

Carl Ryant, who for many years was professor of history at the University of Kentucky, wrote the only other book on Garrett, *Profit's Prophet (1989)*. It was based on his doctoral dissertation of 1968 and was published by his alma mater. I have relied on some of Ryant's legwork, such as looking up Garrett's name change and divorces. But most of *Profit's Prophet's* 94 pages is an analysis of Garrett's books. I had the books. I also had a heavy box of Garrett's magazine work, one year's worth of his diary, some newspaper clips from when he was shot and a small file of his papers preserved at Harvard University, all of which Ryant had had. I also had 24 letters from Garrett to his political soulmate, Rose Wilder Lane, which Ryant had not had. Much of this material fascinated me. But how do you get a biography, even sort-of-a-biography, out of *one* year's diary? Twenty-four letters?

You look for more. Of the diary and personal papers there wasn't more. Garrett's correspondence with his second wife had been lost in a fire. Still I found a few of his letters to other people—some in the file at Harvard and the rest in other people's papers. Most of the letters were unrevealing, but a handful added to the story.

If those were the nuggets, Garrett's books and magazine journalism made up the mound of ore from which I could leach an occasional anecdote or detail. Garrett never wrote a whole piece about himself, but once in a while would make a reference to his past, such as his comments in the *Saturday Evening Post* that he had learned to drive a team of horses at age 10. Ryant had used the most obvious of these bits in *Profit's Prophet.* Two other stories that bracket the Pullman strike—the setting-off of Coxey's Army in March 1894 and the gold run on the New York Subtreasury office in January 1895—are presented in Garrett's fiction, but they are so colorful and exact, and so unlike the rest of his fiction that I believe they are his own experiences. I include them here, and the reader can make his own judgment about them.

Another source has been Richard Cornuelle, who is the only person I have found, 50 years after Garrett's death, who knew him well. It was Cornuelle who gave me Garrett's diary, which is a cornerstone of some of the earlier chapters here, and also newspaper clips from when Garrett was shot. Through email, Cornuelle supplied most of the colorful description for the final chapters, and comments on my manuscript. In 2007 I flew to New York and spent an afternoon with him. He was then 80 and living with his wife in their brick townhouse in Greenwich Village.

Still not enough facts. After gathering source material over several years and pulling out the things I wanted, I sifted through my mound of ore again. It was surprising how profitable this was. Facts that had lain passive jumped out at me. Sometimes it was because Garrett had told a story more than once, which was a signal not to ignore it. For example, in 1916 his diary relates a conversation with Adolph Ochs after a preparedness march. Garrett retells that story in 1937 in the *Saturday Evening Post.* He tells the story of the gold run of 1895 in his column in the *Annalist* in 1913, in a short story in the *Saturday Evening Post* in 1917 and in *The Driver* in 1922. His 1915 interview with Walter Rathenau, which was off the record for his *New York Times* story, is recounted in the *Post* in 1940 and in *A Time Is Born* in 1944.

In his box of papers at Harvard is Garrett's play, "That

Satan Said." The first time I went through the papers I set it aside. I wasn't interested in a play. Six years later I had it in my hands again, and things jumped out at me—starting with the name Ida, which was the name of Garrett's second wife. There were other fragments of Garrett's experiences and beliefs in that play, and I squeezed a chapter out of it.

Much of Garrett's work at the *New York Times* and, years later, at the *Saturday Evening Post*, was editorials with no byline. At the *Post* he was the principal editorialist, and virtually all the writing was his. But at the *Times* he was one member of a council, and for a while I thought his work would be impossible to identify. But sometimes I could tell. It might be the argument, particularly if Garrett was making the same argument in his diary. It might be the use of a Garrett turn of phrase, such as "ecstasy" to describe an economic condition or "Tower of Babel" to describe an office building. It might be a longer phrase. For example, an editorial from the *Times* of June 16, 1915, begins, "War is an imperious customer in the world's markets. It has not time to bargain shrewdly or be polite." In a signed column in *Everybody's*, October 1914, Garrett had written, "War is a sudden and imperious customer in the world's markets, and will not wait its turn." Another case: in "This Prodigal Country," a July 10, 1915, *Times* editorial, the writer pictures America as a country of spenders that grew rich by using capital saved by others. It is the same point Garrett had made in his signed column in *Everybody's* of December 1913.

Also, I had assumed, having worked on a newspaper for several business editors myself, that as business editor of the *New York Tribune* Garrett had been a manager only. But I ordered a reel of microfilm and found that for four months he had a signed column. These columns became the raw material for another chapter.

Another source was Ryant's endnotes. In the 1960s Ryant had interviewed people who had known Garrett. Forty years had passed; Garrett's generation was gone and Ryant had died, but Ryant had left his interview notes in his papers, and I retrieved them. I cursed the sloppiness of his note-taking—and collected a few more facts that Ryant had collected but not used.

Though Garrett had never written memoirs, others had. I was able to find tidbits about Garrett in the memoirs of Gay Talese, Isaac Don Levine, Emma Goldman, Bernard Baruch and John Chamberlain, and in biographies of Baruch, George Horace Lorimer, Rose Wilder Lane and William Randolph Hearst. From David Nasaw's biography of Hearst I learned about a petition that Garrett had written to the Justice Department in 1918. Using Nasaw's endnote, I ordered a copy of it.

The Internet allowed an easy search of Census records, where I found the names of Garrett's brothers and sisters, and a copy of his draft card. On eBay I found a letter Garrett had written explaining how to pronounce his name. Some of the letters I found simply by googling "Garet Garrett" and "letters" (or "papers"). I had never researched a biography, and was pleased to find that one could email the curator of a dead person's papers and, for a few dollars, receive photocopies. In that way I was able to pull things from the papers of Herbert Hoover, Bernard Baruch, George Horace Lorimer, Lincoln Steffens, Frank Fetter, Walter Lippmann, Henry Regnery and George Creel. In January 2008 I drove through a snowstorm to Washington State University, Pullman, to go through the papers of publisher J. H. Gipson.

I have arranged three collections of Garrett's journalism that the Caxton Press made into books: *Salvos Against the New Deal*, *Defend America First* and *Insatiable Government*, and have written introductions to each of them. I also wrote an introduction to 50th anniversary of *The People's Pottage,* reissued by Caxton as *Ex America*. Some of the material here I had used first in those four introductions. My work with

Caxton also led to other finds: its publisher, Scott Gipson, provided more 50-year-old correspondence with Garrett from the Caxton files. Caxton had made a small royalty payment on *The People's Pottage* to a person named Sue Goulet. Her address was an old one, and it was under a previous surname, but it enabled me to find her. She is the granddaughter of Garrett's third wife, and knew of him through her father, who had lived with Garet and Dorothy as a young man. Sue Goulet was delighted to talk of the family connection.

The finding of a relative, the decoding of Garrett's scribbled handwriting, the recognition of a Garrett turn of phrase in an unsigned editorial—all were a labor of fascination. Tracking Garrett also required that I learn of historical figures I had never heard of: Simon Newcomb, Frank Fetter, Francis Amasa Walker, Virgil Jordan and Leo Frank. It required that I read everything I could find of Garrett's work, and the important things, including all of his books, at least twice.

Occasionally the sources disagreed. Garrett's passport application said his eyes were gray. The editors of the *Saturday Evening Post* wrote of Garrett: "He's a small man with alert blue eyes, an apparently inexhaustible supply of nervous energy and the most completely controlled and incisively logical mind we've ever come across."[1]

At the end, there *was* enough information for a book about Garet Garrett. The careful reviewer will immediately spot the holes in it. There ought to be more about Garrett's family and his first two wives, more about his first jobs in Cleveland and Washington, D.C., more about his early years in New York, and so on. Like the fabled stone soup, a biography is made from the ingredients at hand.

Bruce Ramsey
Seattle

[1] *Saturday Evening Post* (henceforth SEP), "Keeping Posted," December 4, 1937, p. 112. His 1925 passport application and photo are in the Garrett papers, Houghton Library, Harvard.

Garet Garrett, 1951

Chapter One

FROM A CAVE

A supplicant Miss Liberty holding out an empty bowl: that was the image on the cover of *The People's Pottage*, by Garet Garrett. I was 16, and was exploring one of the bookstores of the right-wing and unapproved-of John Birch Society, which listed Garrett's blue paperback as one of their "one dozen candles."[1] Garrett had not been a Bircher, having died in 1954, four years before the Society was founded. In his day he had been a member of the mainstream press.

He had an arresting style. It is what one notices first about him. The first essay in that book was about the New Deal. It began:

> There are those who still think they are holding the pass against a revolution that may be coming up the road. But they are gazing in the wrong direction. The revolution is behind them. It went by in the Night of Depression, singing songs to freedom.

The tone was foreboding. The words went on to describe Roosevelt's program in the sort of language one might use to describe a revolutionary consolidation of power. There were two other essays. The third, dated 1952, had a different strangeness. It declared that in undertaking to oppose the Soviet Union and protect the free world, America had

1

changed from a republic to an empire. To me, a kid in the 1960s, that was a left-wing thought, but this could not be a leftist book. The language was wrong.

Who was Garet Garrett?

In his autobiography, *A Writer's Life*, Gay Talese recalls Garrett striding into his father's tailor shop in Ocean City, N.J.:

> I saw many stylish men in my father's shop, but none possessed the jauntiness of Mr. Garrett, who reminded me of one of those continental boulevardiers often photographed in *Esquire*... Garrett usually arrived at the shop with his fedora rakishly tilted forward over his right eyebrow and sometimes with an ebony walking stick swinging at his side, held lightly in his left hand, which was encircled by a leather loop attached to the stick's silver knob. After he had removed his jacket to try on something that my father was making for him, I could see cufflinks gleaming at the end of his shirtsleeves, and the embroidered leather galluses that extended over his narrow shoulders, and the fact that his trousers had three pleats on each side of the fly front... He personified to me the metropolitan splendor to which I someday hoped to escape.[2]

Garrett, he wrote, "would sit sometimes for hours talking to my father about the state of the world" or reminiscing about his days, decades earlier, on the *New York Times*.[3]

Garrett was a raconteur of many tales. He had been on private retreats with Thomas Edison and Henry Ford. He had been a confidant of Herbert Hoover. He had known the economic czars of the United States *and* Imperial Germany in World War I. He had led two crusades, one against the New Deal and the other against American involvement in World War II. He had lost both of them but had left behind a spoor of distinctively written argument. He had once been prominent in American journalism, though by the time Talese saw him he no longer was.

He had not always written with the emotional juice of the first book I read, but he had always written with clarity. H.L. Mencken, who was a master of style, paid Garrett a compliment in an essay pummeling the professors of economics. Consider the subject of foreign exchange, Mencken wrote. "Do the professors make an autopsy of it? Then read the occasional treatises of some professor of it who is not a professor, say, Garet Garrett..."[4]

In its obituary, the *Times* called its former employee a conservative. The political positions for which Garrett was known—pre-New Deal constitutionalism, an America-first foreign policy, economic laissez faire and a gold-backed dollar—were once the stuff of mainstream conservatism. Today those positions would be called libertarian.

Garrett has been called a paleolibertarian, meaning that he is one of the precursors of today's libertarians. But he did not label himself, and was too pragmatic to please a doctrinaire libertarian of the modern sort. He was not categorically for free trade. He supported the Federal Reserve (though not everything it did) and opposed free banking. In World War I he campaigned to suppress the Hearst newspapers and in World War II he reluctantly supported economic controls and the draft. He once called legalized gambling an example of "the European idea of whimsical personal freedom," which was not the freedom that mattered to him.[5] He liked his ideas American. He did credit European economists—Ludwig von Mises, Friedrich Hayek, and others of the Austrian school—but it annoyed him that Americans had to import foreigners in order to explain America's version of capitalism.[6]

But there was a strain of purity in the ideas Garrett cared about. When the social democrats argued that private enterprise had not housed all the people, Garrett replied that private enterprise was not a being with responsibilities. "It is not the function of free private enterprise to house the people," he wrote. "It is the business of people to house themselves."[7] The ideas he cared about, he cared about a lot. He had begun his most opinionated book, *The People's Pottage*, by announcing that he was writing it "with no sickly pretense of neutralism." The book was written in acid, which is why the people who like it like it.

Garrett's writing is a way of seeing the history of the first half of the 20th century through far different eyes than those of the historians who molded the conventional view. In 1935, when Sinclair Lewis imagined a fascist America in *It Can't Happen Here,* he named Garrett as one of the handful of writers that such a regime would surely throw in prison.

What of the man himself? Was there a story behind the repeated names *Garet Garrett*, and how did he pronounce them? The little blue book said that late in life he had "retired to a cave on a riverbank at Tuckahoe, New Jersey, where he lived very quietly with his wife, making notes and comments on the passing show of monstrous human folly." What did *that* mean?

Years later I undertook to find out.

Chapter 1 notes

[1] The other 11 were John T. Flynn, *While You Slept: Our Tragedy in Asia and Who Made It* (1951); James Burnham, *The Web Of Subversion: Underground Networks in the U. S. Government* (1954); Joseph McCarthy, *America's Retreat From Victory* (1951); J.B. Matthews, *Odyssey Of A Fellow Traveler* (1938); Major-General Charles A. Willoughby, *Shanghai Conspiracy: The Sorge Spy Ring* (1952); George Racey Jordan, *From Major Jordan's Diaries* (1952); Arthur Bliss Lane, *I Saw Poland Betrayed* (1948); Sylvester Petro, *The Kohler Strike: Union Violence and Administrative Law* (1961); Col. Victor J. Fox (LCDR Robert A. Winston), *The Pentagon Case* (1958); Alberto Ostria Gutierrez, *The Tragedy Of Bolivia: A People Crucified* (1958); and Rosalie Gordon, *Nine Men Against America* (1958).

[2] Gay Talese, *A Writer's Life,* Knopf, 2006, p. 49.

[3] Talese, *The Kingdom and the Power,* World, 1969, p. 528.

[4] Mencken, H.L., "The Dismal Science," *Prejudices: Third Series*, Knopf, 1922, p. 279.

[5] SEP, "This is Florida," March 20, 1937.

[6] Richard Cornuelle said (in a letter to the author, February 5, 2006) regarding a political label, "if absolutely forced to choose one, he might have said 'pragmatist.'" The same letter is my source on Garrett and the Austrians. Garrett also did not follow the hard-core libertarian position against government schools. In 1953 he wrote an essay in the same length and form as "The Revolution Was," called "Our Leaning Schoolhouse." This essay (held by Caxton but never published) implicitly accepts state education, and attacks the theory and practice of those running it at the time.

[7] "Status for the Poor," *American Affairs,* April 1947, p. 70.

Chapter Two

A HARD CITY

Garrett was not inclined to talk about his youth[1] and only a handful of records survive. He was born in Pana, in central Illinois, on February 19, 1878.[2] His parents, Charles and Mary, were called Silas and Alice by their friends,[3] setting an example of nomenclative flexibility for the boy they named Edward Peter Garrett.

He was the eldest son, the second child of six. The 1880 census shows Charles, 35, working in a tin shop and Mary, 31, keeping house, with two children: what looks like "Clarra," 3, and Edward, 2. By then they lived at Bunker Hill, in southern Illinois near the Mississippi River.[4] In about 1885 Charles and Mary moved upriver to Burlington, Iowa, where they rented a farm. A third child, Gertrude, had been born in 1882; then came Mary in 1884; and at the farm in Iowa came Sarah in 1886 and Thomas in 1890. All the Garrett children survived childhood, being listed in the Census of 1900.[5]

The life in Iowa was tied to the land. Years later Garrett wrote, "I was... handled a team at ten, wore overalls, as all the men did, made by the women out of a striped cotton material called bed ticking." Except for a steam-engine threshing outfit the farm was run by animal power.[6]

His formal schooling ended at the third grade. After that, he said, he read books; today we would say he was home-schooled, which was common in those days.

Though Garrett later referred to Burlington as his "village," in 1890 it was an established town of 22,565. Its pioneers, many of them Germans, had erected a downtown of vaguely European style, with commercial buildings of local limestone and brick, and streets of cobblestone and brick. Wealthier families built brick homes on the bluffs. A one-track railroad bridge had been put over the Mississippi in 1858, and in 1892, when Garrett was 14, it was replaced with a double-track bridge. The railroad was the Chicago, Burlington & Quincy, which was later absorbed into what is now the Burlington Northern Santa Fe.

Garrett's first job in journalism was as a printer's devil—an assistant who mixed tubs of ink and fetched type—at a Burlington paper with the same name as his future employer, the *Saturday Evening Post*.[7] The *Post* of Burlington was a thin, struggling, part-literary publication that reflected the values of its owner and of its day. That included a strong strain of self-reliant individualism. Shortly after Garrett's sixteenth birthday the paper ran a column that might have spoken directly to him:

> My dear boy, you who are first beginning the battle of life by learning some trade, the world wants you and is ready to pay you for your work. It will pay you promptly and well if you are of service to it or it will pay you poorly and slowly if your work is deficient. We are fond of laying all our misfortunes and poverty on the "cold world," because we know the world will never deny it, and it is so much more comfortable to lay all blame upon someone else rather than bear it ourselves. But I tell you, my dear boy, the world wants you and will pay you liberally if you are of the right stuff.[8]

Garrett believed it, and for him it was true.

His future was not in Iowa. Two hundred miles to the northeast was the first real city he knew, Chicago. Its population had doubled in a decade, and in 1890 it had 1.1 million people, many of them fresh from Europe. It was the nation's center of railroading, grain moving and meatpacking. It was a gas-lit city, smoky from the burning of coal, noisy from metal wheels on cobblestones and stinky from the filth. It was the home of the steel-frame skyscraper, and in 1890 had the tallest building in the world—the 21-story Masonic Fraternity Temple—under construction. In 1893 it proudly put on the World Columbian Exposition, which included the world's first Ferris wheel and a brilliant display of the new incandescent lights. The world's fair was a coming-out party for Chicago, a city of new and gaudy wealth. Years later, Garrett wrote of the Chicago of the early Nineties:

> The people's Sunday recreation was to line the Michigan Boulevard and watch the parade of fine carriages. Proud horses in silver-mounted harness, liveried servants outriding, the owners of this magnificently inefficient transportation all with one air pretending to be a little bit bored, whereas they were delighted with the "Ah's" and the "Oh's" that swirled behind them, and returned to their lakeside mansions with their egos uplifted.[9]

The period of optimism and easy profit ended in May 1893 with a banking panic. In the next few years, America suffered the worst depression of the 19th century. "It was terrible," Garrett wrote. "Men in rags, in tied-on shoes, shivering with cold."[10] Parts of the Midwest seethed with populist resentment of the rich. "There were cities and neighborhoods where a fine carriage had to pick its street not to raise a mob," he wrote. "You had then millions of people who never expected to own carriages of their own. They couldn't imagine it."[11]

Garrett left home at the beginning of this period, or during it. Burlington was an "unprogressive place," he thought, and he wanted out. He had had a job sweeping out a little bank, and borrowed some money from "the oracle who conducted the cigar counter across the street." Years later he felt a pang of guilt when he was not sure whether he had paid the man back. [12]

He hopped a freight train for Chicago. He recalled

>...the grand, four-story gas-lighted hotel with half a block of guest chairs and spittoons on the sidewalk in front, and every little while the excitement of a bus careening up the hill from the union depot, the steel shoes of the horses cutting sparks out of the cobblestone pavement. You could not sit in one of those chairs. If you did, a man immediately came to look you over. If you were fairly well dressed, he would ask, "Are you registered?" If you were not so well dressed, all he said was, "Wiggle!"
>
>It was a hard, unfriendly city. If you were hungry, you would let it go for a long time without asking for anything, for if you asked, you were a bum.

Garrett was hungry in Chicago, and did find a way to eat—a way that raised a smile decades later, when he thought about it. He did not report what it was, though he did say he lost his shirt in Chicago because he had washed it in the river and hung it on a bush to dry, and the wind blew it into the river while he was daydreaming. That night he had to go into the rail yard and stalk the outgoing freight with no shirt.[13]

The railroad took him east. In Cleveland, a city one-quarter the population of Chicago, he landed a job at the *Cleveland Recorder,* a strident reform paper. The *Recorder* was bankrolled by former streetcar capitalist Tom Johnson, a man who had been bitten by the Single Tax theory of Henry

George and had gotten himself elected to Congress as a Democrat. The *Recorder* began publication September 9, 1895, and began to fade after 1897, but Garrett did not stay long. He appears in the Cleveland city directory for 1896, the year he was 18, as E.P. Garrett, living at 21 Oakdale Street. By then he was a reporter for the *Cleveland Press*, a much more solid paper.

There is a hint, however, that he was already working as a reporter, or hobnobbing with reporters, at age 16. It is not conclusive, but it is suggestive, and I think it is probably true.

Chapter 2 notes

1 So said Richard Cornuelle, who knew him in his last years, and A.A. Desser, who was interviewed by Carl Ryant on March 13, 1969. The notes of the Desser interview are in the Ryant Papers, University of Louisville.

2 His birthday is shown on his World War I draft registration card, available on Ancestry.com.

3 Carl Ryant, *Profit's Prophet,* Susquehanna University Press, 1989, p. 17. Ryant wrote about Garrett for his PhD dissertation at the University of Wisconsin in 1968.

4 1880 Census, taken June 2, 1880.

5 1900 Census, listing Silas (not Charles), 55, Mary, 51, Gertrude, 17, Mary 15, Sarah, 13, and Thomas, 9, living at Jackson Township, Lee County, Iowa. Silas had died by the 1910 census, which finds the family in Chicago, with Mary calling herself Alice (same age, same state of birth, father's same state of birth), with Gertrude, 27; Marie 25; and Tom, 20. Gertrude and Mary were stenographers and Tom was listed as a clerk, with Alice not working. The 1910 census said she had had six children and all six were still living. In the 1920 and 1930 censuses, Alice was living alone—in Minneapolis and Chicago, respectively. Alice, identified as Garet Garrett's mother and a great-grandmother, made the news in 1929 by graduating from a Chicago grammar school at the age of 81, and announcing her intention to attend high school. She told the reporter she wanted to "brush up on her education" to do some writing. *Havre Daily News*, Havre, Mont., March 20, 1929.

6 SEP, "The Political Curse on the Farm Problem," August 22, 1936.

7 Obituary, Burlington *Hawk Eye Gazette*, November 7, 1954. The *Post* published from 1882 to 1933—at least, those are the years for which the local library has microfilm.

8 Alfred L. Flude, "Notes of an Idler," *Saturday Evening Post,* Burlington, Iowa, March 24, 1894.

9 SEP, "Since the Tower of Babel," October 14, 1933.

10 SEP, "Looking in the Ditch," March 14, 1931.

11 SEP, "Notes of These Times," October 8, 1932.

12 "The 'Money Trust' Again," *New York Evening Post*, April 6, 1912, Financial Section, p. 3. The column is unsigned, he refers to himself as "you" rather than "I," and refers to the town as "Rising Sun"—but the scheme is in Iowa.

13 SEP, "The Youth Document," November 7, 1936.

Chapter Three
THAT UNGUENT KIND OF MUD

In Garrett's novel *The Driver* (1922), his narrator says that on March 25, 1894, "I was one of the forty-three correspondents" at Massillon, Ohio, 50 miles south of Cleveland, covering the send-off of Coxey's Army. This "army" was a march on Washington, D.C., of radicals, hoboes and the genuinely unemployed—a "petition in boots." Its leader, Jacob Coxey, was a sand-and-gravel merchant who had had a vision that the government could restore prosperity by selling zero-interest bonds and spending the money to build roads. Coxey's crusade was the media event of the Nineties.

Garrett's novel described Coxey's men setting out on a cold Easter Sunday:

> The road was ankle deep in that unguent kind of mud which lies on top of frost. Snow began to fall. The followers began to slough off, shouting words of encouragement as they turned back... The marchers were extremely miserable. None of them was properly shod or dressed for it. They were untrained, unused to distance walking, and after a few miles a number of them began to limp in wet, blistered feet. The band played a great deal and the men sang, sometimes all together, sometimes in separate groups. The going

was such that no sort of marching order could be maintained.[1]

The Driver is not *about* Coxey's Army, and there is no need in the plot for this sort of description of it. The book is about a Wall Street speculator who takes over a railroad. Except for the narrator, none of the characters interacts with Coxey's Army, and the narrator doesn't *do* anything at Massillon except file a report and leave—which is what a newspaper reporter would have done. But the description of Coxey's Army serves a function: it is at the beginning of the story, and hooks the reader because it is vivid. It is more vivid than any of the parts about taking over a railroad because it describes a real event. Consider this further excerpt. After the second day of trudging along with the Coxeyites, the reporters reach a town with a telegraph office:

> News is stranger than fiction not in what it tells but how it happens. In a room twenty feet square, lighted by one kerosene lamp, we wrote our copy on our knees, against the wall, on each other's backs, standing up and lying down, matching notes and exchanging information as we went along.
> "What's the name of this town?"
> "Louisville."
> "Kentucky?'
> "Kentucky, no. Hear him!—Ohio."
> "Didn't know there was a Louisville, Ohio."
> "Write it anyway. It isn't the first time you've written what you don't know."
> Then silence, save for the clicking of the telegraph instruments and the cracking of copy paper.
> "Who was the man in the red saddle?"
> No answer.
> Again: "Who was the guy in the red saddle?"

No answer.

Another voice, in the same difficulty, roaring: "Who in hell was the man in the red saddle?"

Now everybody for a minute stops writing. Nobody knows.

Voice: "Call him Smith: the man of mystery, the great unknown."

We did.[2]

Other sources say the Chicago reporters knew who Smith was. But according to the *Baltimore American* reporter's postmarch account, "they humored Smith and called him 'unknown' for the reason solely that it excited interest..." The reporters' articles also ridiculed the marchers. The *Cleveland Press* called the marchers "cranks, leg pullers and tramps," and the *New York Herald* called them "a horde of black and white men, all filthy, famished and ready for any desperate enterprise by which food and shelter might be gained."[3] Writing a quarter-century later, Garrett did not describe the marchers that way in *The Driver.*

The hard core of 11 correspondents who stuck with Coxey's Army for a long time—the United Press man and correspondents for the several New York, Chicago, Pittsburgh and Cincinnati papers—are known by name. The Coxey people, resenting the biased coverage, had called the mainstream media men "argus-eyed demons of hell," a label the reporters enthusiastically applied to themselves. But the names of the rest of the 40-something correspondents (the number varies by account) are not recorded, so it cannot be verified that Garrett was there.

Seeing off Coxey's Army—a crusade for causes Garrett would later oppose—would have been a glorious start for a career in journalism. But if Garrett had been at Massillon at the end of winter, when there was snow on the ground, it suggests that he had left home, and lost his shirt, the previous summer or early fall, when he was 15.

That seems improbable today, but boys left home early in those days.

Garrett did say he was at another event of upheaval in 1894: the strike against the Pullman Palace Car Company of Chicago, which manufactured and leased railroad sleeper cars. Founder George Pullman had been famous for his near-by company town, which provided worker housing, a good school and a free library. But workers went into debt to pay for these things, and in the depression of the 1890s, the company cut wages 28 percent without reducing what workers owed. On May 11, 1894, Pullman's workers went out on a wildcat strike.

On June 26 the strike against Pullman was joined by Eugene Debs' American Railway Union. Within a few days, workers for 29 different roads joined in a boycott by refusing to switch Pullman cars onto trains. The railroads obtained an injunction forbidding Debs and the other strike leaders from supporting the boycott, and they ignored it. On July 4, strikers began tipping over railroad cars in Chicago and on July 6, the peak of the mayhem, strikers wrecked some 700 railcars. President Grover Cleveland ordered in 2,000 federal troops, on the premise that the strike was interfering with the U.S. Mail. The strike was crushed at the cost of 13 dead and 57 wounded strikers. Debs was sent to prison, where he read the works of Karl Marx and became a socialist.

Of all this, Garrett wrote:

Many years ago, during the American Railway Union strike led by Eugene V. Debs, the Chicago switchmen, who were the tough babies, had an artless way of sampling public sentiment. Can you visualize the nut of the bolt that fastens rail ends together? It has eight sharp corners, and one of the old-fashioned kind weighed nearly a pound. The switchmen tied the nut to a leather thong and tied the other end of the thong around the wrist, and then, holding the nut in the hand, ready to throw it, they went up and down Wabash Avenue, saying, "Wid us 'r again us? Say what."

My sympathies at the time were undeveloped. It was a grand shandy all the same, and with a young-ster's love of trouble, I had stood on the Fourteenth Street viaduct cheering the strikers as they overturned box cars with their shoulders. Ten or twelve shoulders could do it, by rocking the car a few times and giving one big heave. Yet toward those switchmen with the captive nuts in their hands I was resentful without knowing exactly why. Long afterward I could formu-late it. What I resented, firstly, was the affront to my common sense of such an oversimplification of the matter. Secondly, it was the difficulty of maintaining a neutral position, in case I wanted to be neutral.[4]

Years later he wrote in a letter, without further explanation, "Have you ever been part of a mob—something like a lynch-ing mob? I have. It is terrible."[5]

Garrett did not write that he had been sent to cover the strike as a newspaper reporter, and perhaps, at 16, he was in Chicago on some other errand. But being a reporter would have given him a reason to be there.

There is one more unusually colorful description from *The Driver*, and I include it as well. It is notable also because Garrett referred to the same event in an editor's column in 1913 and used it again as the backdrop for a short story in 1917. It is the silver holders' run on gold at the New York Subtreasury office in January 1895, at the crescendo of the 1890s depression:

People were frantic to exchange white money for gold. They waited in a writhing line which kept its insatiable head inside the doors of the Subtreasury. Its body flowed down the long steps, lay along the north side of Wall Street and terminated in a wriggling tail around the corner in William Street, five minutes' walk away. It moved steadily forward by successive movements of contraction and elongation. Each day at three o'clock the Subtreasury, slamming its doors, cut off the monster's head. Each morning at ten o'clock there was a new and hungrier head waiting to push its way in the instant the doors opened. Its food was gold and nothing else, for it lived there night and day. The particles might change; its total character was always the same. Greed and fear were the integrating principles. Human beings were the helpless cells. It grew. Steadily it ate its way deeper into the nation's gold reserve, and there was no controlling it... The paying tellers worked very slowly to gain time.

The street was congested with spectators, because the officers of the Subtreasury had just telegraphed to Washington saying they could hold out only a few hours more... Never had the line been so excited, so terribly ophidian in its aspect. Its writhings were sickening. The police handled it as the zoo keepers handle a great serpent. That is, they kept it straight. If once it should begin to coil the panic would be uncontrollable.

Particles detached themselves from the tail and ran up and down the body trying to buy places nearer the head. Those nearest the head hotly disputed the right of substitution. In the tense babel of voices there came sudden fissures of stillness, so that one heard

one's own breathing or the far-off sounds of river traffic. At those moments what was passing before the
eyes had the fantastic reality of a dream. [6]

Was Garrett there? I think he was. The rest of *The Driver*
is clearly imaginary. This scene, and the ones from Coxey's
Army, are real.

Chapter 3 notes

1 *The Driver*, E.P. Dutton, 1922, p. 6.
2 *The Driver,* p. 9.
3 *The Cleveland Press*, March 27, 1894. *Baltimore American*, "Marching
With Coxey," undated. *New York Herald*, datelined Canton, Ohio, March 25,
1894. The last two are in Wilbur Miller's Coxey's Army Scrapbook, 1894-
1931, Ohio Historical Society. Garrett's hometown paper, the *Burlington
Hawk Eye*, covered the first few days of Coxey's Army in articles with no
byline: "Fun With Col. Coxey," March 24, 1894; "Crank Coxey's Craze,"
March 25 and 27; "Goes Marching On," March 28. In "Coxey's Big Fizzle,"
March 29, 1894, the *Burlington Weekly Gazette* wrote, "There is no question that every one of the foot soldiers were tramps. They were ragged,
filthy, and possessed that unmistakable stamp which characterizes the professional pilgrim." The editor of Burlington's *Saturday Evening Post*
declared, "Coxey's army of vags will never reach Washington." March 24,
1894.
4 SEP, "The Labor Weapon," July 17, 1937.
5 Letter to Rose Wilder Lane, about June 1953. Rose Wilder Lane Papers,
Herbert Hoover Presidential Library, West Branch, Iowa. Garrett may also
have been speaking of Cleveland's May Day Riot of 1894.
6 *The Driver*, pp. 86-95. Garrett used the Subtreasury run as a backdrop for
his first *Saturday Evening Post* story, "The Gold Token," January 6, 1917,
and he wrote about it in his editor's column in *The New York Times
Annalist,* April 7, 1913, p. 355.

Chapter Four
A COURT OF TWENTY KINGS

Garrett did not stay long at the *Cleveland Press*. By 1898, at age 20, he had moved to Washington, D.C., where he became a night editor for the old *Washington Times* during the William McKinley administration. It was in Washington that he changed his first name to Garet,[1] which later he said was a youthful pen name he had waited too long to abandon.[2] When asked by a magazine editor how he pronounced his name, he replied, "I pronounce it as garrett, for the room on the top floor, and both the same."[3]

On January 17, 1900, he married Bessie Hamilton. Five months later he had moved to New York, taking rooms with another reporter. [4] Perhaps Bessie followed later, though he divorced her in 1905.

In 1900 Garrett began more than a decade as a reporter on Wall Street. It was a boom time. In Garrett's first year, financier J.P. Morgan was putting together the U.S. Steel Corporation, the world's first company started with a billion dollars of stock. In his novel *The Cinder Buggy* (1923), Garrett describes the lead-up to it, when the independent steel men posed for the financial press. It was, he wrote, "a court of twenty kings, with its rabble and fringe and jesters" in which "no financial editor was safe to go to bed until the Waldorf grill room lights were out."[5] Several years later he wrote in a newspaper column of an entrepreneur of steel wire who, "in an uptown hotel… paused in a game of billiards to announce that he knew of a billion-dollar steel company that was going to be formed. That was the first public reference anybody had made to the United States Steel Corporation, which was brought out in March 1901."[6] Like the description in *The Driver,* these are the memories of someone who was there, though financial reporters didn't have bylines then, and from 1900 to 1902 it is not recorded where Garrett worked.

Who's Who in America records that in 1903 Garrett was a financial reporter for the *New York Sun*, moving on to the *New York Times* in 1906, the *Wall Street Journal* in 1907 and the *New York Evening Post* in 1909. In 1908 he married Ida Irvin, a newspaperwoman three years his senior.

At the *Evening Post* he had a Saturday column, which ran without a byline, but which was clearly his. He used several forms, including a dialog between a bull and a bear, a diary, or day in the life of a Wall Street person, or a mini-essay on a Wall Street type. Some of them were "fly on the wall" pieces, such as a dialog between a bank president and his speechwriter, in which the dialogue was obviously invented. In one case he had a secondhand office desk tell the story of its "life."

And he wrote about himself, at least indirectly. One of his mini-essays was "The Financial Reporter." He wrote:

> The financial news reporter is the only pure agnostic on Wall Street. Everybody else believes more or less; he believes nothing until it happens. His experience is that only about 1 per cent of the things expected ever happen…
>
> The financial reporter's former associates gradually come to think of him as being corrupt and rich. How could a man help getting rich, knowing so many great men who put prices up and down? But a financial news reporter was never known to get rich. He disbelieves too much.[7]

In another column, he tells the story of one of the great market bulls calling a press conference. The man is known to use the press, and the financial reporters are wary. It is winter, and they had been crowding around a fireplace to keep warm, but they all troop to the big man's office, curious as to what's up. The bull announces that he is forming a thing called the Commodity and Securities Valorization Syndicate. This new thing will determine what is a fair price for commodities, and it will have such financial muscle behind its encyclicals that the world will accept them. Prices are, after all, "simply a state of mind," the bull says. His organization will set the state of mind first with commodities and, once having done that, will stabilize the price of securities on Wall Street.

The reporters squint at him. "You'll need all the money in the world," says "the facetious reporter" (which may well have been Garrett.). The great bull says the bankers have pledged $250 million. "What does the syndicate get out of it?" asks "the cynical reporter" (which also may have been Garrett.) The great bull looks hurt, and says the bankers will get nothing for their investment. The work, he says, "will be purely philanthropic."

Not one of the reporters believes it, and the article concludes, "The Commodity and Securities Valorization Syndicate died for want of publicity."[8]

The Wall Street reporter, Garrett wrote, was considered by his uptown city editor as irretrievably spoiled, a practitioner of such bad habits as the anonymous interview. Almost all the interviews in Garrett's columns were anonymous, and some looked to be made up—more literary than journalistic. Others were pure description, such as his picture of the "hoodoo," a man of "departed prosperity:"

> Nearly everybody knows him. He was once a member of the New York Stock Exchange, or the son

of one, or what's-his-name that was Gould's broker twenty years ago. He is most knowing of speech and would easily fool you if you were not warned. All the past he understands, and the why of everything, but for the present and the future he is a source of fatal ideas and a borrower of money...

The Hoodoo is often a man whom everybody likes, speaks well of, and recommends to every one else, with the one reservation—he is a man who unaccountably has not succeeded.[9]

"Unaccountably," "no accounting for" and their variants were favorite words with Garrett. That a thing was not accounted for did not mean there was no reason for it. It might mean the standard explanations did not cover it, or that there was no reason anyone cared to identify. Garrett believed in both intelligence and luck, but intelligence tends to run true and luck, lacking intelligence, tends to run out. In his bylined journalism he wrote overwhelmingly of intelligence, but in his *Evening Post* columns he wrote also of intuition and luck, and his short stories are mostly of luck.[10]

In 1911, Garrett collected "The Hoodoo" and ten of his more literary columns in his first book, *Where the Money Grows*. It could have been twice the size: his *Evening Post* columns had plenty of material he didn't use. It is saucily descriptive, with no political moral.

In his years covering Wall Street, Garrett also made a friend of speculator Bernard Baruch. He described Baruch as "the leader of the radical element on the Stock Exchange," meaning that Baruch favored more rules to protect small players. Baruch later described Garrett as a "small, round, intense dynamo of a man." Garrett was also, Baruch wrote, "one of the few men to whom I could unburden myself. Once, after hearing me express my restlessness with Wall Street, he remarked: 'I keep telling you, B.M., you don't belong in Wall Street; you should be in Washington.' "[11]

Baruch, who was originally from South Carolina, did go to Washington. In 1912 he donated handsomely to the Democratic Party nominee and his fellow Southerner, Woodrow Wilson. During World War I President Wilson appointed Baruch to head the War Industries Board. At his initial appointment, Baruch was accused of using political leaks to profit in the market. Garrett advised him on his statement to Congress, at which he famously identified himself: "I am a speculator."[12]

Baruch professed to be a Cleveland Democrat of the small-government variety, but World War I introduced him to "a revolution in national thinking"—one that, he recalled years later, "envisioned every factory and all raw materials, every business leader and every worker as part of one gigantic industrial army." [13] In 1932 Baruch became an adviser to the next Democratic president, Franklin Roosevelt. Garrett came to care more about political ideas than Baruch did—and to loathe Roosevelt—but he always respected Baruch's practical intelligence. Garrett and Baruch sent brief but warm notes to each other for more than 40 years.

Chapter 4 notes

1 *Profit's Prophet,* p. 18.

2 Cornuelle, Introduction to Garet Garrett's Journal (henceforth GG journal), unpublished manuscript.

3 Reply to Charles E. Funk, editor of *The Literary Digest,* typed at the bottom of Funk's letter of October 12, 1936, which I have in my possession. For years I thought "Garet Garrett" was pronounced GAR-et GARE-et, and I have heard it pronounced GARE-et ga-RETTE.

4 Census of 1900, Roll T623, 1096, P10B, June 7. The Census gets his age wrong, claiming that he was 26 and was born February 1874. The census of 1910 shows Garrett living with Ida in Warren, N.J. Census of 1910, Sheet 4A, enumeration district 125.

5 *The Cinder Buggy*, E.P. Dutton, 1923, p. 340. Garrett also described this scene in the introductory paragraph of "A Tin-Plated Millionaire," *Everybody's*, January 1915. He discussed the floating of the U.S. Steel shares in his short story, "A Luck Leper's Tale," SEP, March 26, 1921.

6 "Mr. Gates," *The New York Evening Post*, August 12, 1911.

7 "The Financial Reporter," *New York Evening Post*, February 25, 1911.

8 "A Great Thought," *New York Evening Post,* November 25, 1911.

9 "The Hoodoo," *New York Evening Post*, October 8, 1910. It is also a chapter in *Where the Money Grows*, Harper & Bros., 1911.

10 One is "A Luck Leper's Tale," about a hoodoo telling a story to his fellow hoodoos. The story is this: a speculator takes a big short position in a stock, which requires him to watch the ticker tape all the following day. He has forgotten that he has promised to spend that day with his mother. He honors his promise. He tells his associates that during that day if his stock begins to rise to sell, but that if it falls, to let it run—and *not*, under any circumstances, to call him at his mother's. The day comes. The stock plummets; his profit, if he takes it, is large. His associates know he would take the profit immediately if he were there. They twist in agony as the profit swells, knowing that it could evaporate at any minute. They are frozen in indecision all day as their friend, in his intentional ignorance, becomes rich. SEP, "A Luck Leper's Tale," March 26, 1921.

11 Bernard Baruch, *The Public Years*, Holt, 1960, p. 2, also Baruch, *Baruch: My Own Story*, Henry Holt, 1957, p. 308; "A Revolution in the Stock Exchange," *The New York Times Annalist,* January 20, 1913, p. 5.

12 Margaret Holt, *Mr. Baruch: The Man, the Myth, the Eighty Years*, Houghton Mifflin, 1957.

13 James Grant, *Bernard M. Baruch: The Adventures of a Wall Street Legend,* John Wiley & Sons, 1997, pp. 102, 142-152, 241; Baruch, *Baruch: My Own Story*, p. 309.

Chapter Five
THERE MUST BE A MORAL

A leftist critic wrote after World War I that Garrett "used to be quite a liberal."[1] He was never any sort of leftist, but to some extent his liberalism is verified in his two earliest bylined pieces, published in 1909 in the middle-class monthly *Everybody's*. He wrote these under the pseudonym John Parr—stocks had *par* value—presumably because he didn't want his freelance commentary to interfere with his newspaper work.

The first was about market manipulation on Wall Street. Garrett acknowledged the value of Wall Street in raising capital for railroads and other great works. Then he wrote, "There is nothing more sordid in Wall Street than the use that is made in the stock market by insiders (directors, bankers and their like) of information accessible only to themselves."

This is the fiduciary problem. Directors are supposed to be working for public shareholders, but they can also buy and sell for themselves. Garrett recognized the problem but resisted jumping to an easy conclusion about it. Instead he included in the story a dialog with his editor:

> "In this article," said *Everybody's* editor, "you have told us in some particulars how the thing is done, but you point us no moral."
> "Is there a moral?" I asked.

"There must be."[2]

Having professed ignorance of any moral, Garrett went to a speculator worth $30 million in gold dollars, and asked him what the moral was. The speculator professed not to understand the question, so Garrett asked it again. The speculator reminded Garrett that insider trading sometimes resulted in a loss. If it was so immoral when he made a profit, the speculator asked, was it moral when he took a loss?

A trick answer. The speculator was rich, because most times he made a profit. Inside information had given him an advantage.

Well, the speculator said, that was the way the market was. He hadn't made it that way. He took it as he found it. If anyone would judge him morally, he said, he would prefer to be judged "by the railroads I have built." This was the best answer there was, though not altogether satisfying.

The second piece from 1909 argued that small margin traders were bound to lose, their nest eggs sucked out by interest and brokerage fees. In it Garrett drew a distinction between speculators and gamblers. He portrayed a speculator, "Blank," who was a chief accountant at a railroad. Blank had inherited some money. He hired an engineer and a retired traffic manager to investigate a different railroad. Blank calculated that the target railroad was selling below market value. He leveraged his inherited money and invested in the stock. He made a big profit—but, wrote Garrett, "Think of Blank's special equipment for the game and the trouble he took to be right."

Garrett's message was that it took intelligence and work to consistently make money in the market, and that professional speculators could not expect to make more than about 25 percent on their capital. Small plungers who played on margin *always* lost. He ended his article by advising the reader, "Put your money into your own business."[3]

Garrett believed that much of the reason for investors' losses was their own impatience and delusion, which no law could remedy. But concerning insider information there was an idea. Two years before, Congress had passed the Pure Food and Drug Act. In the market for packaged food and drugs, in which the buyer did not know the seller, the buyer might be helped by compelling the seller to print the ingredients on the label. This is the same principle under which the Securities and Exchange Commission would require, decades later, that companies going public issue a disclosure statement and that public companies disclose buying and selling by officers and directors. For all his attacks on the New Deal, Garrett never attacked the SEC or the principle of mandatory disclosure.[4]

His 1909 articles were written at the height of the muck-raking vogue. Even then, Garrett resisted wholesale damnation of speculators. Some took advantage, and that was bad, but they were also smart, and he admired that.

For *Collier's* he wrote a piece under his own name about Simon Guggenheim, who controlled the American Smelting and Refining Company (ASARCO). Guggenheim had invested in a copper mine in Chile. Because Chile's currency was not redeemable in gold, Guggenheim was able to pay his workers in cheap money while his mine sold copper on the world market for gold money. ASARCO's Chilean subsidiary was allied politically with Chilean landowners who exported farm products. Each wanted Chile to keep its currency soft.

That meant that in Chile, finance was getting the better of labor. "The reason finance can exact always the larger division is that it is heartlessly intelligent," Garrett wrote. "The Chilean laborer is proud and independent, but too unintelligent to know what is happening to him."[5] Garrett thought the worker deserved a raise, but he was not one to suggest overthrowing capitalism to get it. The Chilean people should press for hard money.

The financial system allowed big people to do big things, but not just anything. In a piece in May 1910, eight months after the death of railroad magnate E.H. Harriman, the *Evening Post* ran a piece called "Conjectural History," which was probably by Garrett. It said that in addition to controlling the Union Pacific, and trying to control the Northern Pacific, which would have made Harriman the "dictator" of one-third the railroad mileage of the United States, at the end of his life he had bought a controlling interest in The Equitable Life. With that, he could have financed quite a dream. But the article doubts whether this would have allowed Harriman to hold and keep such an empire. "Financial history has no difficulty in proving by precedent what happens to over-ambitious financiers who buy up banks to provide the necessary funds for schemes which meet a cold reception elsewhere in the credit market," the article concludes. The result would have been "a general wreck."[6]

Garrett's next move was to be editor-in-chief of the *New York Times Annalist,* a new 32-page weekly tabloid subtitled, "A Magazine of Finance, Commerce and Economics." Priced at 10 cents, it went on newsstands with the issue of January 20, 1913, and would last until 1940. Under Garrett, the *Annalist* published the first weekly stock index numbers. It also had regular sections on railroads, mining, utilities, crops, labor, foreign news, stocks and bonds. Subjects for articles included the question of whether gold was becoming too plentiful to use as money, the Equitable's invention of group life insurance as an employee benefit, the State of Washington's operation of the nation's first workmen's compensation system, and the question of whether antitrust laws should apply to unions.[7]

Nowhere did the publication carry Garrett's name, but the 33-year-old had an editor's column and could expound on what he liked. He was not a muckraker, but there was a streak of reformism in his concerns. In one issue he touched the disclosure issue again, arguing that the New York Stock Exchange ought to require listed industrial companies to publish "such statements of income, assets and liabilities as would be open to analysis" instead of merely a statement of profit in which "only the management knows in what manner [it] has been arrived at."[8]

The *Annalist* debuted in the year when the Constitution was amended to allow a federal income tax. It was also the year Congress passed the Federal Reserve Act. Garrett commented on both.

Years later his verdict on the income tax was that it had allowed government to grow into a giant. In 1913 his concern was narrower. It was that the tax was going to be limited to the top 2.5 percent of income earners, so that the average American had no interest in keeping the rate down. "The ethical value of direct taxation is lost when a very great majority are exempt," he wrote. He also objected to the 10 percent top rate proposed by progressive Sen. Robert LaFollette. It was too high, and punished success. [9] President Woodrow Wilson signed into law a top rate of 7 percent.

Garrett's concern with the proposed Federal Reserve was that it would be made a vehicle for more inflation. But as Congress amended the bill, he began to relax. The new Federal Reserve Notes would be backed 40 percent by gold and would be redeemable—a remarkable promise for a government controlled by the Democratic Party, whose previous nominee had been the inflationist William Jennings Bryan. Wrote Garrett, "It is comforting to reflect that sanity has ultimately prevailed in this country, even economic sanity. On big questions, the people have always voted straight."[10]

In his column Garrett commented on other things. One week it was on the publication of shocking photos of the poor—a thing, Garrett thought, that was shocking only because "never were average people so prosperous as now." Another time it was an elevator operator he had overheard saying he didn't mind wasting the company's time. That annoyed Garrett: if everyone thought and acted that way, the whole country would be poor. Another comment was on the failure of a Pittsburgh bank that had been run by builders. "The builder is always an optimist," he wrote. "He can seldom be trusted as a banker—not that he is deficient in morality, but because his mind is uncritical and oversanguine."[11]

Chapter 5 notes

1 Benjamin Stolberg, "Merchant in Letters: Portrait of George Horace Lorimer," *Outlook and Independent*, May 21, 1930, p. 86.

2 "The Stock Yards of New York," *Everybody's*, March 1909, p. 304.

3 "The Game Gets You," *Everybody's*, April 1910, pp. 499-505.

4 In the July 1948 *American Affairs*, p. 133, he made the parallel between the Pure Food Law and the SEC's "pure securities law"—not to denounce the securities law, but to criticize the International Bank for Reconstruction and Development for requesting an exemption from it.

5 "Guggenheim Finance," *Collier's*, January 6, 1912.

6 *New York Evening Post*, "Conjectural History," May 7, 1910, financial section, p. 1.

7 *The New York Times Annalist*, "What If There Should Be a Gold Deluge?" January 27, 1913, p. 37; "The Washington Experiment," February 3, 1913, p. 90; "May Organized Labor Restrain Trade?" April 28, 1913, pp. 453-454. Weekly index number: Garrett to Lewis H. Brown, undated, about 1942, Garrett papers, Houghton Library, Harvard.

8 *The New York Times Annalist,* June 9, 1913, p. 643.

9 *The New York Times Annalist,* May 13, 1913, p. 547, and September 1, 1913, p. 259. Three years later in the *New York Tribune*, August 15, 1916, p. 10, he argued that the value of the income tax was that it made the people conscious of how much government cost, and that that consciousness should not be "limited to 2 percent of the people."

10 *The New York Times Annalist*, July 7, 1913, p. 3, and September 1, 1913, p. 259. See also September 8, 1913, p. 291; October 20, 1913, p. 387; and December 23, 1913, "Alarm Over Owen Bill." Two years later he was protesting against inflation again, as gold flowed in from wartime Europe. "Each dollar of incoming gold represents a potentiality of between five and six dollars of credit expansion, and there is now more credit in bank reservoirs than can legitimately be employed." ("The Ecstasy of Borrowing," *New York Times* unsigned editorial, September 1, 1915. "Ecstasy," when used to describe a financial peak, is a favorite Garrett word.)

11 *The New York Times Annalist*, May 12, 1913, p. 515; July 7, 1913, p. 3; July 14, 1913, p. 35. Garrett penned a colorful portrayal of the builder as congenital optimist in his short story, "The House a Wop Built," *McClure's,* June 1922.

Chapter Six
YOUR THEORY, WHAT IS IT?

By the second decade of the century, Garrett had become a skilled journalist. His stories were clear and written with flair. Consider his description of Henry Ford, who in 1914 had just raised his workers' pay to $5 a day:

> He is a wisp of withering nerves, no one of which lies amicably against another. He can not be still. He neither smokes nor drinks, nor eats very much, having found a man in a book who lived to be 104 on fourteen ounces of simple food a day. While talking he twists his watch chain, pinches his lips or his nose, and strokes his face. His hands are always moving. They reflect the mind which can hardly wait for a question to be finished. Its decisions are nervous and sudden.[1]

Garrett was a perceptive questioner, neither fawning nor prosecutorial. Ford met Garrett in a little room with a bare desk; after they had talked, Ford suggested they go into the shop. "I don't like this office," Ford said. "I come here only to meet people." If he hadn't liked Garrett, the meeting would have been over. As it was, Garrett spent two days with Ford,[2] some of it for the *Annalist* and some for *Everybody's*. A fragment of that interview made it into his biography of Ford 38 years later.

Garrett had techniques of getting interviews with the unwilling. He recalled approaching the "Tin-Plate Millionaire", Daniel Gray Reid of the American Can Co.:

> "I'm going to do an article about you," I said. "You can't help that. I'll put in a lot of things you won't like, and perhaps some other things that you won't mind. But there is something you can put in for yourself. Down here in Wall Street you stand for a kind of work which the public is beginning to disapprove of. You must have some theory about it. Every man justifies his work to himself, or goes and jumps off the dock. Your theory—your point of view—what is it?"

Reid told his story of the rivalries and suspicions of business. As he relaxed, he mentioned how he had befriended a railroad brakeman and invited him to his high-rise office. Garrett, who had had to use his wits to gain access to that office, thought about why this millionaire had bestowed such a favor on a lowly brakeman. Just as he was walking out, Garrett stopped and turned.

"I'd hate to be rich," he said.

"Why?" Reid replied, not very curiously, and without turning his head.

Because, Garrett said, "Everybody would be trying to get something away from me, and I'd become suspicious even of friends."

In a soft voice, the Reid said, "It is so."[3]

And Garrett put it in his story.

On economic matters Garrett had a brilliant simplicity. In November 1913, while editor of the *Annalist*, he began a monthly column on money in *Everybody's,* writing as John Parr. One of the most common questions from readers was why the government simply didn't print money to spend on public works, instead of borrowing it at interest. It was a variant of the Coxey idea. Garrett explained that money is not wealth, but a claim on wealth, and that you do not add to wealth by creating more claims to it.[4]

Saving was another topic. Others had argued that Americans needed to save in order to create capital for development—and weren't saving enough. Garrett replied that Americans could import other peoples' savings. If Americans had "found it more profitable to borrow than to save," and borrowed the savings of Europeans, maybe it was because they were better than Europeans at creating wealth. *That* was the American strength.[5]

In 1914, World War I began in Europe. Garrett, writing under his own name, penned a prophetic piece for *Everybody's* on the economic meaning of it. "War is a sudden and imperious customer in the world's markets, and will not wait its turn," he wrote. War absorbs goods of all kinds, especially food; it devours labor and stretches credit. Prices, wages and interest rates would all go up, Garrett said—and all of it happened. He predicted that prices would collapse at the war's end, and that happened, too, six years later. Further, he argued, this particular war would make a peaceful America rich.

The idea that burning down a house made the community richer—because it created work for carpenters, masons and laborers—was the fallacy that French economist Frederic Bastiat had demolished seventy years earlier. Garrett was familiar with Bastiat, having quoted him on the fallacy of "the broken window." But rebuilding a house *did* make the carpenters, masons and laborers richer. In the Great War, Garrett wrote, "We are the carpenters, masons, and laborers for whom there is going to be more work than before, though the average welfare of the world, no doubt, will be impaired."[6] He

37

suggested that America, which had always been a net importer of European capital, might even become a net capital exporter—which also happened.

The clarity of these pieces is notable. Years later John Chamberlain wrote that Garrett was the only writer on economics he knew "who can make a single image or metaphor do the work of a whole page of statistics."[7] He could also do it with a character sketch. Consider Garrett's description of Arthur Greaves, city editor of the *New York Times:* "He was a man who waved long, thin fingers in the air and talked out of a loose, sensitive mouth." Or Tom Girdler, the stoutly anti-union boss of Republic Steel: "He is a small bull in a very big field, with only one sound, which is no."[8]

Garrett also took on political topics of emotional hue. One was the rise of Japan as the first non-Caucasian world power—a power that, Garrett said, "will become a manufacturing and trading nation, like Great Britain," and yet was composed of an Asian race Americans feared and, as immigrants, a race against which they discriminated.

Garrett didn't argue for an end to racism. He asked his readers to admit their racism, posing in blunt language and italic type the classic racist question: "Would you consider the thought of your daughter or sister marrying a Japanese?"

"If you answer instantly," he wrote, "you speak from feeling, and simply it is not arguable. If you answer slowly, you speak out of reason. Then it is debatable."

For most Americans in 1915, it was not debatable. (Whether it was for Garrett, he did not say.) Well, then, he argued, if we will not assimilate the Japanese, we should not let them immigrate here. But realize, too, he wrote, that this "cuts to the very quick of their racial pride," He said, "You really must see that."

And over the years, who had bullied whom? "We talk of the Yellow Peril. We hardly know that in China and Japan they talk of the White Peril, and have had more reason to fear us than we have ever had to fear them."

Then—and this was 1915—he wrote:

> Allow this state of feeling to continue, let it be inflamed from time to time by awkward incidents which friends could so easily understand, and then— then if the United States should seem to Japan to be thwarting her economic and political ambitions in Asia she would quickly fight us, not in sorrow for having to do it, but joyful of the opportunity. Then she would seize the Philippines and then might California be afraid.[9]

The subtitle of the article was, "Shall we marry, fight or cooperate with the Japanese?" Garrett's answer was the latter.

Finally, a look at his article on Christianity and war, occasioned by the fact that the Christian powers of Europe were engaged in horrific slaughter.

This is one of the few times Garrett wrote on religion. He described America as a Christian country. He said, though, perhaps speaking for himself, "Many of us make no confession of faith, attend no church and have theories and convictions which a churchman would pronounce heretical; but a little reflection will prove how widely and deeply governed our everyday thoughts and reactions are by Christian precept and counsel."

He asked the reader to think whether the European war, or any war, was consistent with the teachings of Jesus:

> When in the writing of this article I had reached the fullness of that interrogation, it became suddenly as personal to me as I had wished to make it to the

reader. I felt bound to dispose of it on my own account. I felt I must go with it to some dark and silent recess, there to answer or to strangle it.

If he answered it, he didn't say what the answer was. He went off to interview church figures, identified by denomination only. He suggested to them that that by condoning the war they were betraying the doctrine of Christ. They were not much offended by this accusation, or stimulated either. "One said it was a very old thing to bring up," Garrett wrote.[10]

Chapter 6 notes

1 "Henry Ford's experiment in Good-Will." *Everybody's*, April 1914.
2 *The Wild Wheel,* Pantheon, 1952, p. 11. Material from the 1914 interview in the 1952 book included a statement about sweepers picking up tools, p. 11.
3 "A Tin-Plated Millionaire: The Career and Personality of Daniel Gray Reid," *Everybody's*, January 1915.
4 "Everybody's Money," *Everybody's*, May 1914.
5 "Everybody's Money," *Everybody's*, December 1913.
6 "Economics of the Sword," *Everybody's*, October 1914. Garrett had quoted Bastiat in *The New York Times Annalist*, editor's column, March 31, 1913, p. 323.
7 John Chamberlain, Introduction to Frank Chodorov, *One Is a Crowd*, Devin-Adair, 1952.
8 On Greaves: GG Journal, October 20, 1915. On Girdler: letter to Rose Wilder Lane, March 27, 1937. Lane papers.
9 "The Snarl of Waking Asia," *Everybody's*, May 1915.
10 "When Christians Fight, Are They Christians?" *Everybody's*, December 1914.

Chapter Seven
THE CAPITALIZATION OF MIND

Garrett once wrote that in his early twenties, "one took the form of government as a fact to begin with, like the fact of one's parentage, and did not think about it at all."[1] By 1915, when he turned 37, he was thinking about it. That was the year he moved to the editorial council—what today would be called the editorial board—of the *New York Times*, where he wrote house editorials. They were unsigned, but some can be identified as his because they are so close to what he did elsewhere.

He also wrote a journal. It is handwritten in Garrett's faux-Arabic scrawl, almost illegible, on plain yellow paper, and has been translated into civilized font by its owner, Richard Cornuelle. Though it does not delve into Garrett's private life, it is a record of his thinking on his work and the issues of the day. He began the journal when the Germans sank the British liner *Lusitania* in mid-1915 and ended it when he left the *Times* in mid-1916.

Garrett was still something of a progressive in these years. In his journal he complained of "the Tory attitude of the *Times*, which means it being for property first and people next..." In another entry he wrote, "I believe in rate regulation" for railroads.[2] A decade later, he would not.

In some ways, Garrett was already what he would become—for example, a defender of the entrepreneur. When the Ford Motor Co. made a 2,400 percent profit on its initial capital, Garrett wrote in a *Times* editorial:

> In the balance sheet of the Ford Motor Company there is no entry of the item, 'HENRY FORD'... Nowhere on either side of the account is there a hint of one man's mind as the source of the 2400 percent profit... The standard economist also leaves it out in all his theories of ...land, labor and capital.
>
> Cases like that of the Ford Motor Company raise the entire question of the mind in economics... [The company] was not created by capital, for it provided its own capital as it went along... Land was used, but it was paid for by the operations of the concern. The labor was also paid generously, even extravagantly, on any basis of economic computation. It is necessary to believe that mind was the chief factor in the creation of the company...
>
> Ford is but one among those who have made fortunes rivaling his, and by the capitalization of mind.[3]

Where others saw masses, Garrett saw a directing intelligence. He was also a methodological individualist, at least most of the time. While he might say a nation would "think" or "feel" something, meaning it was the predominant feeling, he was not inclined to say a nation would *decide* something. When a colleague started talking about "the Germans" making the decision to attack Warsaw, Garrett wrote in his journal, "The Germans? No. It will be made not by them but for them. One man perhaps will decide it."

It was the same at a newspaper. Some *individual* would decide whether the news from Europe would go on page one above the fold, or inside. "The paper," he wrote, "is made by those who decide." Then he remarked:

I happen to look at Percy Brown. He is asleep again. Percy Brown is a copy reader, in the lowest position at the crescent-shaped copy desk on the other side of the room. He lives at Rockaway Beach and is always much tanned and about to be drunk. He reads such things as fires and small local happenings. When he is not reading copy he is sleeping. I recall an incident of several weeks ago. The German reply to Wilson's note on the Lusitania is in the office. Miller, Mr. O and I were about Van Anda's desk, exchanging solemn looks and restrained remarks, all feeling very grave and apprehensive. Suddenly, Van Anda happened to notice Percy Brown, over there at the copy desk, deep asleep.

"Percy Brown," he said, enviously. "The nations clash and what does he care? He sleeps... If a storm should wash away half a mile of boardwalk at Rockaway Beach he would be no more excited than by the possibility of war with Germany."

Percy Brown decides very little. That's why he is Percy Brown.[4]

The mind behind the corporate thought of the *New York Times* was Adolph Ochs, its publisher. Ochs had begun in the newspaper business much as Garrett had, as a printer's devil in a rural state. Ochs grew up in Tennessee, and had bought a half-interest in the *Chattanooga Times* at age 20. He had made his investment pay, and at 38 had bought control of the faltering, almost-dead *New York Times* with $75,000 in borrowed money. He made it a serious newspaper, and by 1915 had built it into a paper of 330,000 circulation.

Ochs was not, however, a man of hard-edged thought. He was a sentimental man. In his journal, Garrett recounted the story of Ochs declaring unexpectedly that he understood why workers formed unions and why they hated scabs. It amazed Garrett that his anti-union boss would be suddenly sympathizing with workers. Garrett wrote, "I said, 'I wish we could get some of that opinion into the editorial columns of the *Times*, where it would do some good. According to the *Times*, it is never right for labor to get its pay raised, just as it is never convenient for people ever to revolt.' " Ochs said no, "It wouldn't do to take that view in the newspaper." [5]

Much of the journal is about Garrett's colleagues, who were the top editorial men of the *New York Times*. Garrett was 37—young compared with editor-in-chief Charles Ransom Miller, 67; editorial writer Edward Dithmar, 62; and managing editor Carr Van Anda, 50. Only Miller and Van Anda were better-paid than Garrett, who wrote that Ochs, 57, had brought him into the group "because they are old; and the degree of my efficiency is the measure of how I hurt them."[6]

Ochs is the main figure. Half a century later, when Gay Talese came to write *The Kingdom and the Power,* his history of the *Times*, he said, "the most interesting insights into Adolph Ochs himself were to be found in the private papers of a *Times* man named Garet Garrett."[7]

In his journal, Garrett portrayed Ochs as a man of sentiment. "Most of the time he only feels. He begins with a feeling and then 'reasons' in a way to make everything come right with the feeling." Several months later Garrett wrote, "None of us values his mental processes highly... He cannot think his way through a problem." But Ochs could take the other person's point of view, and was "very often right in some unexpected way." Garrett perceived that Ochs was connected to the popular mind in a way the others around the editorial table were not. "The success of the *Times*," Garrett observed, "is very largely owing to the gift he has, the clairvoyant faculty of knowing what the average mind is going to feel, or to think." Toward the end of the journal, he declared that he had figured Ochs out. He wrote, "Mr. Ochs is a crowd."[8]

On occasion, the man of the crowd tries to lead it—and discovers that he is not as much the leader as he had believed. To Garrett, that is what happened to Ochs in the notorious case of the lynching of Leo Frank.

Chapter 7 notes

1 SEP, "The Youth Document," November 7, 1936.

2 GG journal, June 28, 1915; August 13, 1915.

3 "Mental Capital," *New York Times*, June 9, 1915, p. 12. It is unsigned, but it is Garrett's style—and Garrett's thinking. Garrett made the same point about the economists' categories of land, labor and capital in *The American Omen*, Dutton, 1928, p. 119.

4 GG journal, June 24, 1915. Carr Van Anda was managing editor and Charles Ransom Miller was editor in chief. Notice how Garrett always uses "Mr." for his boss, Ochs, and not for his colleagues. Later he did the same in referring to Herbert Hoover.

5 GG journal, May 14, 1916. He retells this story in "The Labor Weapon," SEP, July 17, 1937. In the later version he remembers this as a Labor Day parade, but his journal has it as a preparedness parade on May 13, with no labor representation in it. The quoted remarks in the two accounts are different, but the essence of the story is the same. The *Times* commented on the parade in "The Procession of Patriots," May 14, 1916.

6 GG Journal, July 7, 1915.

7 Gay Talese, *The Kingdom and the Power*, p. 528.

8 GG journal, August 17, 1915; April 21, 1916 and May 4, 1916.

Chapter Eight
A GREAT ENTHUSIASM

L eo Max Frank was the superintendent of the National Pencil factory in Atlanta. In 1913, at age 29, he was accused of murdering Mary Phagan, 13, a factory girl. She had gone into town on a Saturday to collect her pay and to see the parade on Confederate Memorial Day. Later her body was found in the factory's basement bound, beaten, raped and rolled in graphite dust.

The main evidence against Frank was that he had paid her, and was the last person known to have seen her. The other fact is that he was Jewish. One possible motive for charging him was for the Atlanta authorities to erase the anti-black stain from the race riots of 1906. Anyhow, they did charge him, and he is said to be the first white man in the South convicted on the testimony of a black man—in this case, the janitor. Frank's lawyers also tried to play the race card, appealing to the white jury to pin the blame on the black janitor. The janitor may well have done it; decades later a man who had been an office boy wrote that he had seen the janitor carrying the girl's body downstairs, and that the janitor had threatened to kill him if he told. But at the time, there was not enough evidence to make a case against the janitor or against anyone. Nonetheless, after a raucous trial, in which a mob cheered the prosecution and chanted instructions and threats to the jury, Frank was sentenced to death.

The case became a national story because of the lurid details, the background of Southern justice, the ever-present threat of lynching and because this was a white man—and a Jew. Ochs, who was visited on the matter by Atlanta Rabbi David Marx, was convinced Frank was innocent, and in late 1914 the *New York Times* began what Garrett called "a campaign of righteous publicity" to get Frank a new trial. The *Times* was not the only paper to campaign this way, but it led the pack. In December 1914 the paper ran a major story on Frank almost every day of the month. Wrote Steve Oney in a history that is sympathetic to Frank, "Some of the stories, particularly if there was a new development, strove for balance, but by and large, Ochs's sheet was more interested in disseminating propaganda than in practicing journalism."[1]

Garrett allowed that Frank might not have received a fair trial, but he thought Ochs had gone overboard in his defense. Much of the staff thought so, too. Garrett wrote that "the name of Leo Frank is anathema" to *Times* reporters and that the third floor, where the paper was made up, "would vote overwhelmingly to hang him."[2]

Frank's arguments for a new trial were rejected by Georgia's Supreme Court and, on April 19, 1915, by the U. S. Supreme Court. The legal issue was not whether Frank was guilty, but whether he had received due process of law, and the Court ruled he had. Justice Oliver Wendell Holmes argued in dissent that Frank had been faced with "a mob intent on death" and that "mob law does not become due process of law by securing the assent of a terrorized jury."[3] But Holmes had only one other justice on his side, future presidential candidate Charles Evans Hughes, and it was not enough.

By June, Frank was scheduled to be executed. On June 9, 1915, Garrett wrote:

> We discuss the Frank case, which is near to Mr. O's heart. His heart does him more credit than his

head. It is, indeed, a wonderful heart. He believes
Frank is innocent and now wavers in the faith he has
had from the start that an innocent man could not be
hanged. Much to my surprise he asks me to write on
the Frank case. I have never written on it and I have
not followed it, and I remind him of these facts; but
he insists. I say I cannot find anything new to say. He
cannot see anything new either. "But the point to me
is this," he goes on to say. "Under our system an innocent man may be legally hanged." We all remind him
that innocent men have been hanged before and that
the law has survived because on the whole it works
more for justice than injustice... We go round and
round, and at last I promise to write on the Frank case,
without knowing in the least where I shall begin or
where I shall come out.

Garrett's editorial repeated the company line, "We believe
Frank is innocent," while also arguing that the defendant *had*
received due process of law, as the Supreme Court had ruled.
It called on the governor to "exercise his discretion."[4]

On June 21, 1915, it was announced that Gov. John Slaton
had commuted Frank's sentence to life imprisonment. It was
not a popular decision in Georgia. It was the governor's last
day in office—and he and his wife immediately fled the state
for a very long time.

On July 18, a fellow convict cut Frank's throat without
killing him. On August 16, before the wound had fully healed,
came the end. Wrote Garrett in his journal for August 18: "A
mob came to the Georgia prison farm, loaded him into an
automobile, carried him 100 miles to a point near Mary
Phagan's home, and there hanged him to a tree."

Ochs seemed to take the news phlegmatically. "I think I
was the only one at council who was not surprised at Mr.
Ochs' air of reconcilement," Garrett wrote.

What moved Ochs was the report by the *Times'* correspondent, Charles Thompson, who explained the three reasons for the lynching: first, that the governor had been associated with the law firm that defended Frank, so that his act looked like the shielding of a convicted murderer through political favor; second, that the clamor for Frank was an attack on Georgians by outsiders; and third, that the Jews were defending Frank because he was one of theirs.

In his journal, Garrett wrote:

> All this time Mr. O has been insisting that there was no racial feeling in the situation at all, and he believed it because he wanted to believe it; but now suddenly he cannot believe it any longer, and he is in a kind of panic. Thompson's stuff from Georgia, on the aftermath of the lynching, has left positively no doubt of the anti-Jewish feeling in Georgia... Mr. O didn't like it, of course, and yet he knew it was true, and had to be printed. There was no help for it...
>
> The last straw was a telegram from the Macon *Telegraph*, on refusing to print the *Times'* editorial, written by Miller and distributed to the papers of Georgia at Mr. O's request. The editorial called upon the decent people of Georgia to prove Frank's innocence. That was the only way in which they could rehabilitate the name of Georgia.
>
> The Macon *Telegraph*... dispatched a long message to the *Times*, attention of Mr. O personally, and said that for the sake of the *Times* and Mr. O, it would not print the editorial as requested to do, and said that for the sake of the decent people of Georgia and especially for the sake of the Jews in Georgia would Mr. O stop this offensive propaganda. It was the outside interference of the Jews, led by the *Times*, that had

made it necessary to lynch Frank. The Jews in fact were responsible for what had happened to him.

We found Mr. O at council table in a gloomy state of mind. It was time, he said, to begin to consider the newspaper itself. There was a drift of feeling against it in Georgia, and perhaps the idea was beginning to spread that the *Times* was a Jewish newspaper...

I said we should consider a few facts. Mr. O was the most prominent newspaper publisher in the country. He was a Jew. The *Times* had printed more stuff for Frank than any other newspaper and was now the only New York paper with a special correspondent in Georgia. It was clear what a great many people would make of those facts. Also it was clear, and we needn't deny it any longer, that a majority of the people in Georgia approved of the law having been taken into the hands of a mob, because they believed money had been used to thwart the forms of justice.

Mr. O agreed to all this. He has really a remarkable gift of putting himself in the other man's place. He said that if he were a Georgian he would have resented the outside interference. Also, he could see how it looked to a great many people that Gov. Slaton, a law partner of the man who defended Frank, should have commuted his sentence. It was very hard really to meet the argument that Frank had received every legal consideration, which undoubtedly he had.

Well, anyhow, hereafter the *Times* will print only the news of the Frank case. So perishes a great enthusiasm, for the sake of the *N.Y. Times*.[5]

Ochs was hardly the only one shocked by the Frank case. The lynching of Leo Frank was the event that prompted American Jews to form the Anti-Defamation League.

But Garet Garrett was a long way from Atlanta, and his journal shows him little interested in the case as such. His first comment on it, to Ochs, was that he hadn't followed it. Garrett noted in his journal that the *Times'* lawyer, who had read the court documents, believed Frank innocent. Garrett hadn't read them and admitted to a "lack of conviction." His interests were elsewhere. He had begun his journal for that day, June 10, 1915, by writing, "Tonight we shall have the note to Germany. It may be an ultimatum. And in council meeting we discuss the Frank case!"

His sense of journalism told him that the paper had overly favored Frank. There would have been another reason for his disinterest. For an editorial writer at the *New York Times*, the innocence of Leo Frank was not an open question. The only allowable opinion was Ochs's opinion. Why bother, then, to look into it? Garrett did not say this in his journal, but it was implicit in his position. It should be no surprise that after the lynching he wrote, "There is an end of the Frank case, at last. Thank God."

Garrett's interest in the Frank case was in what it showed about the mind of Adolph Ochs, a man with "a feeling for romantic justice," a Jew who had denied the importance of Jewish tribalism, and of Christian tribalism, and who, when confronted with the ugly reality, was shocked into institutional silence.

It wasn't the only issue in which Ochs changed his position and denied he had done it. There was also the story of Gunda, an elephant. Gunda was not happy at the zoo. He pulled at his chains. "Mr. O saw him one day," Garrett wrote, "and was deeply touched." Ochs had the *Times* editorialize that Gunda needed more room. The public responded, and the *Times* editorialized again: give the animal more room! But when the zoo shot Gunda, Ochs said that was all right, too.

"That isn't the position the *Times* took," said one of the writers.

"That is exactly the position we took," insisted Ochs, who let everyone vent and then instructed Mortimer to write something on it.

"That," wrote Garrett, "is the end of Gunda."[6]

Chapter 8 notes

1 Steve Oney, *And the Dead Shall Rise: The Murder of Mary Phagan and the Lynching of Leo Frank,* Pantheon, 2003, p. 457.
2 GG journal, July 19, 1915.
3 *Frank v. Magnum,* 237 U.S. 309 (1915).
4 "The Tragedy of Innocence," *New York Times*, June 10, 1915.
5 GG journal, August 21, 1915. For an account of the Frank case, see Oney, *And the Dead Shall Rise*. For the *Times'* previous denial of religious prejudice, see, "Not Racial Prejudice," unsigned editorial of May 26, 1915.
6 GG journal, June 22, 1915.

Chapter Nine
IN THIS WORLD

Concerning World War I, then underway for a year, Ochs's "paramount feeling," Garrett wrote, "is that this country shall be kept out of war. He wants to think he is for peace with honor, because honor is a word he likes, but really (there is no doubt of this) he is for peace at any price."[1]

That was the attitude natural to businessmen. Disputing a statement by German socialist Karl Liebknecht that Germany's capitalists wanted the war, Garrett wrote, "It cannot be true, not even in Germany, that the capitalist interests want war. Capital is pacific. If there were such a thing in the world as a purely capitalistic state of mind, quite divorced from the human emotions of the owners of capital, it would be for peace at any moral price."[2]

Garrett was not for peace at any price. Though he would later declare World War I "a total loss" for the United States,[3] in 1915 his principal interest was in not wanting his country to be pushed around by either side. He began his journal on May 12, 1915, with the declaration, "I am resolved to shock the [New York Times editorial page] out of its gratuitous support of Wilson... Since the Lusitania disaster he has twice emerged from seclusion to say once, 'Don't rock the boat,' and once, that a nation might be 'too proud to fight.'" What were the Germans to make of this, and for five days without even a statement of protest? They would think, he said, that the Americans "are a pusillanimous people." Which they weren't.

"Pusillanimous" is a recurring word. Two months later Garrett expressed scorn for the president and "the large pusillanimous element" in America.[4] Garrett used "pusillanimous" the same way a few entries later[5] (and would use it that way to describe Franklin Roosevelt's "measures short of war" policy of 1939-1940).[6]

In his May 12, 1915, entry he also expressed his irritation at the president being portrayed as a kingly figure on whom the nation rested its hope:

> In what are we supporting Mr. Wilson? Each day we read that he is praying, that he is thinking, that he is seeking wisdom in solitude, that he wishes not to be disturbed, etc. etc. ad nauseam. Who is Mr. Wilson that he alone should drink the cup of bitterness? Who is Mr. Wilson that he should bear the people's burden away to his private Gethsemane, whence issue these bulletins of his agony? This is the people's matter. We do not require him to bear the burden alone, or, for that matter, at all. Let him recollect the theory of American government, wherein the President's function is the executive function alone. Let him summon Congress, etc.

Garrett was annoyed at his country being stepped on by Germany, and also by Britain. On June 18 he wrote that the *Times* had buried "the news of our disagreement with Great Britain over its right to prohibit trade between the U.S. and Germany through neutral ports." On June 22, he brought it up again, arguing that Britain had no business blocking ships bound to America from neutral Holland simply because those ships carried German goods. On this point he could not persuade his colleagues. "I give up," he fumed in his journal. "The truth, of course, is that nobody wants even to think of emphasizing a difference with Great Britain."

Meanwhile the diplomatic notes had gone back and forth over the *Lusitania*. Garrett had thought Wilson's delay in sending the first note of protest showed weakness, and that the note, which demanded a stop to the sinking of merchant ships, "demanded more than Germany could yield." It looked to Garrett as if "a weak man had done on impulse a strong man's work." Germany sent an evasive reply, whereupon Wilson issued a second note that watered down the U.S. position. Wrote Garrett:

> And now Germany's second note. It is what we deserve. It is an act of urination. And people actually are satisfied with Wilson for keeping us out of war. Great God! This is a stinking acid of peace introduced into our conglomerate psychology.[7]

Maybe America would have to fight. "I have thought we should have to fight against Germany for our faith in democracy—for our social and political philosophy," he wrote. "What she stands for and what we stand for cannot live in peace in the same world."[8]

Ochs was simultaneously pro-British but adamant that the war was not an American affair. Garrett asked him: What if the Allies were about to lose? Then, Ochs said, America would have to get in. Garrett replied:

> "How then can you say that it is no affair of ours? If it is an affair of democracy against autocracy it ought to concern us now; if it isn't, if it is only a quarrel over the Balkan states, why should we take part at all, under any conditions?

He smiles and says, "But the allies are not going to lose."[9]

One reason for Allied victory might be that the Germans were cut off from trade but the British were not. From the United States, Britain was receiving goods on credit. In his journal of Sept. 20, 1915, Garrett raised the issue of war debts. Before the editorial council, he had argued:

> England is now buying more than she can pay for in either gold or credit; therefore, she must have credit to go on buying more, and there is certainly a limit beyond which it will not be safe to give her credit. She has entered upon a policy of unlimited liability, and the war is only one year old.
>
> I am frowned down all around. Why think of these things? British credit is good and unlimited, and that is enough. Besides, we have to lend her in order to keep a market for our goods, wherefore, it isn't a question of whether we can afford to or not. We have got to. And so it is disposed of, with the further remark by Mr. O that if it came to a point where Great Britain had to repudiate her debts it would be more terrible for us than for her, but what that meant I do not know. Neither did he. He was just wondering at a calamity which he had refused to consider possible.

Garrett had presented this theme before in *Times* editorials. In May 1915 he had written, regarding war credits, "It is never safe to lend more than the debtor can reasonably pay."[10] But his thought in September was more pointed than that, and not welcome. And Garrett was right about the war debts, which would become a major subject of his attention in decade and a half after the war. His attitude toward them never changed: he was for the American interest. It pained him when his colleagues obligingly accepted that what was good for Britain was good for America.

A week after Garrett complained in his journal, the *New York Times* printed his editorial arguing that Americans ought to be free to sell to Britain on credit. The editorial was directed at the German-Americans and their supporters, who were campaigning to have private credits blocked. Garrett thought the credits were risky, but he wasn't for blocking them. Americans should be free to shoulder their own risks. American trade, he wrote, had always been open to all. "People could differ emotionally, religiously, ethically, in every way, and yet trade together honestly to their mutual advantage." If American companies wanted to sell to British on credit, that was their business; if they wanted to sell to Germans on credit, that was also their business. It so happened that Germany was cut off from the American market— but that, he wrote, was through "no fault of ours."[11]

From the viewpoint of the 21st century, this seems naïve. *Of course* each side would try to block American trade with its enemy. And these days, it is difficult to imagine American neutrality in a major conflict. It would be out of character. It wasn't, then.

Chapter 9 notes

1 GG journal, July 15 and August 6, 1915.

2 "Capital Is Pacific," *New York Times*, July 2, 1915, p. 10. The editorial is unsigned. I label it as Garrett's because of the argument it makes, and the clarity of its exposition.

3 *The American Story*, Regnery, 1955, p. 216.

4 GG journal, July 10, 1915.

5 GG journal, August 17, 1915.

6 SEP, "Will We Do It," July 6, 1940; "On Going to War," October 19, 1940.

7 GG journal, July 10, 1915.

8 GG journal, July 10, 1915.

9 GG journal, July 15, 1915.

10 "A Credit Limit on War," *New York Times,* May 30, 1915, p. 12. This is unsigned, but there is little doubt that it is his.

11 "Americanism," the *New York Times*, September 27, 1915. In his journal for October 7, 1915, he mentions this editorial as his: "… my long Monday morning editorial 'Americanism,' which the bankers, when they launched their merchandising campaign to sell the bonds to the final investor had reprinted on costly, glossy paper, in a pamphlet."

Chapter Ten
YET I BELIEVE IN IT

In November 1915, when America was officially neutral but leaning against the Central Powers, the *Times* sent Garrett to Imperial Germany to report from the inside, particularly on its economic stamina. The high point of his trip was an interview with Walter Rathenau, the man who had the same job in Germany that Bernard Baruch would soon have in the United States: the government's head of war production. Garrett's half-hour appointment with Rathenau, an industrialist, lasted all day. It was like Garrett's first appointment with Henry Ford: he impressed his subject with the quality of his mind, and the time constraint was lifted. The interview was off the record; in his *Times* report he made only one allusion to Rathenau as "he who might be called the economic dictator of Europe." But a quarter-century later, after Rathenau, a Jew, had been assassinated by anti-Semites, Garrett felt free to describe the meeting:

> It was winter. Snow was falling. He was alone in his office and the temperature was uncomfortably low. We stood at the window looking out, and that made it seem warmer inside. I do not recall how it was that the conversation took a certain turn. Lunch was forgotten. At dark, the snow still falling, as it may

in Berlin all day long without leaving its coat, we were yet at the window.

What had we been talking about? Not the war. I remember that as we went on, the war seemed a thing misplaced in time, meaningless in itself. Whether Germany's resources would permit her to go on for a month, a year, two years—what difference did it make? Sometime it would end, and then the problem would be what it was before. How shall competitive people live together in the world?

Here was a man bending the physical power of Germany to the breaking point in order to wage a nationalistic war, because that was his job, and at the same time dreaming the outlines of an international world... He saw, perhaps, the luminous phantom of it only. There would need to be a change in the philosophy of government, and he had not thought that problem through.[1]

In his 1916 report in the *New York Times* he wrote of the war's terrible inertia:

You get the feeling in Europe that the people are mad and begin to know it, as if they had suddenly come awake in an asylum, all shouting together that they are sane but unable to prove it to themselves, to each other, or to the world outside. And nobody can see a way out. There is a despondent saying that diplomacy in Europe is bankrupt. [2]

These were not the words of a man eager for war. Indeed, Garrett tried some diplomacy himself. He returned from Berlin with a message from the German Foreign Office. The message was, "that Germany wishes to keep peace with the United States, that she is willing to make a reasonable peace,

that she is looking to the United States to act for peace..."
Garrett went to Washington, D.C., to see the president. Wilson
declined to see him, and Garrett ended up talking to Secretary
of State Robert Lansing, who was known to be pro-British.
Garrett confided to his journal, "To none of this was the
Government at all responsive."[3]

In a journal entry after he returned to America, Garrett
wrote:

> We are nearer war with Germany than at any time
> since the sinking of the Lusitania, and for wrong and
> indistinct reasons, without a position, without a theo-
> ry, without faith, simply as a result of piling up irrita-
> tions so high that a war would actually come to many
> persons as a kind of relief. I said this at council today,
> and Miller laughed at the idea... I answered him say-
> ing, "You say we are not on the verge of war with
> Germany, and yet the *Times* in its Washington corre-
> spondence has printed inspired statements from this
> high official of the Government almost openly sug-
> gesting the recall of the German Ambassador. To this,
> Miller replied that the sending of [Count Johann von]
> Bernstorff home would not mean war with Germany.
> But it almost certainly would. [George] McAneny
> said at this point that he had talked during the
> forenoon with Bernstorff, who said the situation was
> very grave. Miller said: "Of course he would say that.
> They are bluffing."
>
> So a great newspaper is made—at least, we are
> under the delusion that we make it. It makes itself. We
> are all irresponsible. And I, knowing what I know
> about the feeling of the German government, from
> having talked with members of it by the hour very
> intimately, and with its understanding, previously
> referred to, in my mind—I am unable to take another

step, owning to the impossible nature of the relations between the United States and Germany.[4]

A few days later he wrote in his journal that he believed in neutrality, though it "is so rare that I sometimes ask myself if it is not an affectation. Yet I believe in it." Three months later he wrote, "I am neither for war nor for peace, except as either one may attend a faith we should have in ourselves." He worried that his country was, however, "fat and slothful and afraid, without either the courage to make war or to abandon the principle of war."[5]

Garrett wrote several times in his journal of his colleagues' nationalistic anger, as if he knew he was susceptible to it himself. On June 2, 1916, he wrote about the case of some "Socialists, Anarchists, Syndicalists or what not" who had held a ceremonial immolation of the flags of each of the belligerents, and also the flag of the United States. The story, printed on page one of the *Times*, inflamed his colleagues. Miller, the editor-in-chief, called it an act of treason and declared that the perpetrators should be imprisoned for life. Ochs said Miller was taking it too seriously. Garrett wrote:

> When they were all through I put in my say. Why shouldn't it be treated as a simple, naïve act of symbolism? The participants had been very earnest, even prayerful. They hardly deserved to be laughed at. They could easily say to us: "Well, how smart are you? ... The world has broken down in war. It does not know how it got into the war nor how it shall get out, but already it is laying plans for a war after the war, and an economic war to follow peace, which means later another physical war, and the whole thing over again. What have you to propose? We propose world brotherhood and an abolition of nationalism. Therefore, as a symbol of what we think, we burn the

flags of all nations." Why should we either laugh at that or wish to put the culprits in jail? ... True, they were probably a dirty lot, unindustrious, averse to bathing, immoral as the world thinks, and not at all the kind of people we should like to associate with, but the world thought all that of the apostles...

When I stopped there was a painful silence, whether of disapproval too deep to be expressed or of simple surprise I could not make out... Mortimer asked if he should write something about the flag burning, and Mr. O nodded assent.[6]

Garrett's colleagues were shocked by his criticism of them. In the next journal entry, Garrett announced his intention to leave the *Times* for the *New York Tribune*. Months before he had written in his journal that the *Times* was so rich that it was "beginning to be a haughty paper." He also complained that it was "too big and unwieldy to respond to the touch of any one man." Ochs believed he had much more to accomplish at the *Times*, but, Garrett wrote, "the fact is that he is afraid to do anything more."

To Ochs, Garrett said his desire was to help in the making of a thing, and the *Times* was so well made there was hardly anything one could do with it. "I was impatient to do things; and it was hard to get anything done on the *Times*—anything new."

"But you will not be as comfortable on the *Tribune* as here," Ochs said.

"I don't expect to be," Garrett replied. "The trouble is, I am too comfortable here. The comfort is killing."[7]

Chapter 10 notes

1 SEP, "War Has Lost Its Pocket," January 13, 1940. He also describes this meeting in *Ouroboros, or the Mechanical Extension of Mankind*, E.P. Dutton, 1926, pp. 45-48, and in *A Time Is Born*, Pantheon, 1944, pp. 161-162.

2 *The New York Times* printed the series January 18-26 and 28, 1916, and reprinted it in *Current History*, Vol. 3, No. 6, March 1916. This quote is from *Current History*, p. 1063.

3 GG journal, February 21, 1916.

4 GG journal, February 21, 1916. George McAneny, 45, was executive manager of the *Times*. He had been president of the Manhattan Board of Aldermen before being hired for the job by the *Times*, and would later go back to politics.

5 GG journal, February 29, 1916, and May 5, 1916.

6 GG journal, June 2, 1916.

7 GG Journal, October 1, 1915; June 5, 1916; February 21-22, 1916; Talese, *The Kingdom and the Power*, p. 170.

Chapter Eleven
ABOVE THE LIMIT

Garrett had declared in 1914 that war produced a net economic loss, and in March 1917, as America stood on the brink of war, he said so again. It was "folly," an "absurd" idea, "that active participation in it can result in a gain in wealth."[1] But if America could stay out of the war and be a supplier only, it could gain from it.

From August 1, 1916, to June 30, 1917, Garrett was business editor of the *Tribune*. For the first four months, his "Finance-Economics" column appeared daily under his byline. These columns provide a picture of an extraordinary time. Europe was in its third year of artillery barrages and poison gas. In America, industry was running flat out, with "the speedometer…above the limit of the dial."

War had doubled the price of steel in one year. America's largest company, United States Steel, was suddenly making fabulous profits. When Steel crossed $100 a share, Garrett wrote, "The imagination is overwhelmed." What was a share worth? On a normal ratio of price to earnings, it should be worth several hundred, but the profit was not normal. The war boom "may continue to happen for six months, a year, two years, or it may stop in sixty days," Garrett wrote. So what was a share *worth?*

"You cannot say what anything is worth," he declared of the stock market. "The sense of values is gone."[2]

Profits on assets bought before the boom could be unimaginable. In the trans-Atlantic trade, Garrett wrote, "vessels built before the war may pay for themselves in one voyage." But if you wanted to order a new ship, the price had gone up.[3] So had the prices of most other things. On the Chicago exchange, the British government was gobbling up wheat, and the price of a barrel of flour was up 50 percent in a year. Garrett wondered whether Americans might sell so much wheat they would run out of bread. Cotton was at the highest price since the Civil War. And, looking back, for American agriculture 1916 was one of the fattest years of the century.

For workers, union and non-union, wages were going up at a faster rate than any time since the Napoleonic war. U.S. Steel had raised wages three times in the year, for a total of 80 percent. Employers railed at the greed of labor, but Garrett wrote that this was futile, and hypocrisy as well. Labor, he wrote, "lives in the present, as most of us do, and takes what it can get because it can get it, as nearly everybody does."[4]

Some gains were illusory, but not all. The boom was real, and not all the stuff it produced was going to the war. American workers—*workers!*—were buying motor cars. And they would continue to buy them, Garrett said. "Every one is consuming more goods of all kinds," he wrote. "More food, richer food, more automobiles, more moving pictures, more transportation, beautiful fabrics, gaudy shoes, and personal adornments. It is not confined to any class."[5]

All this was happening under the gold standard, which in normal times made inflation impossible. But the belligerents were using their gold to buy food and weapons in America. By the end of 1916, the United States had nearly one-half of the world's entire stock of monetary gold. Deposited in a U.S. bank, each dollar of formerly European gold could be used to create several dollars in new American money. Also, America had a new central bank, the Federal Reserve, which, Garrett wrote, had "exercised a powerful, though an indirect, cheapening influence upon the price of credit" by lowering reserve requirements.

American industry had always been a net borrower on world markets. No more. "We are out of debt," Garrett crowed. "We owe the world nothing." As Garrett had predicted, America had become a net lender for the first time in its history. Indeed, it had become the world's only large lender. "It is a new experience," he wrote, "without any of the automatic checks which long experience tends to create." Here was a hint that the American bankers might not know when to stop. Certainly the borrowers were not going to stop. They were at war. Furthermore, Garrett noted, all their borrowing was short-term, a practice that had led to defaults when the railroad corporations had done it. [6]

There had to be a limit to what could be safely lent, but what was it? In one Sunday column Garrett declared, "No country, so long as it is solvent, may repudiate a foreign loan." That was the rule, but would it hold? A few weekends later, he wrote that "the only certainty" about the borrower governments after the war was that "they will not pay more than they can afford to pay." But who would define what they could afford to pay? In another column he wrote that the loans were good "provided the war does not last too long" and provided also that the borrowers "are not beaten." How long was too long? In yet another column he lamented that Americans had not learned to "inquire very strictly into the ability of our customers to repay us." In all this, he was laying a minefield of doubts. What he never asked was: What if America got into the war? How would becoming an ally of the borrowers change their willingness to repay?[7]

Garrett worried about the period after the war. All those war workers would be laid off. Their high wages would be gone. But who was thinking about that? Business wasn't thinking of it. There wasn't time. Never in the past had there been time, either. "The true symbol of our spirit," he wrote, "is the Arkansas settler who never mended his roof. When it was raining he couldn't and when it was not raining there were too many other things to do."[8]

In the fall of 1916 there was a political fight about railroad rates. Garrett had been a supporter of rate regulation by the Interstate Commerce Commission. Two years before, the ICC had allowed a 5 percent increase so that railroads could earn a decent return on capital. Now President Wilson was offering another rate increase if the railroads would support an eight-hour labor bill. The rail unions were demanding a pay increase. Under regulation, a political deal might be reached to charge social gains to the shippers. Just such a deal was being negotiated in public in the midst of a presidential election campaign between the Democrat, Wilson, and his Republican opponent, Charles Evans Hughes.

This was not the technocratic way regulation was supposed to work. It was not economics. It was politics. To Garrett it looked like corruption.

He also noted, "The cost of railroad transportation is rising in this country for the first time. Until a few years ago it had fallen steadily from the very beginning of the railroad era."[9]

Here was Garrett refining his view that government should be kept out of business. But not out of banking. As gold flooded into American banks—gold that bankers said was not needed or wanted from a system-wide view—Garrett argued that the gold should be managed by the Federal Reserve. "Being all in one place, as now every European country's gold stock is, its power of credit could be controlled effectively," he wrote. But, he added, "in banking, however, we are individualists, as in everything else."[10]

It was also in this period that Garrett began considering wartime economic interventions. One was a tax on war profits: "War profits ought to be taxed heavily," he wrote. "They are abnormal and excessive profits, and they are made at the expense of nearly every one, in some degree." In another column he observed that Britain was "controlling prices by edict." He was not enthusiastic about that. He allowed that it might sound good to the average American, but that price control inevitably meant rationing.[11]

Those were technical points. Garrett's big uneasiness was at the artificiality of the boom—that it was a prosperity descended on the people like the weather, rather than something they had done for themselves. And he didn't like the reason for it. Earlier in the year he had written, "It is not good to be the only fat and prosperous people on earth, especially when so much of the increase in our incomes is Europe's loss."[12] He didn't like to see the products of American industry being "shot away out of guns." The whole idea of war and profit together was to Garrett an "abhorrent riddle." He wrote a long, historical digression on it—a strange piece for the financial section of a newspaper—ending with this:

> Who shall be so vain as to suppose that he knows the reason of things or the nature of their sequence? Life is personal. It happens to us unawares, and we react to it as the necessity is. Let us prosper if we cannot help it. Let us discuss the war price of steel."[13]

And so Garrett wrote about the price of steel, and the businessmen lit cigars over it. Still, when the nations of Europe were entrenched in a war of the like humanity had never seen, and for causes supposedly deep and historic, the motives of business troubled him:

> You may chance some day to lunch at the Banker's Club, on the top floor of the Equitable Building, the largest office building in the world. In the smoking room you will find several hundred men, after lunch, sitting in groups of two or more at tables,

and the conversation will be all of the same texture. It will be about money—how to make money, more and more. Here is gathered together each day the finest body of aggressive adventurous intelligence yet evolved in the world, an asset of the most powerful democracy on earth, and what it seeks is profit! Is that all? Is profit seeking the end of business? Second thought forbid. It is not so. What these men are seeking really is their self-expression. Profit is the symbol of success. That is not the fault of any individual. It is a reflection rather than upon the whole of this Western civilization. Our values have been wrong."

It wasn't the money Garrett admired in these men. It was their adventurous intelligence. It was the boldness of their self-expression. And these were qualities best used in a time of peace.

Chapter 11 notes

1 *New York Tribune*, March 4, 1917, sect. 3, p. 5.

2 *New York Tribune*, August 9, 1916, p. 10; September 14, p. 10.

3 *New York Tribune*, September 11, 1916, p. 8.

4 *New York Tribune*, August 21, 1916, p. 8; January 1, 1917, p. 10.

5 *New York Tribune*, November 19, 1916, section 3, p. 5; August 21, p. 8.

6 *New York Tribune*, November 6, 1916, p. 10; October 4, p. 10; January 1, 1917, p. 10.

7 *New York Tribune*, September 3, 1916, section 3, p. 4; September 24, section 4, p. 3; November 5, section 3, p. 5; November 15, p. 10.

8 *New York Tribune*, October 2, 1916, p. 10, and October 9, p. 8.

9 *New York Tribune*, August 25, 1916, p. 10.

10 *New York Tribune*, December 3, 1916, section 3, p. 5. But Garrett was also skeptical of federal officials, observing in the November 15, 1916, *Tribune* that the comptroller of the currency, John Skelton Williams, was a "romantic" who believed in solving all economic problems with cheap credit.

11 *New York Tribune*, August 15, 1916, p. 10; September 11, p. 8.

12 *New York Times,* March 5, 1916, p. 20. The editorial is unsigned, but it exactly matches his thoughts of later in the year, and I assume it is his.

13 *New York Tribune*, October 16, 1916, p. 8.

14 *New York Tribune*, November 13, 1916, p. 10.

Chapter Twelve
THE MOST INSIDIOUS

On July 1, 1917, Garrett took over as the *Tribune's* managing editor, a job that involved overseeing the editorial organization and the printers.[1] He would stay in management less than three years, but many years later, a man who knew him said Garrett had enjoyed his days at the *Tribune* more than at the *Times*. "Garrett was a man of abounding energy and courage, temperamental and decisive, who exercised great influence over the course of the paper," wrote Harry Baehr, historian of the *Tribune*.[2] The *Tribune* would take positions on public issues very different from those Garrett had taken at the *Times*, or for which Garrett would become famous later in life.

There was nothing pusillanimous about the *Tribune*. It was a nationalistic Republican paper that had been pro-war since the sinking of the *Lusitania* in May 1915. When war came, it became a belligerent guardian of national loyalty—with Garrett at the helm. His rhetorical conversion from critic to patriot seems oddly instantaneous from a view of today, when wars are no longer declared and argument against them no longer suppressed by federal law. But it was a different time. When his country went to war, Garrett was on its side unreservedly.

Carter Field, who was the *Tribune's* Washington correspondent during the Garrett years, recalled that Garrett would come to Washington to visit Baruch at the War Industries Board. "Every time," Field wrote, "he would emerge with a brand-new idea about some phase of war production that ought to be investigated."[3]

Editorially, the *Tribune* opposed a proposal for direct press censorship, but it was willing to police its own loyalty—and its competitors'. As did many other publications, it campaigned for suppressing the German-language press, German societies and the teaching of the German language in schools. It also ran a campaign against sedition. This was suggested by Post Office Solicitor William Lamar, who offered the *Tribune* information from the Post Office's files. After some hesitation, Garrett approved the arrangement with the understanding that the government would follow the *Tribune's* exposes with action.[4]

The fruit of this collaboration was an attack on William Randolph Hearst, publisher of two rival papers, the *Journal* and the *American*. On the Sundays from April 28 to June 2, 1918, a time when the German army was making its last great advance on the Western front, the *Tribune* published a series called, "Coiled in the Flag: HEAR-S-S-S-T." Its artists drew the name "Hearst" in snake scales, with a snake's head coming off the top of the "H" and its tail off the "T."

The series was written by Kenneth Macgowan, a specialist in drama who years later went to Hollywood and directed films, including *Lifeboat* (1944). Macgowan, 29, was a Garrett hire, having been introduced to Garrett four months earlier by 28-year-old Walter Lippmann.[5] Garrett probably edited Macgowan's series and as managing editor he would have had to approve it.

The series reminded readers repeatedly that Hearst had opposed American entry into the war. For example, in 1914, Hearst had ridiculed the statement by Sen. Henry Cabot Lodge, Republican of Massachusetts, that the war was a fight for liberty, free government and the rights of small nations.

On the eve of the U.S. declaration of hostilities, Hearst's *American* had said, "Let the Allies fight their own war. We did not start it, and it is none of our business to prosecute it for them."[6] The Hearst papers' line, the *Tribune* said, was "the lie that this is not America's war."[7]

Once Congress voted the declaration of war, the Hearst papers accepted it. They supported Liberty Bonds and proclaimed loyalty to Wilson. But this, the *Tribune* said, was mere "verbal camouflage."[8] Hearst, it argued, was still taking positions that were inherently defeatist. The *American* continued to oppose conscription, saying, "The American soldiers who go to France should go as volunteers."[9] The *American* also said the country was unready to fight and that it should bolster its own defenses before sending money and guns to Europe. It said U.S. war production should focus on a fleet of airplanes and submarines—a sure sign, argued the *Tribune*, that Hearst wanted to keep American boys out of the trenches. In sum, the *Tribune* complained, the Hearst papers wanted "to keep our men, money and food at home under a plea of 'America first.' "

This almost exactly describes the position Garrett would take a quarter-century later in the year and a half before the attack on Pearl Harbor. Then he would be on the side of an organization called America First, and he would say the war in Europe was "not our war." Then he would give respectful attention to Congressmen who opposed conscription, though he would reluctantly support it. Then he would say America was not ready for war, and should defend North and South America first. Then he would propose that the German threat be met by a two-ocean navy and thousands of airplanes. In 1940 and 1941 he would wave the flag for a political position that his opponents portrayed as defeatism.

In 1918 he was on the side of war. In an unsigned editorial of May 12, 1918, the *Tribune* said, "The Hearst newspapers have been the most insidious and dangerous anti-war influence in the country." It noted that Britain and France had barred the Hearst papers from the mails until the American government had prevailed on them to rescind the ban. The series went on to say that in April 1918 the U.S. Post Office had banned Hearst's German-language paper, *Deutsches Journal,* which had been "the munitions dump from which Hearst's American papers drew their most effective weapons."[10]

According to a history of the *Tribune*, Garrett had the paper urge local communities to ban Hearst's publications. At least one town, Mount Vernon, N.Y., did. In Poughkeepsie, people burned bundles of the *American,* and in defense the Hearst papers gave their newsboys little stars-and-stripes flags to wear. The Hearst papers stepped up their support of the war and of the Wilson administration. At stake was not only the newspapers, but also Hearst's political ambitions: in mid-1918 he was thinking of running for governor of New York and also had an eye on the presidency.[11]

Garrett went further. In his biography of Hearst, David Nasaw of City University of New York wrote that Garrett "prepared a brief charging Hearst with treason under the Espionage Act of 1917 and traveled to Washington, D.C., to outline his case to Attorney General Thomas Gregory."[12]

The brief, on 67 pages of plain legal-sized stationery, is not signed by Garrett or anyone else. It does not ask that Hearst be charged with treason—only that his newspapers be barred from the mails. It does make many of the same statements as the *Tribune* series: that Hearst had campaigned to stay out of the war; that once America was in it, he had argued to keep the troops at home; that he had argued that Britain and France were not really allies of the United States and that Japan was a strategic enemy; and that he had said America was free to make a separate peace with Germany. The brief cites as disloyal Hearst's favorable reception to a papal proposal for a negotiated peace. It slams Hearst for arguing, after conscription had begun, for sending volunteers only. [13]

In the conclusion, the brief says:

> Nothing short of an examination of his newspapers day by day in the light of current events treated, as they generally were, with a cunning, insidious German accent will serve to furnish a true picture of the nature and extent of his propagandistic service to Germany. [14]

Nasaw writes that in October 1918, "a federal grand jury sitting in New York City interviewed Garrett and subpoenaed a copy of his brief," but that no charges were brought. By then the war was almost over.

World War I demanded patriotism—and of a stronger brew than World War II—and Garrett, like many others, got drunk on it. A decade later, at a time of political sobriety, he wrote of war as giving people "an emotional image to which they may surrender their reason." During such a war, Garrett wrote, any man undertaking a "destructive examination" of the patriotic image would be denounced for "disloyalty to the tribal idea for which his people are giving their lives."[15]

World War I permanently soured Garrett on overseas wars for high-sounding reasons. It did not, however, erase his concern for national loyalty. At the time of World War I, the Socialist Party, which opposed the war, was more than 90 percent foreign-born, and the Communist Party, founded in 1919, was dominated by immigrants from Russia. These were foreigners trying to overthrow the government of the United States. In late 1919, when Wilson's Attorney General, A. Mitchell Palmer, began rounding up foreign-born communists and deporting them, many Americans raised an alarm over civil liberties. Garrett did not. His history, *The American*

Story, does not mention it, and one would have to assume that he did not strongly disapprove of it.

When World War II came, the loyalty issue came up again. In 1940, after Nazi Germany and Communist Russia had dismembered Poland, the *Saturday Evening Post's* editorial page, edited by Garrett, called for the banning of political organizations "subject to foreign influence," namely those Nazi and Communist.[16] And during the loyalty drive during the first year of war in Korea, Garrett wrote:

> Why do Americans embrace the Communist Party? And this is not the same as to ask why Americans embrace the philosophical idea of communism. That could be understood and there need be nothing alien about it. But an American who joins the Communist Party becomes in fact an alien.[17]

Since those days, we have learned that the Communist Party was, in fact, directed and financed largely by Moscow, which was then an enemy of the United States. To some people, that would make no difference in the rights of its members to advocate and engage in the American public square. To Garrett it did.

Chapter 12 notes
1 Garrett to Lewis H. Brown, undated, about 1942, Garrett papers.
2 Harry W. Baehr Jr., *The New York Tribune Since the Civil War*, Dodd, Mead & Co., 1936, p. 299.
3 Carter Field, *Bernard Baruch: Park Bench Statesman*, Whittlesey House, 1944, p. 163.
4 Baehr, *The New York Tribune Since the Civil War*, p. 336.
5 Walter Lippmann to Garrett, November 14, 1917. Box 11, Folder 445, Lippmann Papers, Yale University.
6 New York *American*, March 23, 1917, quoted in "Coiled in the Flag, HEARS-S-S-S-T: Trying to Scare Us Out," New York *Tribune*, May 5, 1918, Part III, p. 1.
7 *New York Tribune*, May 5, 1918, part III, p. 1.
8 *New York Tribune*, April 28, 1918, part III, p. 2.
9 *New York American*, June 29, 1917, quoted in "Coiled in the Flag: HEAR-S-S-S-S-T," New York *Tribune*, April 28, 1918, Part III, p. 1.
10 "The Roosevelt Challenge," *New York Tribune* editorial, May 12, 1918, part III, p. 2. "Coiled in the Flag, HEARS-S-S-S-T: Hearst's Late *Deutsches Journal*," *New York Tribune*, June 2, 1918, Part III, p. 1.
11 W.A. Swanberg, *Citizen Hearst*, Charles Scribner's Sons, 1961, p. 312; Ben Procter, *William Randolph Hearst: The Later Years 1911-1951,* Oxford University Press, 2007, pp. 66-67, advance reading copy; Baehr, *The New York Tribune Since the Civil War*, p. 343.
12 David Nasaw, *The Chief: The Life of William Randolph Hearst,* Houghton Mifflin, 2000, pp. 269-270.
13 The quote is from Hearst's Garrett-Gregory correspondence, October 7, 1918. Case file 9140-4561, record group 165, stack area 370, row 72, compartment 26, shelf 2. Military Intelligence Division Correspondence, National Archives, Washington, D.C., p. 44-49, 56, 58.
14 Ibid, p. 66.
15 SEP, "Peace-Building," July 28, 1928.
16 SEP, "Fifth Column," August 3, 1940.
17 "Writings of the Apostates," (review of *Men Without Faces: The Communist Conspiracy in the U.S.A.,* by Louis Francis Budenz) *American Affairs,* October 1950, p. 232.

Chapter Thirteen
THE OTHER PART OF HIMSELF

Garrett's romances are mostly unrecorded. He and Ida, his second wife, separated in 1914. She sued him for separate maintenance and he sued for annulment on the grounds that she had had an earlier husband. The annulment was not granted—and he remained married to Ida until 1947, though only on paper. His life was that of a bachelor.[1]

That this was not entirely what he wanted is suggested by a unique document in his papers: a play called, "That Satan Said." As far as we know, it is the only play he wrote and was never performed. It is undated, but its references to Bolsheviks and anarchist plots, and also to the *Tribune,* which became the *Herald-Tribune* in 1924, place it around 1920. The play sheds light on Garrett's attitude toward women and romance, and toward great personal wealth. The careful reader will also find references to Garrett's own life, the most obvious being the play's shrewish woman, who the narrator describes as "a fat, hot little urn, set upon tiny feet, full of wrath and overflowing." Says one of the minor characters, "Her name is Ida. All Idas are like that when they get stirred up."[2]

The play's main character is Rex Bull—"bull" as in "bulls and bears"—who is a cooper's son who left home at age 12 and made a fortune in Wall Street. In the first act, Bull is dealing with requests for money. One is from a newlywed couple from his hometown. Another is from a campaigner against vice. Bull gives the couple a credit for a kitchen appliance. He feigns an interest in the vice crusader but gives him only a dollar. Opening a letter from the National Institute for Pure Government, he scans it and tosses it to his assistant, Jotape. "You join, Jotape," he says. "You believe in pure government."[3]

"I don't fool myself," Bull says. "Giving is vanity. It's the feeling you get out of it yourself—that's what makes you give."

Bull keeps an unmarried girlfriend on a string by providing her with an apartment, a servant and a car. The woman would like to marry him but knows she will not. She moons after his fabulous string of black pearls, which he keeps in a safe in his office, permitting her to wear it only on occasion. The woman is Ida's successor. Ida was dismissed because she became "fat in all the wrong places," and demanding and shrill.

Bull admits to being "a perfect sucker with women, an ass, a perfect damn idiot." As the play begins, Bull's lawyer explains, "A rich man is bound to become callous in the life of his heart. With all his wealth he cannot buy what a woman gives."[4]

Bull has an unexpected visitor who has come to interview him for the Sunday supplements. Her name is Megan. Garrett describes her thus:

> She is small, vital and free. Her face is wide and her eyes have an amused, quizzical expression. Her dress, which is black and daringly simple, with a large white collar, gives her a naïve, unsophisticated appearance. She is fearless, friendly and emotionally intact. Her loveliness is accidental in the point of view, like the prismatic colors in a crystal. It is all in how you look at her. What makes her irresistible is a

contradiction. There is about her an air of elfish inaccessibility, combine with amazing audacity. She is provocative apparently without knowing how or why."[5]

This is the woman Garrett would have wanted to marry: a working woman, "fearless, friendly and emotionally intact."

Bull complains about the people who come groveling for cash, and Megan perceives that his wealth has not made him happy. She says to him, "What would you give to be poor?"

Bull replies that sometimes he thinks he would like to lose all his wealth and start over. Megan shakes her head. "You would only be a rich man without money," she says. What she meant was to have no desire for wealth.

Bull changes the subject, and asks about her. He is surprised to discover that she is a freelance, and has money only when she sells a story. He asks her if she has always had enough to eat. She replies, ecstatically:

> Once when I first came to New York, a year ago or so, I was hungry. That was a wonderful experience. I wouldn't have missed it for anything I can imagine. To be hungry like a wild thing! I suppose you don't know what that's like? [6]

Recall Garrett's story about being hungry in Chicago, and that he did not say how he coped with it. In the play, Megan recalls finding a five-dollar bill on the street.

Bull tests her by draping his string of black pearls around her neck. She allows him to do it, but keeps her professional attention on him. Just then Ida bursts in, shrieks her resentment at Bull, rips the necklace off Megan's neck, spilling the pearls on the floor.

A few minutes later, Bull and Megan are alone again.

MEGAN: Do you prefer them wild or do they get that way?

BULL: They can't help it. I spoil them.

MEGAN. With too much loving kindness.

BULL. How did you know?[7]

Bull goes on about how cruelty makes women tame and kindness makes them wild, and such nonsense, and finally gets personal:

A man wants only one woman. Everything he has in the world he would give to find her—that one, the other part of himself. But she either does not exist or has been so widely scattered by the life accidents of a million years that he finds her in fragments, a glimpse of her here and a thought of her there and never enough in any one place to be satisfied with.[8]

That was Garrett speaking for himself. A few years later, Garrett wrote to an old friend:

You make the same mistake with me that I make with women. A woman is either a saint or a witch, and no middlings; I know better. They are all middlings, only I can't take them that way.[9]

In the play, Bull falls for Megan and she resists him. To another woman, Megan says, "I am not for sale as a wife," and to him she says, "I wouldn't marry you for the world." But in the end he genuinely does lose his interest in wealth, and curses the world, life, death and himself.

Then she takes him. She says, "What's cursed is people's way with money—the way of those who have it and that of those who want it—all thinking it will buy what life has priced in terms of love and sorrow."[10]

There were several women in Garrett's life, but Megan was only a fantasy. She did express Garrett's attitude toward personal wealth, which is not exactly that of "profit's prophet."

Chapter Thirteen notes

1 "Garrett Shot Defying Bandit, Recovery Likely," *New York Herald Tribune*, January 20, 1930, p. 4.; "Hunt Bandit Suspect in Garrett Shooting," *New York Times,* January 20, 1930, p. 14.

2 *That Satan Said,* Garrett papers, bMS Am 1481 (67), Houghton Library, pp. 27, 3.

3 *That Satan Said*, pp. 7, 22.

4 *That Satan Said*, p. 4.

5 *That Satan Said*, p. 20.

6 *That Satan Said*, p. 24.

7 *That Satan Said,* p. 30.

8 *That Satan Said,* pp. 31-32.

9 Garrett to Lincoln Steffens, undated, about 1930, Lincoln Steffens Papers, series II, catalogued correspondence, reel 1, Rare Book and Manuscript Library, Columbia University.

10 *That Satan Said,* pp. 88-89.

Chapter Fourteen
NOTHING WE NEED

In 1915, Garrett had written, "War is transient and has no future. Trade is permanent."[1] But World War I changed Garrett's thoughts about trade.

In November 1919 he quit the *Tribune* and began working on *The Blue Wound*. It is Garrett's take on the history of man leading up to World War I, told mostly as fantasy and parable, with a final chapter of apocalyptic science fiction. The book is narrated in the first person. The narrator, a journalist, meets the mysterious figure Mered (a Biblical name meaning "rebellion"), who takes him through a journey of time and space, like Scrooge in *The Christmas Carol*. The narrator and Mered fly from ancient civilizations to the future of 1950, when Germany starts a war with the United States, spreading fire on the land from New York City to Pittsburgh with a chemical weapon. In Garrett's tale, Germany is able to do this because it has developed a modern chemical industry and America has not.

The message of *The Blue Wound* is that "peace and security lie in self-containment,"[2] meaning national autarky. This was not an idea natural to capitalism, but to war. Garrett turned it around, and applied it to a country that wished to stay out of other people's wars. Be self-sustaining, and you have nothing economic to fight about. Repeatedly when his country was under pressure, he would argue that it could get along without foreign suppliers. In the pit of the Depression in 1933, when the Europeans were playing beggar-thy-neighbor with devaluations and gold repudiation, Garrett wrote, "There is nothing—almost nothing—in Europe that we need." After France fell to the Wehrmacht in 1940 he wrote, "We are the most nearly self-contained nation of modern times."[3]

After World War I, Garrett argued for a connection between the machine, which he called "the will of man engined,"[4] and war. Probably the most philosophical, and abstruse, piece in his 20 years at the *Post* was his 1928 article, "Machine People," an essay on the existential meaning of industrial equipment. He also wrote a book about it: *Ouroboros, or the Mechanical Extension of Mankind* (1926). In this view, the people with machines needed other people, without machines, to supply raw materials and buy the machines' surplus. Before World War I there had been only six machine-wielding countries—Britain, France, Belgium, Germany, the United States and Japan—and they had done that kind of trade. It was fundamentally an exploitative trade, Garrett thought, because the machine people would get most of the benefit out of it. But it had worked. After World War I, however, the machine had broken free of the six countries, and any country could have it. The game of exploitation was up.

Several times Garrett recalled a luncheon in London in which Lord Astor had turned to him and said, "Do you know, as the result of the war many countries now have industries that are not entitled to have them." And Garrett replied: "How does an Englishman determine what countries are entitled to have industry?"[5]

If every country had machines, Garrett feared, each would try to sell each other the same things. In the 1920s Germany was required to pay its reparations to Britain and France in gold. It didn't have gold. And how could Germany earn the gold except by selling lots of machine-made goods to Britain,

France and the United States? But those countries did not want German goods in their home markets. Germany could sell in foreign markets, but those were the same markets Britain, France and the United States were relying on, and they didn't want the Germans elbowing them out of them, either. Thus World War I was followed by an ominous economic rivalry.

Self-containment might be a way out, but was it possible? Garrett had been to wartime Germany. The pundits had said in 1914 that Germany hadn't the resources for a long war, but in December 1915 it had seemed to Garrett that the economically isolated Germans were doing fine. They had replaced copper wire with zinc. They had replaced saltpeter, which had been imported from Chile, with nitrogen fixed from the air.[6] Rubber had been a problem; they had not yet figured out how to synthesize it. But surely someone would engineer that.

For Germany, autarky was a necessity of war. But if trade had been one of the *causes* of war, as Woodrow Wilson had said, and trade in standard machine goods was not necessary, then, Garrett wrote, "the idea of economic necessity, wanton mother of wars, is false."[7] Nations could have self-containment and peace.

Later in the 1920s the thought of war receded, and Garrett considered the more common economic arguments for trade protection. Already he had credited tariffs for jump-starting the American steel industry, the tin-plate industry, and for Japan's rise as an industrial power.[8] In 1924 he argued that America needed to provide a protected market for the cargo ships built with taxpayer money during World War I, else the people's investment would be entirely worthless. In a letter, he allowed that "these are not the right sort of boats" for a modern merchant marine, and that economic necessity for protection was debatable, "whereas the true necessity is political." [9]

In 1928 he suggested controls on capital exports, because private American finance was making sovereign loans abroad without regard to the risks.[10] He did not pursue the idea of capital controls, but it was notable that he would offer it.

Garrett was right about the quality of the sovereign loans: many a small-town American bank collapsed because it had bought too many Argentine bonds. He was wrong, though, about trade. I find national self-containment the least attractive of his ideas, and toward the end of his life he made less of it. Still, he repeated it in *A Time Is Born* (1944), which in part is a rewrite of *The Blue Wound* and *Ouroboros*. In this wartime book he imagined a world of peaceful states made economically self-contained through such technology as plastics, synthetic rubber and gasohol.

If he were alive today, Garrett might be attracted much more than most free-marketers to the idea of energy self-sufficiency. Faced with a foreign war to put the Middle East's petroleum into friendly hands, Garrett would be drawn powerfully to the idea of creating energy at home. He wrote in 1936 in favor of grain alcohol, which he called "the fuel crop,"[11] and one can imagine him today being tempted by biodiesel.

Seldom, however, did Garrett raise the argument of modern protectionists who say Americans cannot compete with low-wage labor. Once time he did was in 1925, when he asked the finance minister of Mussolini's Italy how that country could compete with industrial rivals by producing the same products. The minister's answer was, "A man can live on less in Italy than anywhere else." That idea, Garrett thought, led to a world in which all nations were "sunk in misery."[12] Here was the race-to-the-bottom thesis so popular with today's Left. Garrett presented it as a possibility only, because the world was not sinking into misery, nor was high-wage America having trouble competing.

Sometimes Garrett could sound like a free trader. Describing the world cotton trade in 1927, he wrote: "We meet the low-wage labor of the world with high-wage labor and beat it by superior methods."[13] Late in his career, describing the trade in wheat, he wrote, "It moved with the ease of the tides, by rail to tidewater, by boat to all the ports of the world, supply seeking demand, magnetically... The free grain trade was one of the wonderful mechanisms of the modern world."[14]

In 1950 he made a distinction between free trade and the freedom *of* trade. *Free* trade meant a border without barriers to foreigners. To Garrett foreigners had no rights in the matter; it was an American question, to be decided on the facts at hand, and a barrier might be to the American advantage. The freedom *of* trade was different. That, he said, "means that people should be free to produce and exchange wealth with other people as they please, and make their own bargains at their own risk, with no direct intervention of government."[15] He approved of that. The alternative, to have government take trade out of private hands operating for private profit, would be to operate trade "for national profit in the hands of armed and sovereign states."[16]

Twice, in 1928 and 1940, Garrett argued that the economic motive for war, including a war for markets, was no longer valid. The second of those essays, "War Has Lost Its Pocket," is my favorite. It contains some of his best anecdotes, from his meeting with Walter Rathenau to an interview with a bank burglar—and also some fine argument. Here he responded to the defenders of Germany who said it had had to go to war because its industry was deprived of raw materials and markets:

Never was Germany denied access to raw materials at the world price—the same as was paid by

everyone else... It is true that she has to buy raw
materials and that what she has to buy them with is
her technical skill in the form of manufactured
goods; but that is also true of Belgium, for example.
There were no more barriers in the world against
German goods than against Belgian goods until, in
this country, we raised tariffs against Germany to
compensate for the subsidies she gave her own
exporters...[17]

All of this was part of making an argument that war was
no longer a rational economic enterprise—not for land, loot,
captive customers or captive workers. It was a far different
argument than presented in *The Blue Wound, Ouroboros* and,
later, in *A Time Is Born*. Among nations there could be trade
and peace.

Garrett never reconciled the two arguments, which lead to
opposite conclusions. They do, however, start from the same
place: an urge to stay out of war. After World War I, he never
wavered in that.

In 1928 Garrett provided an unusual blurb of recommen-
dation, as did Baruch. It was for the second printing of *The
Pallid Giant*, a lost-race story of science fiction. Its author,
Pierrepont Noyes, was an official in the occupation of the
Rhineland and son of the founder of the Oneida commune in
New York. Noyes's imaginative novel is forgotten today, but
it is a horrifying story of people who wipe themselves out. It
was said to be the first imaginary story of something like a
nuclear holocaust, but whoever said that hadn't read *The Blue
Wound*.

Chapter 14 notes

1 "Americanism," the *New York Times* lead editorial, September 27, 1915.

2 *The Blue Wound*, G.P. Putnam, 1921, p. 141.

3 SEP, "This Thing of Trade," July 1, 1933; "There Is a Star," July 20, 1940.

4 SEP, "Machine People," April 28, 1928; *The American Omen*, p. 228.

5 *A Time Is Born*, p. 193; see also SEP, "War Has Lost Its Pocket," January 13, 1940. John Tebbel has several pages on this luncheon in *George Horace Lorimer and the Saturday Evening Post* (Doubleday & Co., 1948, pp. 258-260). By Tebbel's account, the luncheon was held by Lord and Lady Astor for Lorimer, his wife Alma and Garrett to introduce Lorimer to George Bernard Shaw. In this version, it was Lorimer who said, "How does an Englishman determine" etc., and Garrett "said nothing through the entire meal, except to make an occasional sour remark." Tebbel reports that as the guests were leaving Lady Astor dropped her mask of politeness and said to Garrett, "Good-bye, you gloomy Gus."

6 *Current History*, p. 1032.

7 *The Blue Wound*, p. 141.

8 Steel: *The Cinder Buggy*, pp. 290-291; tin plate: "This World's Emotional Reaction to the Economic Curse of War," *New York Tribune*, October 8, 1916; Japan's rise: *The Blue Wound*, pp. 81-99; "Ghosts in the Trade Door," *The New Republic*, October 19, 1921.

9 SEP, "Our $3,500,000,000 Nucleus," February 2, 1924; "A Rudderless Merchant Marine," February 9, 1924; "U.S. Ships, U.S. Mud," February 16, 1924; "The Great Meaning of Ships," February 23, 1924; "U.S.S.B.S.S. Suspicion," March 1, 1924. Letters to George Lorimer, October 10 and November 29, 1923, George Lorimer Papers, Historical Society of Pennsylvania.

10 SEP, "A Tale of Thirteen Billions," March 10, 1928.

11 SEP, "The Political Curse on the Farm Problem," August 22, 1936.

12 *Ouroboros*, pp. 66-69. Garrett raised the "race to the bottom" issue in *American Affairs*, April 1946, p. 74, where he noted that average U.S. wages were two and a half times average British wages, and that in trade, "the advantage will go to the low-wage country."

13 SEP, "The Fourth Age of Agriculture," April 30, 1927.

14 "The Debacle of Planning," *American Affairs*, January 1950, p. 22.

15 *American Affairs*, January 1950.

16 SEP, "Socialism in the Red," June 16, 1934.

17 SEP, "War Has Lost Its Pocket," January 13, 1940. The earlier SEP piece referenced was, "What Has Happened to War," August 11, 1928.

Chapter Fifteen
SEIZED US DEEPLY

While he was still at the *Tribune*, Garrett was annoyed by an editorial in the *Saturday Evening Post*. Garrett wrote to the *Post's* publisher, Cyrus Curtis, "The editorials in the *Post* are rotten." [1] A few years later he would be writing those editorials himself.

The *Post* was run by George Horace Lorimer, who had taken it over when it had 1,800 subscribers. Under Lorimer, it would reach 2.9 million. In its prime, when Garrett was a regular freelance contributor, it was the most influential magazine to the middle class. It was upbeat, intelligent and unreservedly American.

Garrett's first work for the *Post*, in 1917, was fiction. It was a short story about a clerk in a bond house who figures out during the gold run of 1895 that the government is bankrupt. Several stories followed, then *The Driver*, which the *Post* serialized. The crucial publication, however, was of his first nonfiction piece, in 1922, about U.S. loans to Europe. It began a 20-year journalistic collaboration, most of it technically as a free-lance. The foreign-loans piece was the first of more than 150 articles—long articles, written for a world before television, when Americans had the patience to read.

Garrett's articles on Europe's debts expressed an American nationalism. Though he would take on other subjects, tracking the debts became a specialty.[2] It was also the subject of his first identified editorial, "Borrowers," which appeared in 1927, and prompted a note from Lorimer saying, "If we could get you to write regularly for the editorial page it would be the best in the country."[3]

The war debts were amounts the U.S. Treasury had lent Britain, France and other governments during and immediately after World War I. Apologists for Europe were saying the Europeans couldn't pay. Garrett argued that they could; their debt represented surplus wealth the United States had produced in a mere 19 months of war. Surely the British and French could repay that sum with interest over 25 years. Besides, at the same time the Europeans were telling the American people they couldn't pay old loans, they were telling Wall Street bankers their credit was good for new ones—and they were getting them. As time went on, the holders of the new, private loans became part of the lobby for canceling the old, government loans.[4]

Reading Garrett's words about the fecklessness and sophistry of Europe, one can hear the Shakespearean adage: *Neither a borrower nor a lender be.* Self-containment again. But his major theme was nationalism. America had made the loans, and it was in America's interest not to accept deadbeats' excuses.

In March 1923, when the Reichsmark sank to 40,000 to the dollar, the *Post* sent Garrett to Germany to cover France's attempt to collect war reparations. The Germans did not want to pay. France had occupied the Ruhr with its engineers, technicians and soldiers in an attempt to force the Germans to pay. The result was an on-the-ground lesson in international finance. Years later, Garrett wrote:

> I was there. From the hotel in Essen, which had been staffed with French cooks and French servants because they were all afraid to touch German food, three army officers and an engineer took me in a

French motorcar to a water tower commanding a panoramic view. They spread out a map on which the industrial plants were marked. Over there was Stinnes, there was Thyssen, there was Krupp. Then we rushed off to visit them. Each plant was surrounded by a high brick wall; and each time we came to a gate, there was a lone German watchman, unarmed, his arm upraised, rotating his palm against us. That was enough. The Frenchmen dared not pass him. Why not? They could call their troops; they could knock down the walls. Yes; but they knew that at a signal a few Germans could wreck the machines, and it would take them only five minutes to do it.[5]

The determination of the Germans impressed him. They hadn't received anything of value from France, they didn't feel they owed the French anything, and they weren't going to pay.

Britain and France were beginning to make noises about not paying the United States. The money they had borrowed had been raised by the sale of Liberty Bonds to the American people. If the British and French taxpayers didn't pay, the American taxpayer would have to pay, because Liberty Bonds were U.S. government obligations. Garrett explained this financial reality to the *Post's* readers, and argued that Americans should not be so indulgently internationalist as to side with the Europeans against themselves. Like those Germans at the factory gates, Americans should defend their own legitimate interests.

To Baruch, Garrett wrote:

Privately, I wish there was some way to get rid of the debts; but to cancel them and give away our face at the same time—that is too much. Sincerely I believe we are trying to do a new thing in the world, and it behooves us to have both pride and theory in the effort, whereas we are fed up instead with a sordid, mean European opinion of our conduct.[6]

To Garrett, and also to Lorimer, the debt issue was a continuation of the whole internationalist way of thinking—that it was America's job to take the viewpoint of other countries instead of its own. He summed it up a decade later:

> It seized us deeply during the war. It carried us into the war. We were going to save Europe from Germany, the German people from the Hohenzollerns, little nations from big ones, and all the people in Europe from the curse of war forever. There were other motives, to be sure. We had money on the side of the Allies, though by such measures as we now use it was very little. Our sympathies went to the Allies. We hated the way Germans made war. Some of us may have been a little afraid of a German Europe. Allied propaganda to get us in had its great effect. Yet for all of this we should never have gone in without the emotional thought images that made a crusade of it…
>
> The allied nations were not interested in our thought images… We could be as romantic as we liked, only so we came in on their side, for unless we did the war was lost. They were not themselves fighting to make the world safe for democracy, nor to end war forever… They were fighting to beat Germany, and with American assistance they did beat her. None of the things we thought we were fighting for came out. What survived was a continuing sense of obligation to save Europe.[7]

From World War I through the 1930s Garrett had the closest contacts he ever would with high politicians. As an executive of the *Tribune*, Garrett had discussed with former Secretary of State Elihu Root and Sen. Henry Cabot Lodge whether to ratify the League of Nations treaty.[8] When President Harding died, Garrett went to meet the new president, Calvin Coolidge. Garrett wanted to discuss the series he was writing on the merchant marine. They talked for an hour—or, at least Garrett talked; "Silent Cal" didn't say much. To Lorimer, Garrett wrote:

> I can't make Coolidge out. He makes very few sounds and the wrong ones. I could easily believe he has more strength than has been revealed. I overran my time and stopped. He said, "Go on." And that was all he said, except to ask me suddenly where I was born... He said one other thing. He interrupted me to ask how I knew a certain thing to be so. I told him. He nodded and said again, "Go on."[9]

Coolidge did not run in 1928. Lorimer's candidate in that election was Herbert Hoover, the mining engineer and hero of war relief in World War I who had been Coolidge's Secretary of Commerce. In March, Lorimer spent an evening with Hoover in Washington, D.C., then wrote Garrett that the candidate needed help. "I wish you could take a day or two off and run down there and give him a little advice about just such things as this *New York Tribune* dinner." Garrett did talk to Hoover, who had grown up in Iowa 50 miles from Garrett's hometown of Burlington. Garrett wrote a colorful piece on Hoover's youth and career, picturing him as a hands-on, can-do manager of enterprises both private and public, an American from the heartland.[10]

Hoover won the presidency, and felt such gratitude to the *Post* that he offered to name Lorimer ambassador to Britain, a post the editor declined. Hoover also sent a post-election thank-you telegram to Garrett, and was a friend of Garrett's for life. [11]

In his 1920s articles in the *Post*, Garrett spoke for American nationalism on issues other than the debts. In 1924, Garrett supported the law shutting down free immigration—a law that stayed in force 41 years. Accepting the world's tired, poor and tempest-tossed was another obligation Americans supposedly had. But immigrants, Garrett argued, did not think like Americans, which made them trouble:

> The new immigration is in a notable degree wage-conscious. Its point of view is proletarian. Previously there had been no proletariat in this country. The word was not current in the language until after the tide of migrating humanity began to rise from the south and east of Europe. There is still in the United States no proletariat but this.[12]

Socialism had been introduced in America by German speakers, and many Americans identified socialism as an un-American ideology. Garrett did; he called it "Old World socialism."[13] At the end of his life Garrett regretted the pre-World War I immigration: it had diluted America's individualist culture. By the 1950s it was politically incorrect to say so, and he had a few paragraphs redolent of racial resentment at the end of a 400-page book. From the viewpoint of the 1950s, the shut-off of immigration in 1924 had been too late. The "copper woman," he wrote, "had done her work."[14]

In 1930 Lorimer asked Garrett what he thought should be done with the Philippines. "I think we should give them up," Garrett said. Lorimer agreed,[15] and sent Garrett there to do a series. He came back with a changed mind. Visiting with the Americans in Manila—and the Filipinos—convinced him that the Filipinos were not ready for self-rule, though educated

Filipinos were demanding it reproachfully. Once again foreigners were trying to make Americans feel guilty, and Garrett wasn't buying it.

But there was a problem with this view. To keep the islands permanently would require Americanizing them, and that project was not going well. The culture of the Filipino was Malay, and it was different from ours. For example, the way a Filipino took to education: "Instead of taking it to be the means whereby one may rise in the world, he takes a degree to mean that he is already risen," Garrett wrote. "Education becomes an end it itself, a patent of caste." To Garrett, who had hardly been schooled at all, such a thought was inside out.

Garrett wrote that what the Philippines needed were "merchants, tradesmen, manufacturers, elementary technicians and skilled mechanics." The American-provided education was producing "an absurd inflation" of professionals and bureaucrats, while the "skilled mechanics are imported from China and Japan."[16]

For a nationalist of Garrett's stripe, the correct position on the Philippines was the one he had begun with: give them up. Let them go their own way and devise their own system. In his final book, written after Philippine independence, he admitted that the moral argument for keeping the Philippines had been specious.[17]

He still saw the Philippine question from an American point of view. Whether our imperialism was good or bad for them was not his first concern. It was bad for us.

Chapter 15 notes

1 *George Horace Lorimer and the Saturday Evening Post,* pp. 122-123.

2 SEP, "Notes on the War Debts," November 25, 1922. He returned to these themes in "On Saving Europe," February 24, 1923; "What a Demagogue Knows," February 7, 1925; "France Mends Her Stocking With Magic Thread," March 28, 1925; "Telling Europe's Fortune," May 23, 1925; "Public Debts and Private Loans," August 21, 1926; "The French Crisis," August 28, 1926; "The Apologetic American," September 18, 1926; "A Primer of Propaganda," January 15, 1927; "The League of Debtors," February 12, 1927; "A Tale of Thirteen Billions," March 12, 1928; "Uncle Sam Learning the Debtor's Lesson," July 4, 1931; "The Rescue of Germany," September 26, 1931; "As Noble Lenders," October 17, 1931, and "Opening the Golden Goose," December 12, 1931.

3 Lorimer to Garrett, November 21, 1927, Lorimer papers, the Historical Society of Pennsylvania. The magazine went to press about a month before the cover date. The obvious editorial to which this refers is "Borrowers," in the Dec. 24, 1927, issue.

4 In the 1940s, Garrett felt vindicated in his belief that Germany could have paid. "In view of what Germany was able to do in preparation for World War II, it was nonsense to say that she couldn't pay reparations on account of World War I," he wrote in "John Maynard Keynes," *American Affairs*, July 1946.

5 SEP, "War Has Lost Its Pocket," January 13, 1940. For Garrett's original report on his visit to the Ruhr see SEP, "The Black Grail of Europe," May 5, 1923.

6 Garrett to Baruch, February 12, 1927. Baruch papers, Princeton.

7 SEP, "On Saving Europe," October 17, 1931. See also *A Bubble that Broke the World*, Little, Brown, 1932, p. 66.

8 *The American Story*, pp. 217-225.

9 Garrett to Lorimer, undated, probably Dec. 13-18, 1923, Lorimer Papers.

10 SEP, "Hoover of Iowa and California," June 2, 1928.

11 *George Horace Lorimer and the Saturday Evening Post*, p. 193; Hoover to Garrett, telegram, November 7, 1928. Garrett papers.

12 SEP, "Lo, the Native American," August 8, 1924.

13 *The People's Pottage*, Caxton, 1953, p. 85. In a short story he also speaks of "the importation of foreign ideas along with hordes of European workers." SEP, "Red Night," April 3, 1920.

14 *The American Story,* p. 396.

15 *George Horace Lorimer and the Saturday Evening Post*, p. 123.

16 SEP, "Our Asiatic Attribute," February 7, 1931, p. 122.

17 *The American Story*, p. 177.

Chapter Sixteen
TAMED A THING

Apart from the foreign debts, Garrett's favorite topic in the 1920s was agriculture—and on that topic he took a much less nationalist approach. [1] Farming, then the occupation of a quarter of the American people, was a domestic issue, and there he was a believer in individualism.

The farmer was lord of his land, suspicious of the city man and his money power, and of the country banker, who was the local conduit of the money power. In the 1890s farmers had campaigned for Bryan and free silver. In 1916 the Wilson administration had given them the system of federal land banks, a measure that had been denounced by the *New York Times*. It was surely Garrett speaking when the *Times* said there was an idea among the people, particularly the farmers, that "they are born with a right of access to unlimited amounts of cheap capital."

> The farmer wants to be subsidized. He wants to be able to command money at low rates of interest, as a free political person, instead of having to borrow it from a banker who can be disagreeable about the details. He doesn't want to be watched like a slave. He wants to be trusted entirely. He is an individualist in his own case, and yet as naïve as a Socialist about

the impersonal, anonymous power of the State to practice unbounded benevolence.[2]

The land banks, Garrett wrote, would create "an enormous inflation of farm land values." Such an inflation was under way already on account of the war, and it continued. War inflated agriculture and peace deflated it. The farmers who had borrowed against their inflated land were left in a precarious position, and in the 1920s there began a campaign for farm relief.

The heartland of the campaign was where the speculative bubble had made the loudest pop—the upper Great Plains. Garrett went there, and on April 12, 1924, the *Post* published his first report on agriculture, "That Pain in Our Northwest."

To illustrate it, the *Post* ran a photo of North Dakota's state-owned flourmill, which had been built during the administration of the Nonpartisan League. The *Post* ran photos of one-horse banks that had been abandoned. Agriculture had cultivated a delusion, Garrett said. There was nothing permanently wrong with it. An adjustment was needed, and did not require help from the government.

Farming interests, hoping for sympathy, were infuriated at the *Post's* criticism. Lorimer received an angry letter from H.A. Nestos, North Dakota's governor, who was particularly incensed at Garrett's description of the early Scandinavian pioneers. Garrett had written:

> They are a strange, unaccountable people, both credulous and suspicious in morbid degree, with the brooding fatalism of a one-crop mentality, a Nordic belief in imitative magic, and no sense of humor.[3]

The governor's other argument was that Garrett had ignored the farmers' progress, and had painted the picture worse than it was.

From his home in Egg Harbor, N.J., Garrett wrote a reply. He didn't defend his line about the strange, unaccountable people with no sense of humor, which was likely an opinion from his boyhood in Iowa. As for the gloom, it was from the farmers themselves. *They* had come to Washington, D.C., parading a disaster. *They* had said the land had been weakened from single-cropping, and that they needed money from the government. The *Post* had pointed out that single-cropping was their mistake, and that they could rectify it.

The governor wrote a calmer reply, and Garrett responded that he would come back later that year.[4] He did, and he made a report on crop diversification. The original crop had been wheat, he wrote, and many farmers had gone too long without planting something else. They had not husbanded the land; they had *mined* it. Now they were ruined. No injection of government credit could save them, because they already owed too much. These farmers would lose their capital. Really they had already lost it. But farming would go on, led by those who had bought land intelligently and farmed it intelligently. What Garrett saw in the Upper Plains was that success and failure were side by side, with only a fence between them. "The difference," wrote Garrett, "is owing, as a rule, to what people have elected to do with their opportunities, their lands and their lives."[5]

Where others saw a "farm problem" that applied to farmers generally, Garrett saw economic conditions to which some farmers had adjusted and some hadn't. The difference between the successful and unsuccessful was partly debt, partly technology, partly management and partly attitude. A North Dakota study had estimated the cost of growing wheat to vary from 80 cents a bushel to $7, depending on the farm. "There is no conceivable price for wheat that would make wheat growing profitable for all of them," Garrett wrote.[6]

The political idea was to help them all. In the mid-1920s it coagulated into the McNary-Haugen Bill, a measure that was supposed to solidify prices so that farmers would not have to bear a loss. But the threat of loss, Garrett argued, was necessary. It was "the only natural restraint upon overproduction."

In the mid-1920s the McNary-Haugen Bill languished, and the agitation for it continued.

Later in the decade Garrett surveyed agriculture again and concluded that its fundamental problem was the farmers who had not learned modern ways:

> They cannot have what they have learned to want—automobiles, movies, plumbing, radiant heat, silk stockings for the women, electric appliances in the kitchen, telephones and radios—without impressing the soil in a scientific manner, increasing their power upon it by mechanical extensions, and adopting the methods of sound business management—that is, to be efficient. And the fact is that agriculture contains a very large number of farmers who are not equal to it. They are the problem.[7]

Congress passed the McNary-Haugen Bill, and President Coolidge vetoed it.

In 1929 Hoover became president. He signed a related bill, the Agricultural Marketing Act, which set up the Federal Farm Board with power to play the futures markets to stabilize the price. Garrett had opposed such measures, and years later he said he had opposed this one.[8] But the *Post* had supported Hoover, and when the law was new Garrett was no more than wary. "Almost unawares we have entered a road of original episodes," he wrote. "No one knows the way of it or the end of it."[9]

In a 1927 piece on McNary-Haugen, Garrett had argued that any attempt to guarantee farm incomes would entail crop controls. "It would mean that a farmer could not break open a new field or change the character of his production without a permit," he wrote.[10] Hoover's law didn't have crop controls, and it failed when the program ran out of money.

In 1933 came Franklin Roosevelt, who brought in the sort of controls Garrett had foreseen. By 1936 the New Deal was paying farmers to keep 30 million acres out of production in order to raise prices. But at the same time, it was trying to bring *into* production millions of acres of desert through irrigation—speeding up a program that had been started by Theodore Roosevelt in 1902. Garrett argued that it made no sense to invest millions to irrigate land where it didn't rain while paying farmers not to grow crops where it did rain.

Everywhere the farmer was the drowning man to be saved. Where in this drama of political rescue was the vision of the hardy pioneer, facing his own difficulties? He was no myth. He had been real. "The fact he is scarce is easily explained," Garrett wrote. "He would never have come to exist at all in a state that had been willing to do everything for him."[11]

By 1938 Garrett had been writing about the farm problem for 14 years. He had seen almost everything during that time. "One thing I have never seen," he said. "I have never seen a good farmer with a good wife in a state of failure."[12]

In 1939 he wrote of his own farm, which he had bought at Tuckahoe near Atlantic City, New Jersey, in the mid-1920s.[13] For years, he said, he had been sharing the work of his farm with a tenant:

> This year I rented the farm to him—the land, the buildings, the power equipment, the livestock, the orchard, the house he lives in, and all, for the total consideration of one dollar plus maintenance... If my advice will only keep him away from the Government lending agencies that are tempting him to go into debt, I daresay he will make some money. As I watch him I notice that he uses the tractor much less and the mules much more, having learned already the three-

mule hitch. Only once have I seen him use the truck to haul cornstalks to idle mules in the pasture, and then I called his attention to it. I notice that he is buying less fertilizer in bags, whereas formerly, when we were halving the cost, he was lavish with it; instead he has bought from a bean grower in the county a great quantity of rotted bean vines at a few cents per ton. Lastly, he hires less labor and puts his own hand more heavily into it.[14]

The farmers who asked for federal relief often pointed to the railroads, which they relied upon and often complained about. The railroads had been the first industry to live with federal control of prices, service and labor relations. Having accepted responsibility for the railroads, the government had acted to keep them profitable, ordering system-wide increases in rates. The farmers claimed that the government had guaranteed the railroads' profit—which, by the 1920s, was substantially true.

The railroads had not begun that way. Some had been given free land, but they were otherwise at liberty. They had grown, Garrett wrote, "by uncontrollable chance and by circumstance." The rates they had charged for hauling seemed to make no rational sense, and many farmers hated them for what looked like discrimination. A haul from Chicago to Seattle was cheaper than Chicago to Spokane, which was *on the way* to Seattle. And yet, wrote Garrett, "in confusion there is rhythm."[15] The freight moved. If you inquired into the why of a certain rate, there was always a reason. It was not disorder really. It *looked* like disorder. (It is the same with airline fares today.)

In the 20th century the government had taken over the railroads' business decisions, promising the shippers fairness and rationality. The result was a wild thing tamed. "When you have tamed a thing you become responsible for it, since it cannot any longer be responsible for itself. You have to feed it, warm it, look to its health and guide it," Garrett wrote.[16] A railroad could no more lower rates without permission than it could raise them. That was what ultimately came of rate regulation, the idea Garrett had accepted a decade before. "In exchange for security, the railroads have delivered their independence, the very life of their industry, into the keeping of the government."[17]

Those words were written not in an article about railroads, but about farming. Garrett's argument was that the railroads had lost their freedom, and that farmers, if they accepted federal aid, would lose theirs, too. Let in the government, he argued, and "you could not sow and reap as you pleased. You would be held to so much of this and so much of that. There might be the blessing of security; it would involve the sacrifice of independence."

Most ominous was that once it was done, the people got used to it. Here he speaks of the railroad men:

> They hate the tame life, of course. Yet it has its points and on the whole they prefer it, no matter what they say. When fierce and vocal longing for the other life is upon one of the older railroad men you can always stop him by asking: "Well, would you abolish the Interstate Commerce Commission?" He faces suddenly the other way, thinks for a while and says, "No. What I would do—" and it turns out invariably to be an ideal Interstate Commerce Commission. He has remembered all at once what the wild life was like to be lived—the strife, the greed, the speculation, the insecurity... There was no mean. There was either ecstasy or panic. The business now may be unprofitable; then it was not solvent. Never before regulation was railroading in general a solvent business.[18]

But it had been a glorious and wonderful business. In the 1920s, farming was still. A man was a lord on his farm. He could grow anything he wanted, in any quantity.

Chapter 16 notes

1 SEP, "Fifty-Year Crisis in Agriculture," April 19, 1924; "Bringing Up The Northwest," October 11, 1924; "Exposing the Farm Problem," November 8, 1924; "The Tale of Uncle Sam's Voyage in an Irrigating Ditch," January 17, 1925; "McNary-Haugenism," April 2, 1927; "Industry, Agriculture & Co.," April 16, 1927; "The Fourth Age of Agriculture," April 30, 1927; "The Land Belonging," May 14, 1927; "Iowa's Debts and Credits," May 28, 1927; "The Revolution in Agriculture," September 29, 1928; "The Corn Belt," October 6, 1928; "Farming With Security and Independence," October 13, 1928; "The New Picture of Agriculture," May 11, 1929; "Farm Relief So Far," June 21, 1930; "The Curse of Plenty," July 18, 1931; "Notes of These Times: The Farmer," November 12 and 19, 1932; "The Boll Evil," December 29, 1934; "Saving Agriculture," October 19, 1935; "Managed Agriculture," November 2, 1935; "Plowing Up Freedom," November 16, 1935; "The AAA Experiment in the Birth Control of Wealth," July 25, 1936; "Agricultural Excursions," August 8, 1936; "The Political Curse on the Farm Problem," August 22, 1936; "Roads Going South," September 3, 1938; "Give Us This Day," June 24, 1939; "The AAA in Its Own Dust Bowl," March 2, 1940.
2 "Subsidizing the Farmer," *New York Times*, May 8, 1916, p. 10.
3 SEP, "That Pain in Our Northwest," April 12, 1924.
4 H.A. Nestos to Lorimer, April 15, 1924; Garrett to Nestos, April 28, 1924; Nestos to Garrett, May 2, 1924; Garrett to Nestos, May 10, 1924. Lorimer papers.
5 SEP, "Bringing Up the Northwest," October 11, 1924.
6 SEP, "Exposing the Farm Problem," November 8, 1924.
7 SEP, "The New Picture of Agriculture," May 11, 1929.
8 SEP, "Roads Going South," September 3, 1938.
9 SEP, "Farm Relief So Far," June 21, 1930.
10 SEP, "McNary-Haugenism," April 2, 1927.
11 SEP, "The Tale of Uncle Sam's Voyage in an Irrigating Ditch," January 17, 1925.
12 SEP, "Roads Going South," September 3, 1938.
13 A letter from writer Elias Tobenkin to Garrett, December 8, 1926, thanks Garrett "for your letter with the quotation from Mr. MacRae." Garrett's letter

quoting publisher John MacRae, dated "Nov. 24," presumably 1926, is stamped, "Tuckahoe, N.J." Elias Tobenkin Papers, University of Texas, Austin. Garrett's letters regarding his "Pain in the Northwest" article, written in April and May 1924, are datelined Egg Harbor, N.J.

14 SEP, "Give Us This Day," June 24, 1939.

15 SEP, "The Natural History of Railroads," October 3, 1925. See also "Taming the Railroads," October 10, 1925, and "The Railroad Apple," October 24, 1925. Garrett explored the effect of government control of railroad labor relations in SEP, "Peace on the Rails," September 3, 1939.

16 SEP, "Taming the Railroads." October 10, 1925.

17 SEP, "Farming with Security and Independence," October 13, 1928.

18 SEP, "Taming the Railroads," October 10, 1925.

Chapter Seventeen
THE NATURAL DESIGN

Americans were a people who practiced self-reliance, individualism and capitalism. Some connected these to a belief in God, though Garrett thought it more likely they were connected to the weakening of religion in the 19th century and an increased interest in "compensations here, upon this earth." But even if God were as the old faith imagined Him, and we were indeed His children, Garrett argued, He would prefer children who took care of themselves to "those who continually importune Him for favors."[1]

For Garrett, the essential American idea was self-reliance. In the 1920s he wrote that in America, "If a man...says the state owes him a living, he is ridiculed; if he insists, we know there is something wrong with him. He is a failure, a ne'er-do-well, a nuisance."[2]

Self-reliance had been the imperative in Garrett's youth, and he always believed in it. As an old man he wrote, "Let the people be; let them make their own mistakes and absorb their own troubles. Few Americans now living have any idea how strong that conviction was."[3]

Individualism was part of that, and capitalism was the system that accommodated it.

Garrett's views on individualism and capitalism are similar to Ayn Rand's, and his first real novel, *The Driver* (1922), has been compared to her *Atlas Shrugged* (1957). Rand's novel is set in the core industries of the early 20th century—railroads and steel—and has a hero named John Galt.[4] Similarly, *The Driver* concerns railroads and has a protagonist named Henry Galt; a capitalist. Garrett described Henry Galt in these words:

> His mind was not on money, primarily. He thought in terms of creative achievement.
>
> There are two regnant passions in the heart of man. One is to tear down, the other is to build up. Galt's passion was to build... Works enthralled him in light of their own magic. To see a thing with the mind's eyes as a vision in space, to give orders, then in a little while to go and find it there, existing durably in three dimensions,—that was power! ...
>
> His theory, had he been able to formulate one, would have been that any work worth doing must pay. That was the ultimate test. If it didn't pay there was something wrong. But profit was what followed as a vindication or a conclusion in logic... The profit would mind itself.[5]

Garrett's Galt doesn't exude the radicalism of a Rand hero, but he is still an industrial achiever. In the 1930s, when American literature became an acreage of the downtrodden, Garrett complained that such characters had gone missing in it, and that the literary critics "have no heroes."[6] Like *Atlas Shrugged*, *The Driver* also takes place in a time of economic collapse, in its case the depression of the 1890s. Based on the life of E.H. Harriman, it is the story of a speculator who buys control of a railroad when prices hit rock bottom, and others are in despair. It illustrates Garrett's argument that depressions end when entrepreneurs "spend money courageously when there is a surplus of things that nobody else wants."[7]

You could take that as part of an argument for capitalism, but not a moral argument, as Rand's novel was.

The Driver is not a good novel. Garrett's friend Bernard Baruch wrote in a review, "I am not competent to express myself upon its merits as a novel," but that "the great interest and the great worth of the book lies in its practical teaching on economics." More than 20 years later, John Chamberlain wrote that the book's characterization was sketchy and its psychology one-sided, and that "no critic would argue that it is even a good second-rate novel." Chamberlain found it memorable because "it gave the sense of the drive of an age." [8]

Garrett's next novel, *The Cinder Buggy* (1923), subtitled *A Fable in Iron and Steel*, is the story of the first entrepreneurs of steel who, in the 1870s, challenged the producers of iron. It is much like *The Driver*.

Garrett followed this with *Satan's Bushel* (1924), an evocative fable of the life and economics of wheat and, like *The Blue Wound*, not entirely a novel. Its central character, Dreadwind, is hardly more real than Mered. Through the story, Dreadwind dogs the real protagonist, a shadowy figure named Absalom Weaver who wanders the wheat country dispensing both wisdom and grief. At one point Weaver gives a very Rand-like speech to a group of farmers, dissuading them from the idea of agricultural cooperatives:

> "This natural elm," he began, with an admiring look at the tree, "was once a tiny thing. A sheep might have eaten it at one bite. Every living thing around it was hostile and injurious. And it survived. It grew. It took its profit. It became tall and powerful beyond the reach of enemies. What preserved it—cooperative marketing? What gave it power—a law from Congress? What gave it fullness—the Golden Rule? On what strength was it founded—a fraternal spirit? You know better. Your instincts tell you no. It saved

itself. It found its own greatness. How? By fighting. Did you know that plants fight? If only you could see the deadly, ceaseless warfare among plants, this lovely landscape would terrify you. It would make you think man's struggles tame. I will show you some glimpses of it.

"I hold up this leaf from the elm. The reason it is flat and thin is that the peaceable work of its life is to gather nourishment for the tree from the air. Therefore it must have as much surface as possible to touch the air with. But it has another work to do. A grisly work. A natural work all the same. It must fight. For that use it is pointed at the end as you see and has teeth around the edge—these.

"The first thing the elm plant does is to grow straight up out of the ground with a spear thrust, its leaves rolled tightly together. Its enemies do not notice it. Then suddenly each leaf spreads itself out and with its teeth attacks other plants; it overturns them, holds them out of the sunlight, drowns them. And this is the tree! Do you wonder why the elm plant does not overrun the earth? Because other plants fight back, each in its own way."

He goes on to describe the grass, the bramble and the honeysuckle, each silently selfish and naturally armed. Plants, he says, need to be fiercer than animals, because an animal can run. A plant cannot. A plant has to fight it out where it stands.

"The farmer is like a plant. He cannot run. He is rooted. He shall live or die on the spot. But there is no plant like a farmer. There are nobles, ruffians, drudges, drones, harlots, speculators, bankers, thieves and scalawags, all these among plants, but no idiots... Until you fight as the elm fights, think as the elm thinks, you will never be powerful and cannot be wise."[9]

All of Garrett's book-length fiction of the 1920s champions individualism in one way or another, sometimes on a plane of ideas. Consider this passage from *The Cinder Buggy:*

> The fact of oneself is an amazing unlikelihood. The biological chances against one's getting born as one is, plus the chances against any particular organism getting born at all, must have been billions to one. Yet here one is… Luck is the happy chance. The right thing happens when it is needed. It strains a point to happen. Why it happens in streaks, why it happens more to some than to others, why to a darling few it happens importunately— these are questions one asks in a rhetorical sense. There is no answer. Luck and genius may be two aspects of the same thing. Luck happens and genius happens, and there is no accounting for it.[10]

Many Americans resented the inequality of luck. Garrett did not. The difference between rich and poor, he wrote, was the result of "the disparities inherent in the human material"[11]—how smart men were, how hard they worked, what risks they took, and how well they husbanded what they earned. "The many spend," he wrote, "and the few save."[12] Inequality was a fact of nature; it was *natural*.

In that sense, Garrett's justification of capitalism was like that of Herbert Spencer, who had posited a theory of natural rights.[13] Garrett and Spencer both argued from a Darwinian premise, but Garrett applied the idea of natural selection to the system. Capitalism was dynamic, *alive*. It had arisen from life. "Never was it imposed on life as a system, or at all," Garrett wrote. "It grew out of life, not all at once but gradually, and is therefore one of the great natural designs."[14]

Garrett's views were filtered through his experience as an economic journalist. When, for example, he defined inflation as "an appropriation of private property by the arbitrary right of the state to debase its currency,"[15] he was thinking of what he had seen in Germany, where savers had been pauperized and borrowers—the farmers, the tycoons and the government—enriched.

Garrett had absorbed the writings of the economists, including some Americans not much remembered today. His authority on money was Simon Newcomb, who had brilliantly analyzed the three types of official paper currency during the Civil War—greenbacks, state bank notes and national bank notes—and declared that it was "the actual volume of the entire mass of currency... which determines the depreciation of the whole."[16] Newcomb was an astronomer by trade, and is mostly forgotten as an economist, but he was one of the thinkers who formulated the quantity theory of money, which became the foundation of the monetarist school led by Milton Friedman.

Garrett had also read Francis Amasa Walker, a Civil War veteran, president of the Massachusetts Institute of Technology and prominent exponent of bimetallism. John Chamberlain called him "the first really important American economist." Walker had refuted the British idea, accepted by Adam Smith, of the wage fund—the idea that wages could never rise because the enterprise needed all the money.[17] To Garrett the discarding of this Old World apology for poverty was the special achievement of American capitalism.

The system did have an egalitarian aspect. Natural inequalities were allowed, but the old, artificial inequalities were swept away. "In the American social philosophy there was no principle of caste," Garrett wrote. "What a man could do well, for that he was esteemed."[18] That meant as long as

120

you did what you could, you were respectable. "To be poor is no disgrace," Garrett wrote in 1947. "In the whole civilized world that was only true here."[19]

Chapter 17 notes

1 SEP, "This Is Well-Being," December 26, 1925.

2 *The American Omen,* Dutton, p. 23.

3 *The American Story*, p. 129.

4 That the two novels each had a protagonist named Galt was noted by Ryant in *Profit's Prophet*, p. 116. In *Reclaiming the American Right*, Center for Libertarian Studies, 1993, pp. 199-205, Justin Raimondo pointed out another parallel. Garrett's novel twice uses the line, "Who is Henry M. Galt?" Rand's novel begins with the line, "Who is John Galt?" The John Galt question, repeated many times in *Atlas Shrugged*, expresses a mystery and also a sense of existential frustration, as in, "Aw, who knows?" One of Garrett's uses is vaguely like that. Raimondo argued that it was "too much to believe that the use of the same rhetorical device could have occurred by happenstance." Really it is only vaguely the same device. "Galt" is a name that sounds like "gold" and "gilt" and might be chosen by two different writers for an exemplar of capitalism. "Galt" was also a name in the public mind when Garrett wrote his book, as it was the maiden name of President Wilson's wife, Edith, who married him when he was in office. Garrett also wrote a short story about a capitalist cornered by an anarchist assassin, and named the capitalist "Gault." (SEP, "Red Night," April 3, 1920.) Rand and Garrett were close politically and were contemporaries, but there is no record that either took note of the other—all of which proves nothing. Raimondo may be right. Jeff Walker also argues that *The Driver* is part of the "disowned ancestry" of *Atlas Shrugged* in *The Ayn Rand Cult*, Open Court, 1999, pp. 305-308. Garrett denied the premise of *Atlas Shrugged*, more than 30 years before Rand conceived it. "Capital cannot strike," he wrote. "That is an inherent weakness." *New York Times Annalist,* July 21, 1913.

5 *The Driver*, pp. 188-189.

6 SEP, "The Lost American," March 28, 1936.

7 *The Driver*, p. 272.

8 Baruch's comments were from a book review in the *Philadelphia Public Ledger*, December 23, 1922. A copy is in the Bernard Baruch papers, Vol. 4, A-G, Seeley G. Mudd Manuscript Library, Princeton University. Chamberlain's comments were in his column, "Books of the Times," *New York Times,* May 2, 1944, p. 17.

9 *Satan's Bushel*, E.P. Dutton, 1924, 72-74.

10 *The Cinder Buggy*, p. 201-202.

11 SEP, "The Wealth Question," August 31, 1935.

12 Ibid. For Garrett on thrift, see also *The Blue Wound*, pp. 37-44.

13 See Herbert Spencer, "The Great Political Superstition," *The Man Versus the State,* Caxton, 1940, pp. 195-205.

14 SEP, "The Balance Sheet of Capitalism," May 10, 1934.

15 SEP, "The French Crisis," August 28, 1926. For Garrett's reporting on the German inflation, see SEP, "While Germany Wept," April 21, 1923; "Why Germany Drowned Her Credit," SEP, April 28, 1923, and "Dangers of Inflation," *The Annals of the American Academy of Political and Social Science,* July 1923.

16 Simon Newcomb, "A Critical Examination of Our Financial Policy During the Southern Rebellion," D. Appleton & Co., 1865, p. 210. In "Everybody's Money," *Everybody's,* May 1914, Garrett recommended Newcomb's *The Principles of Political Economy* (1885) as "the best and most readable book" on economics written by an American. A decade later, in "Edison's Idea for a New Kind of Money," *New York Times,* July 16, 1922, section 7, p. 1, he said Newcomb's book was "A classic textbook, perhaps the finest in any language." A quarter-century later, in *American Affairs* (April 1947, p. 67), he wrote that it was "still the finest statement there is of the laws that govern the production and exchange of wealth."

17 Garrett credited Walker in *The American Omen*, p. 41. Chamberlain noted that Garrett was one of the few who had done so. Chamberlain, *The Roots of Capitalism,* Liberty Press, 1959, p. 154.

18 SEP, "Hoover of Iowa and California," June 2, 1928.

19 "Status for the Poor," *American Affairs*, April 1947.

Chapter Eighteen
REIGN OVER US

All of Garrett's fiction is about work, industry and making a living. Some of his short stories turn on the absurdity of life, but his serious concern was with man's struggle to create such things as the steel industry, the auto industry, railroads, steamships, electric power, mechanized agriculture and modern finance. To socialists these were faceless, inhuman, mechanistic things to be tied down and made human; to Garrett they were living creations. That was one of Garrett's similarities to Ayn Rand. He didn't picture industrialists in the romantic light she did, because, for one thing, he knew them. He did picture the act of creation, and sometimes the thing created, in such a light.

Garrett's last novel, *Harangue* (1927), is about leftist egalitarianism. It was the idea that, as one of the characters says, "Life shall be level. The values of existence shall be horizontal. No one shall have more to eat or wear or enjoy than another." [1] The novel imagines some people who champion this idea, and what happens when they put it into practice.

The title "Harangue" is not descriptive, and it is a fair bet that the publisher came up with it. In its serialization of the novel, the *Saturday Evening Post* used a better title, retained in the book as a subtitle: *The Trees Said to the Bramble, Come Reign Over Us*. This is a reference to a parable in the Book of Judges in which the woody plants try to elect a ruler, and none

123

of the productive plants, busy growing olive oil or grapes or figs, wants to rule. The only willing ruler is the bramble, a master under whose rule the productive plants will suffer. [2]

In *Harangue* the characters are more finely drawn and the literary method more modern than his earlier novels. Garrett was not a great novelist, but he was competent, and this is easily his best. Reviewing it for the *New York Sun*, Henry Hazlitt praised it highly, though still he said it was "an economic treatise disguised as a work of fiction."[3] "Economic" is too narrow a word here; "social" would have been better.

Six years before the real revolution in America—the New Deal—*Harangue* imagined a socialist takeover of one state. Garrett's story was based on the takeover of North Dakota in 1916 by a socialistic group called the Nonpartisan League. It financed itself through thousands of postdated checks, and when it took power it had the state build a people's grain elevator and a people's bank. In *Harangue*, Garrett named the political group the Freeman's League and the state New Freedom.

The story begins with a conclave of intellectuals explaining themselves—and in fiction they can be made to bare themselves to the author's will. Garrett's character Fitzjerald, who plays the role of the honest socialist, explains how democratic civilization is made up of people who think they are better than others and other people who think they are just as good:

> "The I-am-betters are hard put to it. In the last resort they become ludicrous. I think I am better than money changers, shop keepers, meat packers, superior to the great cult Rotarian. I know I am better than a coal digger. But if these others—I mean the money changers, shop keepers, meat packers, Rotarians, press me hard—and they are always coming up—if they begin to know too many things as I know them

and to prate my language, then I am obliged to go and live near or among coal diggers in order to keep my contrast clear. To conceal from myself what I am doing I am very likely to ally myself with them against the cult Rotarian, whom they envy and I am contemptuous. I become their champion. I talk of up-lifting them. Deity stuff. I am much more likely to fool myself than to fool them. I am not a coal digger. But I may start a revolution."[4]

Garrett was said to have a "fondness" for the Industrial Workers of the World[5]—the Wobblies—whose syndicalist doctrine rejected state socialism and embraced a kind of left anarchism. In *Harangue* he wrote of the I.W.W. as peculiarly American—and for Garrett, that was praise:

They stand also for adventure, vagabondage, the truant life, combat, the stone of David, ganghood, sharing, love of destruction, outlawry, secret power, signs and cabals. These are values and attitudes that lie close to the wayward spirit and belong naturally to youth. Imagine a fraternity of men in whom the spir-it of youth has not been overthrown by self-discipline and wisdom and who for that reason are unable to make the commonplace adjustments to reality; imag-ine again that they were conscious of their maladjust-ments and propose to make society over in accord with those values and attitudes of youth. There you have an engaging picture of the I.W.W. In that aspect it is or was a romantic order, peculiar to this country notwithstanding its grand big name, and one that could not have come to exist anywhere else in the world.[6]

Garrett did not admire the Wobblies' juvenile values, but he saluted their authenticity. In *Harangue*, the Wobbly, Semicorn, is an earthy egalitarian, the son of a miner. At the beginning of the story, when Garrett introduces his cabal, Semicorn sits silently in a rich woman's parlor as the college-educated socialists rant against bourgeois values. Then he rises and berates them for being all talk. "We fight for it," he says. "I been in jail for it."[7]

To Semicorn, the rich socialists are altogether too precious to accept equality with real workers. They would create a society, he says, that had its own "scissorbills, bosses, pie in th' sky capitaliss jus an so you could feel better than somebody." (A scissorbill, Semicorn explains, is "a man who thanks the boss for his pay check.")[8]

Nonetheless, Semicorn agrees to become the cabal's newspaper editor—which is what Garrett would have been in a revolution he was part of. Semicorn staffs his newsroom with Wobblies, some of them former typesetters. He runs the Freeman's League paper like his own troop of cavalry, and inevitably is confronted by the head socialist. The leader says to Semicorn:

> "I know Wobblies. The trouble is, they can't play any tune but their own. They play that one wrong. Each man sings it to suit himself. Very bad for the tune. That's why you get nowhere. Free speech is all right in matters of personal opinion. But where you've got a practical purpose in view you might as well have free trombones in a band."[9]

Semicorn agrees to run the paper as a League mouthpiece for as long as he agrees with the League—a period, he figures, that will, by and by, come to an end. It soon does. As the Freeman's League loses power and the anti-socialists regain it, Semicorn takes it upon himself to assassinate the state's leading capitalist. The new government arrests Semicorn, convicts him and sentences him to death. His comrades arrange a breakout from prison, but he refuses to run and is hanged. Semicorn is mistaken but honorable—and to the end, an example of American individualism.

None of the radicals, however, represents mainstream America. Says the honest socialist, Fitzjerald, at the book's end:

> "The people are not radical here. They are conservative. The soil is young, the hour is young, opportunity is young. Radicalism in this country is a pale ferocity. A personal attitude disguised as a social intention. If you are really a radical you have something the matter with you. There was nothing the matter with the people of New Freedom. They were too young to have anything the matter with them. They had no impulse to destroy anything in principle. What they did want and all they wanted was increased participation in the material benefits of the order that is. Which is not radicalism."[10]

Though Garrett believed the socialists were wrong, his condemnation in *Harangue* lacks the bite by which he would later condemn the New Deal. His tolerance was not only in fiction. In 1923, in Berlin, Garrett met with left-anarchist Emma Goldman, who had been deported from the United States as an enemy alien. She asked him for help with the McClure newspaper syndicate regarding a manuscript about her experiences in Soviet Russia. He wasn't able to help her.[11]

In 1929, while spending a month's vacation in Carmel, Calif., he struck up a friendship with the old progressive muckraker Lincoln Steffens, who had written for *Everybody's* before the war, when Garrett had. Steffens recounted a lunch at the end of this month with Garrett and a woman in which

Garrett said, speaking of Steffens, "Do you know, God damn it, I hate to have about anybody or anything the God damn sentimental feeling I have toward that man."

In the early 1930s Garrett invited Steffens on a cross-country road trip, and also supplied an enthusiastic blurb for the dust jacket of Steffens' autobiography. The Steffens archives have four letters from Garrett in which he tries to bridge their political gap with personal sentiment and an assurance that political differences need not matter. In one he writes:

> Every night I pray to get my prejudices back. All murdered in the sobriety of tolerance. From trying to disbelieve what I was born to believe, I end, like you, in believing nothing. There is not one damned thing I am sure of; neither is there one damned thing you are sure of, for all your make-believe to the contrary.
>
> I think—you see, I have to say, I think—it is much more important to believe something than that what you believe should be right. For else, the tension fails, and without the tension and the conflict even that which might turn out to be right cannot prevail. I don't like the kind of world you are talking about. I don't want to live in such a world. But the only way for you to get it is by overcoming. If there were nothing to overcome, such as me, your world would be born like a wet dream, and if you lived to see it you would wipe it off.[12]

Chapter 18 notes

1 *Harangue*, E.P. Dutton, 1927, p. 240.

2 Judges 9: 1-15.

3 Henry Hazlitt, "Radicalism in Fiction," *New York Sun,* February 26, 1927.

4 *Harangue*, p. 23.

5 Notes of a phone call by Carl Ryant to Abraham Albert Desser, federal mediator, Federal Mediation and Conciliation Service, September 24, 1968. Ryant papers, University of Louisville. Years later, Garrett wrote a sympathetic review of Ralph Chaplin's *Wobbly* (1948), the story of an I.W.W. member who became disillusioned with communism. Garrett began his review with the line, "In the American heart there is a soft spot for the rebel." ("Autobiography of a Native Rebel," *American Affairs,* October 1948, pp. 238-239.)

6 *Harangue*, pp. 103-104.

7 *Harangue*, p. 27.

8 *Harangue*, pp. 26, 30. To the I.W.W., a scissorbill was a migrant worker who refused to join their union. H.L. Mencken, *The American Language Supplement II*, Knopf, 1948, pp. 677, 777.

9 *Harangue*, p. 113.

10 *Harangue*, p. 239. Garrett had portrayed farmers as unradical as early as 1912. In "A Western Sketch," *New York Evening Post,* Sept. 21, 1912, he reported from Phillipsburg, Kansas, that farmers were doing well and were not much excited by the Bull Moose insurgency.

11 Emma Goldman, *Living My Life*, Knopf, 1931, chapter 54. In 1923 Doubleday published her memoir, *My Disillusionment in Russia*.

12 "God damn it" letter: Lincoln Steffens to Ella Winter (his second wife), July 1, 1929, Ella Winter and Granville Hicks, editors, *The Letters of Lincoln Steffens*, Vol. II, 1920-1936, Harcourt Brace, 1938, p. 836. Road trip: Lincoln Steffens to Erskine Scott Wood, February 3, 1931, *Ibid*, p. 888. "Every night I pray" letter: Garrett to Lincoln Steffens, undated, Steffens Papers, Columbia University Rare Book and Manuscript Library, Series II, Catalogued Correspondence, Reel 1. One of the four letters mentions Magdalene Davis, the woman Garrett was dating when he was shot in 1930.

Chapter Nineteen
WE ARE ASSERTING

The 1920s was the last decade in which Garrett was optimistic about America. He showed it in what he wrote about American business and what he wrote about the American road.

Business was the subject of his last book of the decade, *The American Omen* (1928). Written at the height of prosperity and before the storm clouds were overhead, *The American Omen* is Garrett's interpretation of American capitalism in the 1920s. The picture he draws is one of enlightenment, which comes with the increase in capital per worker:

> The more your investment is in machines, the greater your stake in the man who touches them, in his general well-being, in his manner of living, his conscious and unconscious attitudes. You see clearly what the head of the United States Steel Corporation means when he says the true problem of modern industry is how to gain the loyalty, the cooperation and the understanding of the individual man. Not men in general—the man.[1]

Business had to take a responsible attitude toward the consumer, too. Garrett remembered the old days:

When sugar was sold in barrels—and that was in our own childhood—sand in the sugar was the staple almanac joke. Who put it in no one ever knew. It had to be either the grocer or the refiner, and they accused each other. Now sugar is sold on the refiner's reputation, in sealed packages, and anyone proposing to put sand in it would be examined for lunacy.[2]

By the 1920s, management had become a thing to be studied at schools of business administration. Rotary was spreading the gospel of Service. Personnel had become a corporate function. Public relations had become both a function and a business. In all this was a certain razzle-dazzle and bunkum. Treating the worker as an individual might depend on whether the worker was a manager, a clerk, a tool-and-die maker or a drudge with a broom. It also might depend on how easy it was to find a replacement. Yet there was truth in it, too: business *had* changed since the 1890s, and it would continue changing in the ways Garrett said.

One thing he spotted was the practice of managing inventories of parts so that they were used the same day they arrived. He thought it was very smart and called it "hand-to-mouth buying."[3] In the 1980s it would be proclaimed as a new thing and called "just-in-time" inventory management.

In *An American Omen* Garrett also commented on profit, and its function in modern capitalism:

To make a great profit you have to increase the total product of wealth more efficiently than your competitor. Having made the great profit in that way, it is rightfully yours to consume. You may remove it from the business and do anything you like with it. But unless you return it to its source—the greater part of it—the source will dry up. Why? Because if you do not pursue that line, another will, and he who does will presently have costs lower than yours, and your profit will cease.[4]

An example was Henry Ford. He had made an immense profit. But, wrote Garrett:

> In what form does it exist? A house to live in, what his household has consumed in living, the Wayside Inn, a quantity of antiques and the *Dearborn Independent*—these are the things Ford has taken for himself personally, and the cost of them in proportion to the wealth he created is trifling...
> He says himself, "All anybody can get out of this is a job."[5]

Meanwhile the people had the motor car, the second example of Garrett's optimism.

Garrett loved to drive. "It expands the ego," he wrote in 1916. Driving "tremendously gratifies and extends the sense of one's personal importance." It was a feeling he shared with his fellow countrymen, who, he wrote, were "perhaps the most egoistic in the whole world."[6]

By the early 1920s Americans had more cars but, Garrett wrote, "the worst highways of any country in the civilized world."[7] The cars were created by private enterprise and the roads by the government, and the government was behind. The roads were particularly bad in the West. Really they weren't highways at all. In 1919, a U.S. Army convoy called the Transcontinental Motor Train had taken 62 days to travel on the straightest road from Washington, D.C., to San Francisco.

Ten years later it had all changed. Congress had passed a highway bill. The new U.S. highways weren't all paved, and Garrett wrote of passing another car in West Texas through a swirl of dust. In Mississippi he crossed the Tombigbee River

on a flatboat that would hold five cars, and the car owners had
to wait while the flatboat owner finished his dinner. But by the
end of the 1920s, it was practical to take cross-country road
trips, and Garrett took them.

As in all good travel writing, his accounts tell much about
the author. For example, he viewed the economy as an organic thing. Here he describes the Kansas City rail yards, seen
from a high tower:

> From every direction come freight trains like
> jointed worms, some a quarter of a mile long. First
> they lose their heads and tails. Then they break into
> car parts, and thousands of cars, all at one time, go up
> and down from track to track, each seeking another
> that has a directional affinity. As they find one anoth-
> er in that principle a train forms, and when it is long
> enough it receives from somewhere in that appalling
> confusion the head it needs and the right tail, and
> departs, knowing its way.[8]

Seeing the steel mills of Birmingham, he wrote of the
teams of men like specialized cells in an organism. Some were
making steel but not knowing who wanted it; others, not
knowing how to make it, had found someone to buy it and
knew when they needed to have it.

These are economic things described in terms of nature.
Garrett also described natural things in terms of economics.
On his way to Florida, he noted the first palm trees at the
northern edge of their range. To Garrett they were *marginal*
trees, like the marginal farmers on poor soil or the marginal
workers that had jobs only when business was good. Thinking
these things, Garrett wrote: "There is no world of any kind,
animal or vegetable, without its irreducible fringe, as if in
every separate design, social or organic, there might be a law
of tapering benefit."[9]

Tapering benefit: a Garrett phrase.

Garrett was a hard worker, and looked askance at people with easy lives. Going south, he viewed the warming climate:

> The relation of the North Carolina backwoodsman to the soil is still what it must have been always—insolent and wheedling. Just enough is plenty. Nature is soft, good-humored, a little too easily persuaded, like a woman more to be desired for herself than to be recommended for good housekeeping. As it is not altogether good for a man to love that kind of woman, or better to have one that nags him to enterprise, so neither is it well for him to find Nature in this pleasurable mood, never provoking him to arrogance or to wrestle with her for mastery.

At Los Angeles, the "great seacoast city not made by the sea" but by Midwesterners, the climate was also easy. "Here, if anywhere, the American might learn indolence," Garrett wrote. But the Midwesterners were not indolent. Many of them, having made their grubstake on the Plains, had intended to loaf in L.A., but eventually their Puritan consciences had gotten the better of them. "The retired capitalist plays golf until the sight of a golf stick gives him a feeling of depravity," Garrett wrote. Then the capitalist starts a company and is not retired anymore. The Iowa farmer comes to grow a few orange trees but, "in a few years, he is a large orange grower, up to his neck in it." Soft living is on offer, but "the creative passion defeats it."[10] The difference is not in the place but the people.

Garrett had been brought up on the land, and had a feeling for how people entwined their lives with it. His own farm was at the edge of an area that had once been a pine forest. The forest had been carelessly logged off, much of it for charcoal that had been made sloppily without kilns and used to smelt bog iron. The iron men had extracted the value and moved on. "Nature either would not or could not replace the pines," Garrett wrote. "What came instead was a race of dwarfed oak trees, perfectly useless." It was a desert really. People called it the Pine Barrens.[11]

That was in the East, which was old. The West was new. Venturing north of San Francisco, Garrett was swallowed by the redwoods—and coughed up:

> As you stand in a redwood forest you may believe that all questions of wonder have been sometime answered. It is the same emotion that touches you alone in a great cathedral. All doubts resolved. Perfect refuge in dogma. Everything already answered. And suppose the answers are wrong. Do we know that any answer is right? You will whisper, as in any cathedral, and notice that little sounds are elongated, magnified, and have a distorted perspective. You will know why forest dwellers were superstitious and mystical, and what a pleasure it would be to go back to naïve super-stition, if only one could. Forest dwellers were obliged to think up. Man on the seashore was the hor-izontal thinker.
>
> There is a last sensation. Driving a motor car through the redwoods, you will find yourself going faster and faster with a strange sense of elfish delight; you yourself invisible and without substance, taunting the trees with your power of movement, because it is the only thing you can think of to taunt them with, and they have made you feel so small. The diameter of your life cycle is inferior to theirs, but you do not have to stay always in one place.[12]

Motoring across America in the 1920s, Garrett considered the weakness of the economic explanation for works of marvel. There had been no economic necessity to create Los Angeles, he thought; there was no natural harbor there, and people could have left that place alone. Later he would say the same of Wichita: they could have left it in buffalo grass. New York might just as well have been built on Staten Island, which he thought a more logical place for it. Arriving in New York from a transcontinental road trip, he beheld the skyline. It was the end of the 1920s, and the skyline was nearly completed for the following half-century. Nowhere else on earth was anything like it. Could the Manhattan skyline really be an expression of rational decisions to maximize profit? The buildings did serve an economic function. They had been created by entrepreneurs—but was the motive for making them *that way* primarily economic? Garrett considered John D. Rockefeller and his proposed Center:

> When a man so rich that private profit can no longer be of the slightest interest to him buys a whole block in the midst of New York City's terrific congestion—buys the land at its fabulous price—purposefully to raise there a group of towers, then the idea that the passion for vertical architecture is an effect of land values begins to waver. [13]

Garrett's explanation for skyscrapers and Wichita and Los Angeles was simpler: "We are asserting our power."

Chapter 19 notes

1 *The American Omen,* p. 52.
2 *The American Omen,* p. 165.
3 *The American Omen,* p. 111.
4 *The American Omen,* p. 145.
5 *The American Omen,* p. 144.
6 "Finance-Economics" column, *New York Tribune*, November 10, 1916, p.
7 *The Cinder Buggy*, p. 123. This is repeated almost verbatim in SEP,
"West Coast, East Coast," November 2, 1929.
8 SEP, "West Coast, East Coast," November 2, 1929. The description of
Birmingham is from SEP, "Travel Notes," September 28, 1929.
9 SEP, "Points South," August 9, 1930.
10 SEP, "Los Angeles in Fact and Dream," October 18, 1930.
11 SEP, "Travel Notes," September 28, 1929.
12 SEP, "West Coast, East Coast," November 2, 1929.
13 SEP, "Travel Notes," October 12, 1929. Garrett ran (and had probably
written) an anonymous piece in the *New York Times Annalist* about how the
skyscrapers of the day—the tallest was the 51-story Woolworth Building—
did not pay: "What Hinders a Tower of Babel," November 17, 1913, pp. 613-
614. And in the *New York Tribune*, he had written of the tall buildings of
Kansas City: "They are personal monuments, named for the men who built
them." "West of East," August 6, 1916, sec. 3, p. 4.

Chapter Twenty
LIKE THE MISCHIEF

Here an intermission from thoughts and controversies, and a short account of the most bizarre moment of Garrett's life.

On January 18, 1930 a Saturday night in New York, Garet Garrett was shot by a masked gunman. The first-day stories in the *Times,* the *Herald Tribune,* and the *World* were sketchy because Garrett had refused to talk to reporters and had given only a brief story to police, who were not called to the scene by the restaurant.[1] But the *Herald Tribune* and the *Times* worked the story and came out on the second day with detailed accounts of what had happened to their former employee.

Garrett, 51, had invited to dinner an advertising woman named Magdalene Davis, described by the *Times* as "a brunette in the early thirties, of cultivated appearance, well and tastefully dressed."[2] Also in the party was Frederick Simpich, 51, described as "a stocky, greyish man of intellectual appearance and a man-of-the-world bearing." Simpich was an old friend of Garrett's. He had been a U.S. consul in Baghdad and Guatemala, and a newspaperman in Shanghai and Manila. His companion was Hazel Humm, a half-Chinese bacteriologist who had once worked at the Mayo Clinic. She was to be Simpich's guide and interpreter so that he could write a story on the Chinese theater in Pell Street.

The restaurant, at 357 West Fifteenth Street, was called by the *Times* Chez Madelon and by the *Herald Tribune* Chez Madeleine. They never did agree on it. The place had only a handful of tables. The next day's *Herald Tribune* said it was "an establishment for which no accurate descriptive phrase has yet been invented." It might be called "a dignified speakeasy"—this was during Prohibition—without the "speakeasy art effects." The *Herald Tribune* noted that the guests "belonged to a social layer which dreads the notoriety of being connected with shooting scrapes even in the most respectable speakeasies."

Dinner cost $2.50, with brandy fresh from the ships in port at $1 a glass. Commenting on the restaurant—and the shooting—Garrett said, "You get a wonderful dinner at this place, but it costs like the mischief."

From the *Herald Tribune:*

> The holdup men gained entrance by using the bootlegger's password... The dinner was nearly over when the three holdup men appeared on the parlor floor at 9:55 o'clock. In a rather soft voice a man with a revolver and a handkerchief over the lower part of his face said, "Stay where you are, ladies and gentlemen. Keep your seats."
>
> This phrase cut off Mr. Garrett in the middle of a sentence. He was sitting facing the front windows...The three holdup men were scattered through the room behind the party...All conversation stopped. Mr. Garrett could see...the consternation on the faces of the others, but he did not look around at the intruders. Instead, he rose in a characteristic way, both hands thrust into the pockets of his evening jacket,

and when on his feet he turned without undue haste and faced the man who was threatening him with a pistol.

"What's this?" exclaimed the writer, in a tone that conveyed nothing except the utmost peevishness. He acted like a man bored, vexed and annoyed...

"Oh, what's this? What's this all about?" he repeated in the same exasperated voice. According to witnesses his behavior was that of an irritable executive who had just been hit by an office boy's paper wad.

Mr. Garrett refused to take the pistol seriously. He was still advancing with an expression of contempt on his face, as if dealing with badly behaved boys, when the bandit pulled the trigger. The writer staggered and then fell before the fourth shot.3

Garrett had been hit with steel-jacketed .25 caliber rounds. The *Times* reported that one was embedded in the flesh of his left thigh; one perforated his lung, causing blood to flow into his chest cavity; and one pierced his neck and grazed his windpipe.

Simpich and Davis helped Garrett to the street and took him to the hospital in a taxi, while Humm, who was hysterical, was sent home. Simpich and Davis then went to the police precinct, where they were questioned for hours. The motive was a problem: after shooting Garrett the men had fled. Their .25 caliber guns were lighter than usual for hold-up men. One witness recalled Garrett saying that nothing had made so many enemies for him as his recent articles in the *Saturday Evening Post* about the stock market crash. Another witness reported that at the hospital, Simpich had leaned over, patted Garrett's wrist and said, "I'm sorry, G.G." A police detective interpreted this as "a sign." The police also thought the crime might have been of passion. Garrett was still legally married, and his estranged wife, Ida, attempted to visit him and was turned away. She didn't buy the robbery thesis. "There's something funny about this," she said. When the police questioned Garrett about the crime-of-passion theory, he threw at his interrogator's head what is described by various newspapers as a dish, a porcelain cup or a small porcelain spittoon.

The police also searched the speakeasy for liquor, but the *Herald Tribune* reported, "not a drop was found." It said that New York City detectives, even armed with passwords, "had never been able to set foot within the Chez Madeleine."

None of the suspects was identified by witnesses. After leaving the hospital, Garrett was called in to finger Charles Meehan, 27, but could not. Meehan walked up to him and said, "Thank you, Mr. Garrett. Another man wouldn't give me a break like this." The *Times* reported that Garrett "smiled, said nothing, and left the courtroom."[4]

Six weeks after the shooting, President Hoover sent a note to Garrett thanking him for an article in the *Post* called "The First Hoover Year," adding, "I hope that by now you have fully recovered from your recent indisposition." [5]

Garrett's vocal cords had been permanently damaged. From then on, he spoke with a rasp.

Chapter 20 notes

1 "Garet Garrett Shot 3 Times by Café Thugs," *New York Herald Tribune,* January 19, 1930, p. 1.

2 "Garet Garrett Shot in a Café Attack," *New York Times,* January 19, 1930, p. 1.

3 *New York Herald Tribune,* January 20, 1930, p. 4. A.A. Desser, who knew Garrett, told Carl Ryant that Garrett said he'd stood up because he didn't think the gunman would shoot, and because he resented the intrusion on his dinner. Ryant notes of March 13, 1969. Ryant papers.

4 "Garrett Fails to Identify Suspect," *New York Times,* February 28, 1930, p. 14.

5 Hoover to Garrett, March 6, 1930. President's Personal File, Box 113, Hoover Presidential Library; SEP, "The First Hoover Year," March 1, 1930.

Chapter Twenty-one
WHO BEATS DEPRESSION

It is remarkable that two-thirds of a century after the Great Depression its cause is still the subject of contending theories. The free traders say that it was an ordinary recession made terrible by the Smoot-Hawley tariff. The Chicago school argues that the Federal Reserve worsened an ordinary recession by allowing the money supply to shrink by one-third. The Austrians posit that the Fed had made credit too cheap in the 1920s and encouraged entrepreneurs to make bad investments.

Garrett's answer was closer to the Austrians', but he didn't quite fall into their camp. The hard-core Austrians are against central banking, arguing that an all-private system with purely commercial concerns would be more stable. Garrett was not opposed to the Federal Reserve. He did not believe in free banking. That was the system America had before the Civil War, and he said it had been chaos:

> There was Boston money and Maine money and New York money, all of it better than Tennessee money or the red-dog money of Indiana; there were 1,600 kinds of paper money, all circulating together, and the worst was saddlebag money, so-called because the banks sent agents through the country to peddle it in exchange for farmers' notes. If a bank

failed, as it very often did, its money was worthless, because it was secured by nothing more than the general credit of the bank.[1]

"Banking," he wrote, "is not like the grocery trade. If a man fails in the grocery trade he loses only his own capital; if he fails in the banking trade he loses, besides his own capital, also other people's money."[2] And if democratic and populist America made it as easy to start a bank as a grocery store, which it nearly did, then, Garrett argued, banking had to be policed.

Garrett allowed that regulation was bureaucratic and inexact, and guaranteed nothing really. Also, the regulators were fragmented. America had 48 state systems plus the national-bank system. Allowing a bank to choose between federal and state charter allowed it to choose the least oversight—and by the 1920s lack of oversight was a problem. Bankers had created non-bank subsidiaries as hiding places for their delinquent loans, which made the banks' published accounts unreliable. The poor depositor, wrote Garrett, was left with "no certain way... to distinguish between a bank where his money will be safe and one where it will be in jeopardy."[3]

In contrast, Britain and Canada had only a handful of big, old banks run by gentlemen of ingrained prudence. They didn't need regulators peering over their shoulders. Their banks didn't fail. But a British-style credit oligarchy would not be tolerable in America. And that meant that in economic cycles, which Britain and Canada had also, the Americans had the additional burden of runs, collapses and frozen deposits.

By the 1920s Americans were used to that. It was not new. Something new had made the plunge that started in October 1929 especially harrowing.

The monetarist explanation—that the Fed had allowed the money supply to shrink too much—was made after Garrett died. It was logical as far as it went, but it was inherently a paper-money argument, a case for more inflation. In the 1920s, bank credit had increased by $14 billion, which was almost three times the value of all the coin and bills then in circulation. This was inflation, Garrett said, even though it didn't feel like previous inflations, which had erupted as speculation in commodities. This time, he wrote, "it was all in securities."[4] In any case Garrett would have rejected any argument to heal the economy with inflation. That was incompatible with the gold standard and with good sense.

Decades later, the free traders would argue that the cause of the Depression was the Smoot-Hawley tariff.[5] Garrett didn't think so at the time. Even in the good years, foreign trade had amounted to only 7 percent of national output.

In his view the principal problem had been credit. Though he rejected free banking, Garrett's explanation of the Depression—reckless lending—echoed the Austrians' theory. The new thing about this lending was that much of it— some $15 billion in gold dollars since World War I—had been overseas. "We inflated Europe with enormous loans," Garrett wrote. America had run a trade surplus of about the same amount. Simply put, America was lending the world the money to buy its goods. To service the loans, gold flowed back to New York. After a few years the United States had more than half the world's monetary gold. That was an imbalance, and dangerous. Gold was needed in trade, not in a "dead lake." In 1927, the Fed pushed interest rates down in New York so that the Bank of England would borrow back some of that gold. That was a favor to the British, and also to some others whose benefit was not intended. A gaggle of South American governments, national and local, used the break in interest rates to float bonds that were peddled to small American banks.

In 1929 came the Wall Street boom. It had an appetite for credit, and hoovered up the nation's savings. American credit was thereby diverted from the Germans, the Argentines and the Bank of England, so that in 1929, loans to foreign countries fell by half. In borrower countries, Garrett wrote, "the effect was one of terrific deflation." Their purchases of American goods sharply declined.[6]

The credit to the stock market went into the fire. "Not only did billions of paper turn suddenly worthless in our hands, but we lost at the same time our foreign markets," Garrett wrote years later.[7] The Smoot-Hawley tariff, which came eight months after the Crash, took away foreign entry to the U.S. market. Garrett argued that the tariff was an effect of the collapse, not a cause of it, though he did not deny that it made matters worse. The principal problem, he thought, was the debt itself, and for that, blame had to fall on those who had created it. In a nutshell, the story of the Crash was that during the Great War, America had replaced Britain as the world's lender of surplus capital, and had done a bad job of it.

Then, the question of recovery.

America had had depressions before. One had hit in the 1870s, after the paper-money inflation of the Civil War. Back then, industry had complained for years that it could earn no profit. But after a dip, at the same time as the bellyaching, production had increased. *Some* producers were earning profits, and some entrepreneurs were investing. Really what was happening, Garrett wrote, was that old capital was being wiped away. "New capital, founding the principles of modern industry, was taking its place."[8] That had happened again in the 1890s.

In the sharp depression after World War I, Garrett had argued that the collapse in prices presented a chance for business to invest and produce its way out.[9] He had been right; in 1921 President Harding's government had done nothing to rescue the economy, and industry came back on its own, and in less than two years. In December 1929 Garrett said it again: it was a chance to invest. [10]

A few weeks after the Crash, President Hoover scheduled a meeting with industrialists—and to prepare for it, he called in Garrett. Years later Garrett recalled the "dreary week-end at the White House with Mr. Hoover."[11] The idea Hoover reached the following Monday was to keep wages up, and not cut them as had been done in previous recessions. It had not been Garrett's solution. Garrett would have advised them to cut costs, and learn to live in the new structure of prices.

Hoover's solution didn't work. But Garrett wasn't right, either, about it being time to invest. Two and a half years later, in mid-1932, it was. Everything of economic value had been beaten down: stocks, bonds, land, buildings, machines, labor. Banks were awash in liquidity. *Somebody* had to be making use of cheap productive assets. Garrett went on the road in New England looking for Depression-beating entrepreneurs, and he found them:

> In nearly every community, certainly in every one of the principal industries no matter how deeply, as a whole, it may be sunk in depression, you will find a plant working night and day to fill its orders. Often this will be a small plant in the hands of a man whose attack upon adversity has carried him into some new ground of opportunity. If it is a large plant, it will be yet not so large as to exceed one man's power of personal dominion; and this is without exception. Always there is the man who did it—the one man.

One such entrepreneur was manufacturing a rake better than other rakes. Another had found a new way of merchandising curtains. Another had undertaken to deliver cut cloth for women's dress goods, custom ordered, to New York buyers within two weeks. Such was the individualist answer to the Depression.

The man who beats depression is in every case a pattern breaker who has in him the business passion. He wastes no more of his own thought matter on universal solutions, or on how, by some act of monetary legislation or government policy, prosperity may be restored at one stroke; he gets all his energies free to act upon one problem. [12]

That was the old way of thinking, and in the early 1930s there was much of it still; but there was also a new way, a politically progressive way that looked to experts and leaders to save the society as a whole. Garrett wrote:

Lately in one of the embarrassed Midwestern cities, a banker addressed the people by radio on the extravagant follies of government... The title was, "If I Were King"... Twenty years ago, speaking on this same subject, would this banker or any banker have employed that title? In the first place, it would never have occurred to him; secondly, if it had occurred to him, he would have dismissed it at once for fear he would be misunderstood or ridiculed. Instead of saying what he would do if he were king, he would have told the people what they should do to mend their own government. Thus, unawares, a change has taken place. The nature of it is pervasive. How deep it goes, no one yet knows.

What Garrett saw in much of America—and this is *before* the election of Franklin Roosevelt—was:

People wishing for some power to descend upon them from above and make everything right by edict...The right thing must be done. How can people themselves think what the right magic is? How could they perform it if they could think of it? Therefore, let the Government think of it and do it.[13]

The people were ready for the New Deal.

Chapter 21 notes
1 SEP, "A Story of Banking," August 8, 1931.
2 SEP, "A Story of Banking."
3 SEP, "A Story of Banking."
4 SEP, "'America Can't Come Back,'" January 23, 1932.
5 See Jude Wanniski, *The Way the World Works*, Basic Books, 1978.
6 SEP, "Uncle Sam Learning the Lender's Lesson," July 4, 1931.
7 "The Mind of American Business on Free Competitive Enterprise," *The Economic Record,* July 1944, p. 39.
8 SEP, "The Fourth Age of Agriculture," April 30, 1927.
9 "The Wage Curve," *The New Republic*, June 22, 1921.
10 SEP, "Wall Street and Washington," December 28, 1929.
11 *The American Story*, p. 237.
12 SEP, "Notes of These Times," August 6, 1932. The line, "the one man," is much the same as Garrett's conclusion about corn farmers in the depressed 1920s. He wrote, "In every type of farming… success and failure are side by side. And there is no one formula for success. One may do it with power machinery, another does it with horses, another with horses and tractors together. One does it on cheap land, and one does it on dear land. In every case it is the man who does it—and he does it with his head." SEP, "The Corn Belt," October 6, 1928.
13 SEP, "Notes of These Times," October 8, 1932.

Chapter Twenty-two
NOT A DOLLAR

Franklin Roosevelt took office March 4, 1933. Years later, Garrett wrote:

> There had never been a President remotely like him... Power flourished in him, and multiplied itself, until he had more than any other President ever possessed or wanted. Some of it he got from a spellbound Congress... Some of it he seized, some of it he got by outsmarting the law, and some of it by thinking of things no law had had the forethought to forbid.
>
> And yet you could not say that he had an evil lust for power like Lenin, Mussolini or Hitler; it sometimes seemed more as if he enormously enjoyed playing with it, just to see what would happen. He was not cruel; he was perhaps too civilized to be sinister... But no Constitution that had ever been written could chain this Roosevelt down.[1]

Garrett gave him his hundred days of grace, and then some. His first blast at the new president in the *Saturday Evening Post* did not come until the issue of August 12, which was put to bed in early July. The country, Garrett said, had "embraced a dictatorship, with no conscious intention, no serious debate about it, by implied consent, all in one hundred days."[2] His tone was skeptical, but with final judgment held in reserve. He wrote to Hoover concerning his article: "The reactions to it have been on the whole much less adverse than I had expected."[3]

As 1933 unfolded Garrett grew more alarmed, as did his boss, George Lorimer. "Up until that time," wrote Lorimer's biographer, "the *Post* had been primarily an organ of entertainment and enlightenment, notwithstanding its political campaigns. Now Lorimer frankly abandoned that concept of it in favor of an open and continued attack on the enemy."[4] The *Post's* enemy was the New Deal, and its artillery piece was Garrett. He was 55, and starting a battle against a president he would come to loathe.

Garrett made two broad cases against the New Deal, one economic and the other political. But first there was the matter of the currency, which involved economics and politics both, and a moral point besides.

For two decades Garrett had commented on the workings of America's modified gold standard. He had not been a champion of gold particularly. In 1922, in *The Driver,* he had mocked the quasi-religious battle between the silver people and gold people in 1896. "Money is not a thing either true or untrue," he had written. "It is merely a token of other things which are useful and enjoyable. Both silver and gold are sound for that purpose." In theory, a country might keep the supply of paper money corralled by fiat, but in a democracy, Garrett argued, the central bank needed an excuse to say "no" to the clamor for cheap credit. The Federal Reserve's requirement of 40 percent gold backing on Federal Reserve Notes was an excuse like that. It was "an arbitrary fact," Garrett wrote. Perhaps it was even a "fetish," which is what the inflationists called it, but it was a fetish "that ultimately serves rational ends." The point was to control the money supply. Do that, Garrett wrote, and people "may prosper under any theory of money."[5]

But when Franklin Roosevelt took the gold and left the people with fiat money, it was no longer an academic question. It was an act of federal authority, and Garrett found it deeply troubling. His immediate objection wasn't so much to fiat money itself, but the purpose of the change, which was to redistribute wealth and to remove institutional shackles on the state. When journalist Dorothy Thompson argued that it didn't matter, Garrett wrote in a letter:

> It is dangerous for one to know as much as Dorothy Thompson knows without knowing a great deal more... She does not know, for example, what gold was for in the modern case. It was not to pay with; it was not to settle international balances with. In the modern case it had but one function, really, and that was to limit credit expansion. That was no fiction. It was one of the few realities in the whole world of banking and finance. Bankers cannot be trusted to expand credit in their free judgment; governments cannot be trusted to expand it as the necessity occurs to them. Both must be limited by something they cannot control. And that was the gold standard.[6]

Deeper was the issue of honesty. In his campaign, Roosevelt had promised the voters to maintain a sound dollar. He hadn't specified what that meant, but in the politics of the day it was taken to mean a gold dollar. Then, as president, Roosevelt had issued an executive order calling in the gold and U.S. Treasury gold certificates held by the people. "They thought it was for the emergency only," Garrett wrote, "and they would get it back later." In exchange, the government paid out gold-backed Federal Reserve Notes. Then after the government had the gold and the people had the paper, the government said paper dollars were no longer as good as gold.

155

This was repudiation. Every Federal Reserve Note had engraved upon it, "Redeemable in gold on demand." The Treasury had sold bonds and promissory notes engraved with the promise to pay "in gold coin of the present standard of value." Several billions of this debt had been sold after Roosevelt was elected, and some of it after he had taken office.

All these promises were broken.

The dollar had been severed from gold before. During the Civil War the Treasury had printed the first United States Notes and declared them legal tender. These were the "greenbacks." Some courts had gone further and said they were legal tender for old contracts, in one case a contract calling for payment in gold coin. Economist Simon Newcomb had condemned that ruling specifically, saying it was "as wrong as if Congress had changed the size of the bushel measure and decided that old contracts for the delivery of wheat must be made in the new measure."7 But that is exactly what the New Deal did, and the Supreme Court said the government had the authority to do it. All private contracts calling for payment in gold dollars were to be settled in paper dollars.

The default was international. An American railroad had sold bonds to investors in Holland. The contract gave the investors the option, at maturity, of receiving the principal in dollars or guilders. They chose guilders—and the U.S. Supreme Court ordered payment in dollars. In Garrett's eyes, the Dutch investors had been swindled—not by the railroad, but by the U.S. government.

Garrett's article about it was called, "The Crisis Is Moral." Another of his articles about the gold repudiation was called "The Great Moral Disaster," which is what he thought it was. What the government had done went to the very heart of all business. He wrote:

All our economic undertakings above the level of solitary savage existence come to rest at last upon the security of words. Hence the importance of documents, bonds, statute books and records, lest people should dispute afterward what the words were. Then what if a sense of security in words should fail? What if it were no longer possible to trust the word of a government, that of your own or of any other; or to trust the word of a bond, the word of the law, the word of a contract, the word of a platform? ...It requires no reflection to be able to say what the effect of this would be upon the sense of economic security.[8]

The moral disaster was worldwide. Britain had defaulted, too—and not only on the gold backing of the pound, but also on debt payments of $180 million a year to the United States. France also defaulted on its debts to the United States. In the 1930s came a whole string of defaults.

Really it had started in Germany. In 1923 its government had printed up Reichsmark bonds and sold them all over the world, then ran its currency into the ground. It had done this on purpose to defy the Allies, who had insisted in the Treaty of Versailles that Germany pay for the war. The response of the American government and of international finance was to step in and bail Germany out. In 1934 Garrett looked back and thought: They shouldn't have done it. If they had refused to lend, they would have had to write off the war reparations immediately. But none of the following loans would have been made, and lost—and the reparations were lost anyhow. And the precedent wouldn't have been set that default was a strategic option. But the precedent had been set, and in ten years defaults had spread from Germany to the world.

The economic result was uncertainty. "The saving of capital tends to cease," Garrett wrote. "Why? Because capital must be saved in terms of paper money, and nobody knows

157

what that paper money will be worth."[9] There was also a political effect: financial power had moved into the hands of governments. Loans would be made, or not made, for political reasons.

Garrett's position did not imply that he was opposed to private default of unpayable debt. "Default is an act complete, a red mark across the slate," he wrote.[10] But only those who really could not pay should default. Default should be an act of necessity.

The repudiation of gold, in Garrett's view, had never been necessary. At the time of default, the U.S. Treasury had one-third of the monetary gold in the world. The dollar was good. It was even good after the Roosevelt administration tried to beat it down: when the Treasury declared a policy of buying (but not selling) any and all gold at $35 an ounce—a price that implied a 59-cent dollar—the fiat dollar vacuumed up gold from all over the world. With the onset of World War II America was also the safest country, which attracted more central-bank gold. By 1940, Garrett wrote, the U.S. Treasury owned almost *three-fourths* of all the monetary gold. And what good was it to the American people? "The Government controls it entirely," he wrote. "It is illegal for private persons to touch it. There is not a dollar of gold money in circulation."

He permitted himself to fantasize.

When the war is over and the mind of the world inclines to restoring peaceful trade, the very first want of all will be for a kind of money everybody can trust. No fiat money can be trusted. The world of no government can be trusted.

But if there were then one country—and it could only be this country—with gold currency resting not upon the engraved word but upon gold itself, the money of that one country would be the paramount money of the world.[11]

The dollar would indeed become the paramount money of
the world. But it would remain fiat money. The golden anchor
was gone.

Chapter 22 notes

1 *The American Story*, pp. 257-258.
2 SEP, "The Hundred Days," August 12, 1933.
3 Garrett to Hoover, August 22, 1933, Post Presidential Individual file, Box 67, Hoover Library.
4 *George Horace Lorimer and the Saturday Evening Post*.
5 *The Driver*, p. 88. The fetish: "Discussion of the Edison Money Plan," *New York Times*, July 16, 1922., section 7, p. 1. Any theory of money: SEP, "This Is Well-Being," December 26, 1925. Garrett also said, "Almost any monetary system would work if you could leave people out," in *The Wild Wheel*, p. 141.
6 Letter to Rose Wilder Lane, undated, Lane papers, Hoover Presidential Library.
7 Simon Newcomb, *Principles of Political Economy*, Harper & Bros., 1886, p. 152.
8 Dutch investors: SEP, "The Crisis Is Moral," August 12, 1939. The quote is from "The Great Moral Disaster," August 18, 1934. The case of the Dutch investors was *Guaranty Trust Co. of New York v. Henwood,* 307 U.S. 247, decided May 22, 1939. It concerned mortgage bonds sold in 1912 and payable in 1952.
9 SEP, "Pieces of Money," April 20, 1935.
10 SEP, "'America Can't Come Back,'" January 23, 1932.
11 SEP, "Gold Marbles," November 16, 1940.

Chapter Twenty-three
NOW IS FORBIDDEN

Always the strength of the American economy had been the willingness of people to try something new, to give up the old, and to make the best of whatever might come. The result was not stability, but that was all right. An economy was not a finished mechanism like a clock; it was a live thing, the actions of living people, all trying to survive and get ahead. Garrett had ended one of his road-trip articles by writing: "Americans embrace change. And this, perhaps, is the final secret of American power."[1]

In economic policy, the New Deal aimed to reverse the most recent change, and beyond that, to impose stability.

Under the New Deal, government would offer crop supports for tillers of the land, a dole for idle labor and the hope of rescue for sunk capital. The idea was to insulate the people from the pain of change. That was a mistake, Garrett thought. "If you overcome the sensation of pain by anesthetics, how shall the economy know when it is sick or why?"[2]

Beyond pain relief—which Americans now accept as normal—the New Deal also contained the more radical idea of a steady-state economy. This was never explicit policy, but it was a recurring theme. Capitalism had run out of creative juices. Anyway, most of the changes made by capitalism had been unnecessary, frivolous and even wasteful. People needed security. What John Maynard Keynes called the "animal spirits" and Garrett called the "wild wheel" of capitalism should be sedated in the name of stability, order, social security and, for the farmers, "an ever-normal granary."

To Garrett these were "all the ideals of a finished world."[3]

The institution that most clearly embodied this was the National Recovery Administration, set up in 1933. It was run by Gen. Hugh Johnson, who had helped write the conscription act in World War I, and had been the Army's liaison with Bernard Baruch at the War Industries Board. Johnson's task was to restore prosperity by raising prices to new official minimums. In the NRA regime, investment to expand capacity would have to be done by permission only, because new investment might undercut others. As on the farm, the New Deal would manage prices by managing production. All this was to be voluntary, sort of. Companies were urged to sign up, and once enough of them had done so, the NRA wage and price codes were enforceable on everyone. Joiners were encouraged to display the agency's symbol, a blue eagle grasping lightning bolts and a mechanical gear, with the slogan, "We Do Our Part." There were parades about it, appeals to patriotism and pressure to boycott "chiselers."

To Garrett, the attempt to cure the Depression by raising prices, either by inflation or Blue Eagle price codes, was backwards. The right way to deal with a new economic reality was to adjust to it; if prices fell, the smart producer should cut costs, perhaps by wage cuts and debt repudiation but most boldly by investing in new machinery. This was the way it had always been done. He wrote:

> Those that were able to reduce their costs could go on; those that were unable to do it, wanting either the capital or the courage, or wanting both, would have to quit...The high-cost producers with their old equipment were ruined. But that is how industry, when governed by a law of ruthless competition, got rid of

its obsolescence. In every depression the forward part of industry was made over new.

Such a thing now is forbidden...The new idea is that prices must rise first. Production must be limited until they do.[4]

In his message to Congress of January 1934, with business in a grim state, Roosevelt referred to "the unnecessary expansion of industrial plant" as wasteful and antisocial. He said, "We must make sure that as we reconstruct our life there be no soil in which such weeds can grow again."[5]

The president of the United States was comparing new industrial plant and machine tools to *weeds!* It was bizarre, though in Garrett's experience it was not quite new. He had had a whiff of such a notion before. In 1925, in Britain, he had seen capital and labor thinking along these lines:

Each pursues the idea of monopoly. Both are controlled by a common fallacy, which is to suppose that the divisible product... may be increased by limiting the output... A bricklayer does half as much as before the war, thereby exploiting the monopoly enjoyed by the building-trades unions. A coal miner's output is about one-third what it is in the United States. Capital also limits production, by means of rings and federations, fearful of losing its profit if output is uncontrolled. Thus a vicious circle of limitations.[6]

Garrett had found the Britain of 1925 to be a land of "acute social anxiety," a society "totally absorbed in the act of taking [its] own pulse," an unvigorous country of old men in boardrooms and workers on the dole. In 1936, incredibly, this sickness had come to America. "People all alike have been thinking as introverts... Where has been any thought of making any new attack on the environment, a new conquest of reality?"[7]

There were some thoughts. The Supreme Court shot an arrow through the Blue Eagle in 1935. That is when economic revival began, but more tentatively than in past recoveries.

In October 1936, Garrett visited Detroit. From 1929 to 1932, auto production had plunged 80 percent. In 1935 it had begun to recover and in 1936 the automakers were having their first good year in a long time. The new cars looked radically different from the 1929 cars. They had bigger engines, more features, and actually took more labor hours to build. And their price had gone *down*.

Garrett wrote his report in the first person, in a way that 40 years later would be called the New Journalism. He called himself the Old Reporter. He stationed himself at the Detroit Athletic Club, where the motor men had hobnobbed since the days of the Dodge brothers. His aim: to explain why the auto industry was leading the economic recovery.

All afternoon, auto men came and went at his table, and Garrett put the question to them: Why were they succeeding? They had exciting products, they said. But it was more than that, Garrett said. That was the manifestation of something deeper. An idea. They were *competitive*. That was it. Still Garrett was not satisfied. *Why* were they competitive? What had made them so? It was Henry Ford, several said. Yes, Garrett replied, it was Ford. But also Walter Chrysler, who had bulled into the Big Three in the 1920s, and General Motors, which had surpassed Ford. It wasn't *only* Ford. What was it, then? Finally, the auto men, exasperated, turned on Garrett: "You've asked us a lot of questions. How do you answer your own question?"

"I may be coming to one," said the Old Reporter. "Tell me this: in the Blue Eagle days, why was the automobile industry the one that refused to write or to accept from the NRA a code that would mean to exchange a bargain on hours and wages for the right to fix prices, limit production, and be exempt from the antitrust laws?"

"We believed in competition."

"You wanted to be free," said the Old Reporter. "That was the point." [8]

Ford had been the only big automaker to reject the Blue Eagle, so Garrett was stretching a point here. His more general point was that each industry attracted a certain personality. In the first third of the 20th century, the auto industry had attracted men with a kind of wildness. "The auto industry was what it was because the men were like that," Garrett wrote.

Garrett's point was lost in the events around it. His account of Detroit's recovery was printed at the beginning of 1937, when the United Auto Workers began its assault on General Motors and Chrysler, and when the New Deal was pushing against the Supreme Court. The unions would win and the New Deal would win—and the economic recovery would collapse.

When the Depression deepened in the winter of 1937-38, Roosevelt blamed "economic royalists" for sabotaging his recovery. Garrett blamed the New Deal, which he said had "crippled the free competitive system."

> For five years there has been no American system. What we have been watching is the experiment of trying to make a captive capitalism work, conducted by a Government that only half believes in it and has not the daring to destroy it.[9]

Garrett explained better than anyone else that the New Deal's central economic doctrine, the inducement of recovery by pushing prices up, did not work. Nor did it increase "purchasing power" for unions to push up wages in a depression.

High wages prevented workers from being hired at all, which lessened production and therefore *lessened* purchasing power. These policies delayed economic recovery in the United States compared with countries abroad. Such recovery as was achieved in 1935-36 collapsed in the depression-within-a-depression of 1937-38, which occurred in the United States and nowhere else.

The New Deal's vision of a steady-state economy is forgotten, even by dyed-in-the-wool Democrats. So has its approach of protecting prices, raising wages and restricting output. After the Asian economic collapse of 1997 the economists of the Democratic administration of Bill Clinton advised the South Koreans to let prices fall to their natural levels, cut costs, and compete. It was anti-New Deal advice, and it worked.

Chapter 23 notes
1 SEP, "West Coast, East Coast," November 2, 1929.
2 "Comment," *American Affairs*, January 1950.
3 SEP, "Fifth Anniversary N.D.," March 5, 1938.
4 SEP, "Washington Miscellany," December 16, 1933.
5 SEP, "Fifth Anniversary N.D.," March 5, 1938.
6 SEP, "Signs in England," May 16, 1925.
7 SEP, "Signs in England," May 16, 1925; "The Lost American," March 28, 1936.
8 SEP, "The Detroit Principle," January 2, 1937.
9 SEP, "Fifth Anniversary N.D.," March 5, 1938.

Chapter Twenty-four
THE WORD IS 'FEAR'

Garrett fought against the New Deal on two grounds, he wrote, "one minor and one major." That the economics didn't work was the minor ground. To the Austrian-school economist Frank Fetter, he wrote, "It's no use saying this or that won't work, or *won't work here.* Many things that we hate may work."[1]

The major ground for opposing the New Deal, Garrett wrote, was liberty. It was the rising power of the president, the "contempt for the restraints of constitutional law," the beguilement of the individual to surrender his responsibilities to the state. The sequel, Garrett worried, would be "some form of elective despotism."[2]

Much of it turned on the meaning of a few words in Article 1, Section 8, of the Constitution, which grants to Congress the power "to regulate Commerce... among the several States..." The Commerce Clause had always been interpreted to mean transactions among people in different states, leaving dealings between two people in the same state beyond federal authority. That included dealings between an employer and employee, both in the same state.

There was also a legal doctrine that every adult American had a constitutional right to sell his labor without limitation. This was very much like the right of abortion proclaimed in *Roe v. Wade* 40 years later. As with abortion, the right to sell one's labor was not spelled out in the Constitution, but the Supreme Court had perceived it in the hints and shadows. As with abortion, to sell one's labor was to make a very personal decision. They might have called it "a worker's right to choose," though actually they called it freedom of contract.[3]

By creating a law to regulate wages and union membership nationwide, the Blue Eagle violated both the Commerce Clause and the freedom of contract as understood at the time. In 1934 Garrett wrote, "Many of the things the New Deal proposed to do were of doubtful constitutionality, as everybody well knew; the Government, nevertheless, was resolved to do them. And so it hired lawyers, very subtle with words and periods, to find holes in the Constitution and ways to go around it."[4]

This they did.

In 1935, the Court struck down the National Recovery Act, killing the Blue Eagle, and also the Agricultural Adjustment Act. But it had sided with the government in the cases brought by the owners of gold bonds. Its resolution was weakening. And the New Deal kept the laws coming: the labor law of the Blue Eagle was re-codified in the National Labor Relations Act. The old AAA was replaced by a new AAA. Then came Social Security. None was constitutional under the old doctrines.

After his landslide victory in November 1936, Roosevelt launched a torpedo at the Court. He asked Congress to enlarge the number of seats so that he could fill them with like-minded justices. Congress resisted, but the Court had already decided to buckle. In decisions made in December 1936 and announced in the spring of 1937, it accepted a minimum wage law, a national labor law and the Social Security law. The Court's fight against the New Deal was over. Henceforth, in the matter of economic regulation, the federal government could do what it wanted.

We are used to that power, today. The power is immense and potentially destructive. It is rarely, however, in leftist hands. Business has large influence over it. During the New Deal, business was the class enemy. The president publicly called businessmen "royalists" and "brigands." Government power was sudden and threatening, its purpose transformative. And it was *new*. People read about it in the same newspapers in which they read of Hitler's belligerence and Stalin's show trials. The destination was not clear.

The New Deal is known today for the institutions that have survived: the Securities and Exchange Commission, the Federal Deposit Insurance Corporation, Fannie Mae, and so on. We forget the national directive to plow under cotton and kill little pigs; the Blue Eagle's price and production controls; the aggressive raising of taxes while unemployment was above 15 percent; the retained-profits tax, which had the explicit purpose of forcing companies to pay out earnings rather than reinvest them; and Tennessee Valley Authority, which was then a front in a war against private power—and all in a pervasive intellectual climate of leftism.

Many of the things the New Deal did made little economic sense. But perhaps, Garrett wrote, the New Deal was not really about economics:

> From a progression of acts it may be possible to deduce a fundamental policy, only provided the acts are consistent with one another, or consistent as a whole with a controlling principle. But the acts of the New Deal bewilder that process. In the entire book of the New Deal's self-revelation and self-exegesis there is a certain paragraph that would reconcile all of its acts, not one with another but with one principle of contradiction. It is the passage in the last annual message in which suddenly the President speaks of the new instruments of governmental power that have

been created, and then says of this new power that it is such that as in other hands "would provide shackles for the liberties of the people." But it is in his hands. Well, conquest of power for purposes of all-doing—that in itself could be a controlling policy, and such a policy, impossible to acknowledge, would involve many inconsistencies of immediate policy, because the peaceable course to the seizure of great political power is a zigzag path.[5]

Political centralization was the policy, and the economics came after. And sometimes very bad economics. The New Deal made investors reluctant to invest. In 1935 Garrett wrote in the *Post*, "Wealth is looking for holes in which to hide itself; it is running to and fro in the world, seeking places of asylum, and willing to pay for them."[6] In 1936 he wrote in a letter, "There is nowhere in the world such a thing as certitude of money. The whole affair is in a state of chaos. And yet they all prate of restoring enterprise and trade."

In 1938, he wrote about a dinner with private-sector men. Here, at 60, he refers to himself again as the Old Reporter:

"Listen, you economic royalists," said the Old Reporter. "I've been listening to you for three hours. Do you realize everything you have expressed in that time could have been expressed in one word?"

"What word is that?" the public-relations man asked.

"It is a word," said the Old Reporter, "that I have been trying to think of for three or four days. A single word to define a new fact in the relations between people and Government. The word is 'fear.' You are all afraid of the Government...

THE WORD IS 'FEAR'

"This thing we speak of, calling it fear, is new, isn't it?" the Old Reporter continued. "I've been thinking about it a good deal in the last few days. I've been trying to contrast the Washington I'm looking at now with the Washington I first knew. I've brought it down to the attitude of the ordinary citizen toward the Government. How has that changed? When I first came to Washington, the attitude of every man here, of every man who came here on any errand, was that the Government was his Government. He supported it. He had something to say about it because he paid the bill. The ways in which the Government could touch him were definite and limited; he knew what they were and submitted to them in a voluntary manner, and if it tried to touch him in any other way he knew how to put it in its place. That was fine. At least, I think it was. But that feeling is entirely gone. Where will you find any trace of it left? In place of it is fear. No man is sure what his immunities are... No man knows how, tomorrow, the Government may touch him or what he can do about it."[7]

Pro-New Deal historians would question why private investment collapsed in the 1930s. They were not inclined to accept the explanation business gave, which was "lack of confidence." To them, it sounded like a public-relations man's reason. Years later, historian Robert Higgs of the Independent Institute documented it in a study of opinion polls and the extraordinary divergence between short-term investment, which recovered in the mid-1930s, and long-term investment, which did not. Higgs called the lack-of-confidence phenomenon "regime uncertainty,"[8] which is another name for political risk. People did not invest long-term because they believed long-term investments were not safe.

171

"Regime uncertainty" was the final reason why, in America, the Depression lasted until the onset of World War II.

The transformative impulse ended with the war. Government still occupied most of the social territory it had seized; its legacy was a permanent increase in taxes, spending and the power to make rules. The entrepreneur lost part of the control of his business. The worker lost the unquestioned right to bargain for himself and to receive his full pay. The farmer lost his freedom to plant what he wanted in his own dirt.

"The people were willing," Garrett wrote. "They were not coerced. They were writhing in economic pain. Many forgot and many seemed no longer to care that unless they absorbed their own troubles instead of unloading them on a paternalistic government they would never again be as free as their fathers were."[9]

Even the capitalists were more willing than their defenders wanted to admit. To Hoover, Garrett wrote: "Almost I am persuaded that business itself has done more harm to capitalism and to its principles of liberty than all the demagogues."[10]

172

Chapter 24 notes

1 SEP, "Not on the Ballot," November 2, 1940. Garrett to Frank Fetter, October 10, 1937. Frank Fetter papers, Courtesy Lilly Library, Indiana University, Bloomington, IN. Frank Fetter, 1863-1949, a native of Indiana, developed a theory of interest rates entirely based upon time preference. He was credited with being "the leader in the United States of the early Austrian School of Economics" by Murray Rothbard in the introduction to *Capital, Interest and Rent: Essays in the Theory of Distribution,* Sheed, Andrews and McMeel, 1977.

2 SEP, "Not on the Ballot," November 2, 1940.

3 The key freedom-of-contract case was *Lochner v. New York* (1905). The parallel between *Lochner* and *Roe* is stated in Justice Rehnquist's dissent in *Roe.* A difference, of course, is that the worker's right of contract did not involve killing a fetus, though it might involve undercutting another worker.

4 SEP, "The Great Moral Disaster," August 18, 1934.

5 SEP, "National Hill Notes," February 29, 1936.

6 SEP, "The Wealth Question," August 31, 1935.

7 SEP, "A Washington Errand," January 22, 1938. Garrett has a passage much the same in "Ex America," *The People's Pottage,* 1953, pp. 96-97.

8 Robert Higgs, "Regime Uncertainty," *The Independent Review,* spring 1997, pp. 561-590. Reprinted in Higgs, *Depression, War and Cold War: Studies in Political Economy,* Oxford University Press, 2006, pp. 3-29.

9 *The American Story,* p. 386.

10 Garrett to Hoover, undated, Post Presidential Individual file, Box 67, Hoover Library.

Chapter Twenty-five
TO THE FIGHT

I n the election of 1936 Garrett aided the Republican presidential nominee, Alf Landon, not with a puff piece in the *Post*, but with direct advice, written after a meeting with Landon in Topeka on August 7. Garrett's six-page memo to Landon, offered free of charge, is preserved in the papers of *Saturday Evening Post* editor George Lorimer.

Garrett advised Landon to attack on two points. First, Roosevelt had run up the national debt. Landon should demand that the government stop borrowing:

> Instead of promising to balance the budget, declare: The government will borrow no more money for any reason, in peace and war. (If you say, not even for war, that means paying for war as we go, which is bound to be a restraint upon the impulse to war.) What is the result of borrowing no more? ...The extension [of the] Federal government is stopped... The government is made solvent... The integrity of money may be established.[1]

Second, he advised Landon to keep saying that Roosevelt had not abolished unemployment. The unemployment count had gone down, but only by the amount that public payrolls

175

had gone up. Landon should point out the only way known to create real work:

> The free competitive system shall be restored unconditionally...The profit motive shall be released... The spirit of adventure shall be called up again... If subsidies are yet needed, it is production that shall be subsidized. Turn men's thoughts to new industry. Destroy the only great industry that has appeared under the New Deal, which is the industry of relief.

"Challenge the idea that there has been a recovery," he said. There had been only a revival, a greater production of things in ordinary use. A recovery implied the resumption of progress, the creation of the new. He wrote:

> There has been no recovery... Recovery, with ten million unemployed? Recovery, with money at one per cent? The cheapness of money is a sign of disease. It means we have ceased to perform creative works for the future. It means we are creating no new industry.

That was an overstatement: as Garrett reported a few months later, the auto industry was creating new models and having some success at it. There was *some* recovery by 1936, but by historical standards it was anemic. And Garrett was right about interest rates: business was not interested in borrowing.

But Americans on government relief were feeling better, and Franklin Roosevelt looked to getting their votes. Garrett advised Landon to appeal to people still working, who were supporting those not working, and to the bank depositors whose money the government was borrowing.

Garrett advised Landon to attack, attack, attack, and "defend nothing."

Garrett was not optimistic that Landon would take his advice. This is clear from a second document preserved in the Lorimer papers, a confidential memo on Landon the man. In it, Garrett described the Kansan as a good listener. If Garrett made a point, Landon would absorb it. But, Garrett wrote, "it is like dropping it down a dry well. There is no splash." Landon, he wrote, was a man of no gestures:

> If he were a dog he would not be a terrier... If he were a savage he would be the first to make friends at the settlement and embrace the new religion for practical reasons; but in a crowd of men going over the top under fire he would be neither first nor last... All his success so far has been from stroking life the way the fur lies.

Then came the clincher: "What obviously is wanting is power. There is no feeling of power in him."

Landon was an anemic public speaker. H.L. Mencken, who traveled awhile with the candidate, and supported him for the same reasons Garrett did, lamented that Landon recited most of his speeches, often accenting the wrong words. Rather than pumping up his audiences, Landon let them down. He did not make a forceful stand against the New Deal, but caved in on farm relief and a number of other things. Wrote Mencken, "He was too mild a fellow for it."[2]

As the election drew nearer, Garrett wrote to his closest confidante in the 1930s, Rose Wilder Lane:

> I'm so sick of politics that I have an acid chemistry in my stomach. A parade of competitive masks and images. The people are not so much fooled; but they have to vote, wherefore they vote cynically, or as

parasites, and the thing goes on. I still haven't a guess as to the outcome. I've provided some ammunition, and everybody sounds grateful, Landon, Knox, et.al., but they use it to make Roman candles, not really to shout anything. I think I told you, the plan of campaign is Landon's own. His idea is, estrange nobody, and to get elected by a vote against Roosevelt.

In the next letter, he wrote:

It is the hardest intelligence test we ever faced. Roosevelt will get the entire moron vote. Most intelligent Republicans will have to vote the Republican ticket in spite of Landon. I am sick with disappointment. All he has said is that he will go on doing as much for people as they expect the New Deal to do for them, only in a Constitutional manner, and it will cost less. *Merdes.*

Landon was trounced. Roosevelt won every state but Maine and Vermont, and the Democrats emerged holding 76 percent of the seats in the House of Representatives and 79 percent of the seats in the Senate. Garrett wrote to Lane:

As a reporter who worked at his trade, and as an intelligent person, I am too humiliated to have an opinion about anything. Everything I believed about my own people was wrong. Everything I have written in the last four years was absurd.

Two letters later:

I have been trying to find out why I take it so hard. I don't know. What vanity to suppose that what one thinks or says is of any importance, or can make any difference. So it was vanity. I get that far, and it does not help. Why should I care what happens? Why should you? Your philosophy that whatever happens, life transacting itself against it saves you. It doesn't. You have what I have—a sense of great loss.

By the next letter, he looked outward:

Our fighting base is gone. Formerly we could say the people had never voted for the New Deal. That was a strong fighting position. Now they have voted for it in a positive, overwhelming manner. Then what? Shall one go on telling them they are wrong, or that they shall see, or that they have lost the world without knowing it, that they threw it away, and so on? Certainly not.

Where is the new base? I don't see it. Where is the fighting position? I haven't any; no one else seems to have one. Hearst and Smith and Rockefeller embracing it. The Republicans saying they must reorganize the party on a liberal platform. As for me, I believed something. What I believed has been rejected. According to my own argument, what people reject they have a right to reject; what world they want they have a perfect right to bring to pass if they can.

I realize now that it is not arguable and never was. You are or you ain't, and that's how you were born. My neighbors used to come in to get me to tell them what was the matter with the Townsend Plan. I told them; I took pains to tell them; I made it simple. Each time when they were gone I realized that I had not touched them. It wasn't that they didn't understand what I said. It was that what I said didn't interest them. They were thinking of something else. We were talking about different things. They wanted manna

179

and water out of the rock. I wanted people to stay hard and fit and self responsible, for the sake of going on. And in my folly I was trying to prove to them that the Townsend Plan would wreck the economic scheme. What did they care about the economic scheme? They would be dead before the result. Meanwhile, $200 a month. Do you see the trouble—I was right and they were right. So with the New Deal. For those who want that kind of world it is right. For those who don't want that kind of world it is wrong. And, again, it simply isn't arguable.

He still had his beliefs. In another letter he wrote:

I wish you would do an essay on the importance of prejudice. I am building a series of wakes—one for each prejudice I have buried.[3]

Chapter 25 notes

1 Garrett to Landon, August 12, 1936. Lorimer papers. The date of the meeting, August 7, is from the *New York Times'* story of that day, "Landon Will Meet Aides in Buffalo," p. 8.
2 H.L. Mencken, "Coroner's Inquest," Baltimore Sun, November 9, 1936, reprinted in Mencken, *A Carnival of Buncombe*, Johns Hopkins Press, 1956, p. 335.
3 All the letters to Lane are from the Rose Wilder Lane Papers, Herbert Hoover Presidential Library, West Branch, Iowa.

Chapter Twenty-six
ONLY HALF A SHELL

Garrett had met Rose Wilder Lane November 20, 1923, while returning from Britain on the steamer *Leviathan*, where they had talked for hours. They crossed paths again in 1928, when Garrett wrote the profile of Hoover. In the article, he had said:

> A book about him by a California woman, a writer of some excellence, was so displeasing to his sense of values that he bought it up, together with the plates, and destroyed it. This he did not do so much because the facts were wrong; they were treated in a glamorous manner, and that he hated.[1]

The book was Lane's *The Making of Herbert Hoover* (1920). To her, the article implied that she had accepted money to suppress her book, which she had not.[2] She sent the *Saturday Evening Post* an angry telegram, which associate editor Adelaide Neall forwarded to Garrett. He replied that he had taken the story from Hoover, had had no idea who the California woman was and had never heard of Lane's book. Neall replied: "Just why Miss Lane has gotten so excited I cannot see, as the paragraph as it reads is not at all libelous." (And clearly it is not.) Lane seemed to want an apology from the *Post* that did not name her or the book. Neall admitted to

Garrett that she should have edited out the identifier "California"—but the *Post* did not print an apology.[3]

Seven years later, Garrett and Lane were fast friends.

Lane had grown up in Missouri and absorbed the same frontier values as Garrett. She had written a biography of Henry Ford—*Henry Ford's Own Story* (1915)—as well as the one of Hoover. She had written fiction based on frontier life. Briefly attracted to communism, she went to the Soviet Union, breathed the Marxist air and spat it out. By the 1930s she had become, she said, "a fundamentalist American." She would later write the *Little House on the Prairie* books, working from outlines by her mother, Laura Ingalls Wilder.

Some of the Garrett-Lane correspondence is preserved in the Herbert Hoover Presidential Library at West Branch, Iowa. Though Garrett wrote with a thick-nibbed pen dipped in bottled ink, and his penmanship is at war with understanding, once decoded it provides an unusual clarity. It is as if mud on a window had been rubbed clean in just one spot. Lane's letters tend to be cautious, and somewhat formal; Garrett's bare his soul. In the mid-1930s, he wrote:

> I'm buying a small press on which, when the worst comes, I can print a paper of my own. I learned it when I was a printer's devil. I can set type and run a press. Do you want a job? I could teach you the trade in a few weeks...
>
> P.S. For the name of my paper, what would you think of CROSS ROADS. Owned, edited and printed by me. Advertising rates: none.

After Landon's defeat he wrote:

> Maybe I shall take a long drive. Meanwhile, I'm converting an old Model A into a power plant, setting up a saw rig, tinkering. There is nothing I can think of

more satisfactory, by the way, than feeding wood into a buzz saw. It's good for the dumb rankles.

As 1936 came to an end, he wrote:

Spengler, who says many things that are both so and untrue, says optimism is cowardice. Pareto, who says many things that are true and yet not so, says people do not behave as if they were rational.

Faith may be a quality of the liver.

Signs of decay in our part of the human race—the whole western part—are these: Love of soft living. Hope of security. Moral numbness. Dread of responsibility. Sentimentality. Present mindedness.

Anyhow, I wish you a merry Christmas.

In the summer of 1935 Lane had joined Garrett for a two-week drive through Illinois, Kansas, Nebraska and Iowa as he interviewed farmers about the New Deal. In Pope County, Ill., they talked to proud farmers who were being enticed with promises of federal houses and jobs—and the threat of federal condemnation—to sign over their land to Rexford Tugwell's Resettlement Administration for $7 an acre. Lane recalled later that the land was not eroded and the farmhouses were simple, "a few without electricity or plumbing," but some with, and all the places cared for by their owners. "None of them wanted to be rehabilitated," she wrote. "None of them would speak to Garet or me until we proved that we did not come from the Government. Garet was dumfounded when men surrounded the car and demanded that proof; luckily he had it, by chance."[4]

Lane noted that the Resettlement Administration's project manager was a member of the Communist Party, which made her think of what she had seen in Soviet Georgia. She called the program "Communist Terror in Illinois."

Garrett didn't quite call it that—at least, not in the *Saturday Evening Post*. ("Neither Lorimer nor any other editor would print it"—the full story—Lane wrote.) Garrett did describe meeting "a woman, seventy, who had helped her man clear the ground by taking herself one end of a cross-cut saw." Now the government wanted to "resettle" this woman and her ailing husband somewhere else, and "rehabilitate" them.[5]

The resignation of many of the farmers made Lane furious. At the end of her trip with Garrett, she penned a libertarian blast of her own. Called "Credo," it was published in the *Saturday Evening Post* of March 7, 1936. It was the seed of her book of political theory, *The Discovery of Freedom* (1943).

The interest between Garrett and Lane was not exclusively political. "There is just a hint that what began in business led to a brief romance," wrote her biographer William Holtz. "She was nearing fifty now, he seven years older—short, fat and balding, with a voice husky from an old bullet wound and missing some fingers as well... In this bed of sympathetic principle, something like love bloomed, crusty and irritable on his side, quietly supplicating on hers."[6]

Garrett wrote her:

> Do you know the fish,—the shell fish,—that has only half a shell and lives against a cliff for the other half? I can pronounce it and so can you, the name, I mean, but I cannot spell it and neither can you, unless you remember it from a bill of fare, which doesn't prove it to be right. I cling to the cliff. Only two things can pry me off. One is death and the other is a female. That is why I hate females. I know what this strange fish is thinking. He wonders why anybody would want to pry him loose, that is, he wonders why anybody should want him to eat. It is a weak fish. The only strength he has is his weakness, his half-shell-

ness, his incompleteness. He is tough and to the refined taste coarse, but these qualities, which should be somewhat in his protection, are of no use whatever because when they are discovered it is too late, for him and for everyone else. When he dies he drops into the sea, and it was a hell of a little to have lived for, and he can't help it...

Life is an ass. I've told you that. It is so in all senses, personal and impersonal.

What do I want you to do? Nothing. You are not that kind of shell fish. And if you were, what would be the use of sticking side by side to as sea cliff? And for all of this I'm in a great rage at you. If we were in the kitchen I'd throw a plate at your head...

In another letter he wrote:

Rose dear, it is more than I can understand. You shake me in the fixed principle of my life. I am angry and happy. We two! We ought to be in a row boat somewhere in the middle of the Pacific or on a distant island. I want to see you and yet I dread it.

After this heat, the letters move back to politics and work. Lorimer, who had run the *Saturday Evening Post* since the turn of the century, announced his retirement in December 1936. He had been bothered by a sore spot on his tongue; it was cancer, and he died of it in 1937. In one of his last notes to Garrett, Lorimer said he was under doctor's orders not to talk, but that he would be pleased for Garrett visit him. "You do the talking," Lorimer said. Garrett would miss him deeply. Years later Lorimer's biographer said of Garrett, "His loyalty and devotion to Lorimer were touching, particularly because other old friends and associates I talked to were not always so.

Garet was very anxious that I give the best possible impression of the Boss."[7]

Wesley Winans Stout was promoted to editor-in-chief. Garrett suspected the campaign against the New Deal was over, but it was not. Early in 1937, Garrett wrote Lane:

> I was thinking to cut out, because apparently the Post was leaning away from the fight. But now Stout wants me to get into the labor story, and that changes my feeling about him and about the Post. Anyhow, I'm going to do it.

Garrett had always written favorably of the skilled worker, the "aristocrat of labor," who could "think with his hands." One of the heroes of *The Cinder Buggy* was that kind of worker. Of the unskilled worker, likely an immigrant, Garrett had little to say. Once he had referred to him as "the economic unit in its lowest form."[8] In a moment of gloom, he wrote Lane, "Who do the work are slaves. They know it and we know it, and in a democracy it cannot be mentioned."

But at least in America that worker was paid more than in Europe, and if he wanted to, he could join a union. It was all right for unions to ask for more money, but when they reached for control of the production line, Garrett was against them. Still, he honored the strong, and had to admit the vigor of the new union leaders. In early 1937, he interviewed John L. Lewis of the United Mine Workers, who was organizing the steel industry for the CIO. Garrett wrote Lane:

> It would take 5,000 words to tell you what I make of him. Powerful, intelligent, subtle, ruthless, remorseless, probably sinister, with amazing poise and self-control... During four hours of hard conversation he has been apparently spontaneous, unthink-

ing, unguarded, almost naive. He listens. He never [admits] a weak position, but says, "Well, what of it?"

In Garrett's next letter, he wrote:

I ask myself what I should do if I worked on the assembly line. Would I join Lewis? I wish I knew. I think I'd go with Lewis, even hating any kind of union. Why? I cannot be sure. Probably from seeing people go in and out of the Detroit Athletic Club. I know that gang and it's fine. But if my acquaintance with it were confined to seeing it go in and out, I'd go with Lewis. Worse still, if my acquaintance with it were confined to what it says or to what it knows about itself, I'd be for Lewis now. It's fine for reasons it does not know.

For Garrett, the final attraction of capitalism was not that it allowed people to get rich, or workers to have high wages, though it did those things, but that it respected the liberty of the individual. Before the economic was the political, and before that, the philosophical— and Garrett was a philosophical individualist. To Lane he wrote: "In principle I believe that the less we act upon the lives of others for good or evil— the less the better. Each one saves himself or he is not saved."

Garrett used to say that any thinking person should be a philosophical anarchist. That is what Lane was, and she took it further than he did. There is a certainty in Lane about such questions as the existence of God, the rights of man, about what is and must be, that is absent in Garrett. Both recalled fondly the pre-World War I time of economic laissez faire. Lane declared it was the system that fit the true nature of man. Garrett preferred it for himself, and argued that it was the system in which strong people like Baruch and Ford did best, and that had made the nation strong. Years later, after he had died,

Lane complained in a letter that Garrett had "spoiled every-thing he wrote" by trying "to fight for individualism on an always semi-collectivist basis."[9]

Garrett would not follow an idea for the sake of consistency. To Baruch, Garrett wrote:

> Do you recall that we have often made the distinction between intelligence and wisdom? It is intelligence that wants to solve all the problems at once; it is wisdom that knows better. Some day I shall be tempted to do an essay on excess cerebration, by which I mean only too much intelligence and too little wisdom.[10]

Years after Garrett and Lane had died, Richard Cornuelle, who had known them both, wrote, "I think he considered her an irritating ideological libertarian. She once told him she couldn't understand the fuss about repetitive work on the assembly line. She found knitting and the like relaxing."[11]

In the late 1930s an issue was coming that would divide them—World War II. Though they both opposed America volunteering to fight, their thinking about what their country *should* do was quite different. Their correspondence—at least, that part that is preserved—breaks off in 1940 and starts up in 1953, after Garrett had remarried, and has a less familiar tone.

Chapter 26 notes
1 SEP, "Hoover of Iowa and California," June 2, 1928. Leviathan: "Ocean Travelers," *New York Times,* November 25, 1923, p. 8.
2 William Holtz, *The Ghost in the Little House: A Life of Rose Wilder Lane*, University of Missouri Press, 1993, pp. 189-190.
3 Adelaide Neall to Garrett, June 6, 1928. Lorimer papers. Holtz, *The Ghost in the Little House*, pp. 190.
4 Lane to Jasper Crane, January 30, 1957, in Roger Lea MacBride, ed., *The Lady and the Tycoon*, Caxton, 1973, p. 169. Here Lane puts her trip with Garrett in 1933, but the Resettlement Administration wasn't formed until 1935, and Garrett would not have delayed his report by two years.
5 SEP, "Plowing Up Freedom," November 16, 1935.
6 *The Ghost in the Little House*, pp. 260, 268. Garrett's draft card from World War I noted that two fingers on his right hand had been cut off.
7 Lorimer to Garrett, August 16, 1937. Garrett papers. John Tebbel to Carl Ryant, December 15, 1967. Ryant papers, University of Louisville.
8 *New York Tribune*, "East of West," August 1, 1916.
9 "Any thinking person": letter to the author, February 5, 2006; God: Lane to Jasper Crane, July 5, 1948, *The Lady and the Tycoon*, pp. 32-39. Lane's comments: Lane to Jasper Crane, August 25, 2955, *The Lady and the Tycoon*, p. 125.
10 Garrett to Baruch, December 31, 1943. Garrett papers.
11 Letter to the author, February 1, 2006.

Chapter Twenty-seven
ITS RIGHT NAME

Franklin Roosevelt had first sounded a note of war with his "quarantine the aggressors" speech in 1937. The public reaction was negative, and he backed away. And yet as Adolf Hitler pushed closer and closer to war, Roosevelt returned to a martial theme. Years later, Garrett wrote:

> To wend his contrary way toward war without a single false step and at the same time to keep an unwilling people with him was a feat of statecraft for which Mr. Roosevelt was peculiarly qualified in mind and character. It took daring, rare subtlety, an intuition for right timing and the entirety of his power to cajole the mass mind. That was an extraordinary power, beyond reason or analysis, and almost infallible.[1]

In early 1939, five months before Hitler and Stalin jointly began the war in Europe, Garrett noted "the steady onset of the idea that we shall have to save the world for democracy again." He wrote, "You can feel it… The American character is inhabited by a strong crusader spirit. Many voices, for different reasons, have been calling to it, and it responds."[2]

Garrett feared a repeat of World War I, in which America talked itself into someone else's quarrel. He thought his country needed to match Germany's power—to build an "incomparable" navy in the Atlantic and another in the Pacific, and "an impervious antiaircraft wall." But he did not want to *pick a fight* with Germany. That was the difference. Germany was a land power in Europe. America was an air and sea power in North America. Geography gave us an option the French didn't have. The interventionist voice was saying that America had to help England and France, because the Rhine was America's "first line of defense" against Nazism. "The thesis was false," Garrett wrote. "Our first line of defense was not in Europe. It was here." The Rhine was *their* first line of defense. [3]

That was a selfish attitude, but all countries had the right to be selfish about their security. Britain was selfish. "Never did Great Britain fight for anything but her own, which is right in this world," wrote Garrett in a letter to economist Carl Snyder, "and would that we had that kind of intelligence."[4]

Unless America was willing to go to Europe and destroy German militarism there, Garrett wrote, "we may as well make our minds up now that we shall have to live in the same world with it..."[5] It is the same phrase he had used in World War I—to "live in the same world" with Germany—but he reached the opposite conclusion. One world war was enough.

Garrett had written an occasional editorial for the *Post*, and in May 1940 he was named chief editorial writer. From that perch he laid down a barrage of copy in favor of a military buildup but against open opposition to the Axis and an alliance with Britain.

Roosevelt's position was that America should help defeat Germany through "measures short of war," meaning selling weapons and supplies to Britain. The idea was that Americans would not have to fight. Garrett argued that declaring for the Allies, which Roosevelt had done, was engaging in the rhetoric of war, and that selling them munitions was an act of war. Roosevelt was getting America in while telling the people he was keeping them out. In the late summer of 1940 Garrett wrote, "If [America] should come awake one morning to read in the newspaper headlines, or hear by the radio, that it had walked backward into war, it would take it no doubt as having been somehow inevitable from the first, and yet nobody would be able to say quite how or why it happened."[6]

In the campaign for intervention, he wrote, "Nothing was called by its right name."[7]

In the presidential campaign of 1940, Roosevelt and his Republican opponent, Wendell Willkie, were both publicly for selling war material to Britain but against going to war. "The basic purpose of our foreign policy is to keep America out of war," the president had said. A month after Roosevelt won the election, Prime Minister Winston Churchill notified him that Britain had run out of money. It could no longer pay cash for American munitions. Roosevelt asked Congress to approve Lend-Lease, a law allowing the president to give weapons and supplies to any country he deemed essential to America's defense. The law was passed, and Roosevelt declared Britain, Greece and China essential to America's defense.

Lend-Lease was America's commitment to defeat the Axis. It was, wrote Garrett, the real declaration of war. After it passed, the fight against intervention was over.

"From May 1941 on, the *Post* was no longer isolationist," wrote Ryant in *Profit's Prophet*. "While it regretted the necessity of going to war, it believed the nation would do so."[8] A more accurate reading of Garrett's editorials is that he never admitted the necessity of going to war but believed that his country had already done so.

On the eve of the attack on Pearl Harbor, Garrett wrote in the *Post*:

> Whether the noninterventionists were right or wrong is now a question that belongs to history. Their cause is lost. But they were never confused, never

involved in a moral dilemma. It was not our war. That is what they believed... Their assumptions and premises ought to have been debated in a dispassionate manner, on grounds of grand strategy. Could we stand upon our own hemisphere and defend it against all aggressors, or are we obliged by military necessity to take the war to Hitler?...

But the question was not debated in that manner. It was debated in terms of an idea that must have been all the time taking shape in the President's mind and now appears fully clothed in these magnificent words: "The American people have made an unlimited commitment that there shall be a free world." ...A war to make the whole world free...[9]

And once America undertook *that* obligation, where would it end?

"We understand the crusader passion, even though we seldom share it," wrote Garrett, "but when the crusader begins to think, we lose him entirely. He ought not to spoil it by thinking."[10] In other words, if the American government had decided to fight Germany, then *do* it—but let's not explain ourselves by embracing a doctrine that commits us to an endless string of wars into the future.

For all his opposition to World War II, Garrett's sympathy was never with the dictatorships. In December 1939 he had worked on a plan to raise $50 million on Wall Street for Finland, which was being attacked by Germany's partner, the Soviet Union.[11] Nor was he dismissive of the aggressors' power. In 1940, when Rose Wilder Lane asserted that Nazi Germany's state-controlled economy did not have the productive potential to sustain a long war, Garrett disagreed. He remembered World War I, and how long the Germans had held out. Besides, long-run staying power was not the only thing: France had been overrun in a few weeks. "The art of war has been revolutionized," he wrote, "and with it the time factor."

In mid-1940 he wrote an editorial endorsing conscription. It was full of reluctance. America had never had a draft before the onset of fighting, and its president was promising the people to keep them out of any foreign war. The Roosevelt government had a long record of dissembling about its intentions, and the idea of a draft, Garrett wrote, seemed to conjure among the Congressmen "forebodings that could hardly name themselves." He shared these feelings, and most of his editorial was an exposition of them. But a volunteer army was unscientific and inadequate, he wrote, and he ended by capitulating to necessity.[12]

When Lane chastised him for it, he replied: "Don't abuse me. Argue with me. What is the good of being free if you cease to exist? Survival is an important value, whether you think so or not." He concluded, "The German power has to be matched, else there is no living in the world. To match it, as I keep saying, a people must put from one quarter to a third of its national income into armaments."[13]

He also rejected the position, taken by libertarian Isabel Paterson in *The God of the Machine* (1943), that the wartime U.S. economy should be run without price, wage or production controls.[14] Garrett had covered these issues during World War I, and sided with his old friend Baruch, the former czar of war production.

Garrett explained his position as follows. Suppose, he wrote, the government needed steel, and its demand plus the private demand totaled more steel than the industry could produce. The free-market answer was for the government and private users to bid against each other, to push the price up, and for some entrepreneur to see the rising price as a signal to build another steel mill. "True, it would work that way, given time," Garrett wrote. But, he added, "while waiting for new steel mills to be built, we might lose the war."[15]

In war, government was not simply another customer for steel or any other product. It went to the front of the queue, and it bought whatever it needed. It had to. It was in everyone's interest that it did.

Garrett knew more than most what would have to be done to fight Germany and Japan. He also thought that preparing to fight, but not talking or acting to *pick* a fight, was the best policy. It was not the policy that was followed.

When America was attacked at Pearl Harbor, the *Post* supported the war and called for victory. But the magazine was so identified as isolationist that Garrett was forced out in March 1942, along with editor-in-chief Wesley Stout and, after 33 years, associate editor Adelaide Neall. Garrett got the news in the middle of a project on the Detroit automakers and the war—a piece the magazine no longer wanted. "A new editorial management marched in this week to take charge," crowed pro-interventionist *Time*, which said Garrett's "brooding editorials afforded the nearest thing to a bible of the isolationists." In a note to Hoover, Garrett lamented that the *Post* had "lifted up her garments to the New Deal."[16]

Garrett was 64. As in World War I, once his country was officially at war, he was on its side. He tried for a job with Donald Nelson, head of the War Production Board, and didn't get it. "What I want more than anything else is to get into the war," he wrote a friend, "Washington is out. Even if I could work there I am not wanted because of my anti-New Deal history." A few months later a recruiter for the U.S. Civil Service Commission asked if he was interested in a $6,500-a-year job to write on economic problems. He said yes, replying, "I am entirely at the disposal of the Government, for anything it may wish me to do, for the duration of the war." A month later the recruiter wrote, "Matters did not turn out as has been anticipated." There was no government job.[17]

He had turned down two private-sector jobs. In October 1942, Garrett wrote to Baruch, "None of the writing I might want to be doing on my own account would be likely to help win the war. So therefore, unless something unexpected happens, next Monday yours truly will be in overalls at work in a local ship yard, building Army freight boats, ten hours a day, six days a week... You didn't know I was a ship's carpenter, did you? Well, I'm good enough and I'm taking my own tools."[18]

A month later he was spending the weekend in bed. "The shipyard job is out in the open weather and seems to be getting me down," he wrote. "I am expecting to be transferred to a machine shop job, inside. Just to be doing something with my hands gives me a sense of relief. I can listen to the news with more fortitude." He ended with the salutation, "Damn Hitler."[19]

Baruch wrote back the next day, "I think it is silly of you to be doing the kind of work you are doing now."

Garrett once quoted Lane saying that an intellectual was a man who couldn't do anything with his hands. In his last years he was still using his home forge to hammer out an iron collar for one of the pilings in his pier on the Tuckahoe River.[20] He also made wooden furniture.[21] But war work in a commercial machine shop was too much. He soon went back to writing.

Chapter 27 notes

1 *The American Story*, p. 301.

2 SEP, "Who Cultivate War," April 8, 1939.

3 SEP, "Design for Freedom," November 11, 1939; "Will We Do It?" July 6, 1940.

4 Letter to Carl Snyder, undated, Hoover Institution files, Folder Ts U.S. G 239. The letter uses the same language as Garrett's editorial in the March 29, 1941, *Saturday Evening Post*, suggesting that it was written in late February or early March 1941.

5 SEP, "While Yet There Is Time to Think," September 7, 1940.

6 SEP, "While Yet There Is Time to Think."

7 SEP, "The Peril," May 24, 1941.

8 *Profit's Prophet*, p. 91.

9 SEP, "Review," December 20, 1941.

10 SEP, "Now One War Aim," April 12, 1941.

11 He tried to enlist Herbert Hoover: Phone message to Hoover, December 27, 1939; Post Presidential Individual file, Box 67, Herbert Hoover Library. Garrett noted the failure of the Finnish bond issue in a letter to Baruch, March 4, 1940, Baruch papers, Princeton.

12 SEP, "Conscription," September 28, 1940.

13 Garrett-Lane letters, Hoover Library.

14 Isabel Paterson, *The God of the Machine,* Caxton edition, 1964, Chapter 22, "The Energy Circuit in Wartime." My juxtaposing of Garrett and Paterson is not meant to imply that they dealt directly with each other, only that they are representative of opposing points of view.

15 "Comment," *American Affairs,* October 1950.

16 "Stout Out," *Time,* March 23, 1942. Garrett to Hoover, March 15, 1942. Garrett papers, Houghton Library, Harvard.

17 Letters from Gerald Graze, recruiting representative, U.S. Civil Service Commission, Sept. 18 and Oct. 23, 1942; Garrett's reply of Sept. 21, 1942; letter to Lewis Harold Brown, June 25, 1942, all in Garrett papers.

18 Baruch papers, Princeton University.

19 Garrett to Baruch, November 16, 1942. Baruch papers.

20 Richard Cornuelle, letter to the author, November 11, 2005.

21 "Ex America" pamphlet, Caxton, 1951. Blurb about Garrett.

Chapter Twenty-eight
BECOMES THE RADICAL

Garrett's mind turned to the road his country would take once the war ended. A premonition of that was in his own work, and he missed it.

In 1936 Garrett had written of the "composite face" of government—the *look* of the people who compose the federal state. It had changed in the New Deal revolution of 1933 from a Republican face to "a face unknown." Wrote Garrett, "It was not a political face at all. Its character was academic."[1] These were the people like Rexford Tugwell and Henry Wallace.

With the coming of war, the composite face of Washington began to change again:

> You could see it changing in the hotel lobbies, the dining rooms, the anterooms of government and the galleries. Slowly, like a trick of the movie film, the refined profile of the political dreamer faded out; it was overlaid by the profile of the doer and the know-hower. Not the dollar-a-year man only, though his number steadily grew, but those also who came in his train, such as the engineer, the scientist, the technician, the production man, the organizer, and lo, with many scars upon him, the rugged individualist again...[2]

That was the sign that the New Deal was over. Not
reversed, not undone, but over. But Garrett, who had lost his
position at the *Post* and had time to sit by the Tuckahoe River
and think, did not see an ending. Roosevelt had made a truce
with American business in order to fight Hitler. That was all.
That the war would be over in three years, Roosevelt dead,
Vice President Wallace out and the political flavor of the
country utterly changed were things Garrett could not know.

World War I had ended with deflation, strikes and anarchist bombs in America and Communist rebellion abroad.
World War II was bigger; common sense said its social effects
would be worse. "In one unpredictable moment the war will
end," Garrett wrote. "In that moment we shall face the
extreme problem... The government will take control, and
thus, in the name of emergency, we shall arrive at a planned
economy."[3]

It was not an isolated thought. In November 1941, poll-
sters for *Fortune* surveyed the directors of the 750 largest U.S.
companies and the presidents of every company rated AA-1
by Dun & Bradstreet. Respondents were asked to imagine
four economic systems after the war:

First, a free-enterprise economy, as before the war, with
intervention to take care of specific problems.

Second, "an economic system in which the government
will take over many public services formerly under private
management but still leave many opportunities for private
enterprise." Call it a mixed economy.

Third "a semisocialized society in which there will be little room for the profit system to operate." This is what the
Labour Party had in mind in Britain.

Fourth, an economic dictatorship as in Germany.

Asked which they preferred, 91 percent opted for free
enterprise. Asked which they expected, 7 percent said free

enterprise, 52 percent the mixed economy, 37 percent semi-socialism and 4 percent dictatorship.[4]

Garrett was worried. The anti-New Deal newspapers—and there had been a lot of them in the 1930s—were mostly cowed by the government. In 1940, Roosevelt had slandered the America First Committee as a Trojan horse, and interventionists had smeared it as a Nazi front. It was neither of those things, but after Pearl Harbor every group that had been anti-New Deal and antiwar was subject to brownbaiting. Garrett had been shut out of the *Saturday Evening Post. Harpers* had declined to take his work, as had *Collier's*, and though *The Reader's Digest* was an ally, it did not print original work. The United Features, McNaught and NEA syndicates rejected his proposal of a syndicated column.[5] Wrote Garrett:

> There are ten or fifteen well-known writers who now find themselves marked, as if they were on a blacklist. Some of them compromise by avoiding the subjects on which they cannot write as they believe; others, we understand, have resorted to the use of fictitious names in order to relieve the editors of a sense of liability—meaning the liability that now attaches itself to the name of a writer whose history is anti-New Deal.[6]

Garrett wrote this to a group of like-minded men in August 1942 in an attempt to finance the mass publication of 18 pamphlets to promote capitalism and constitutional government after the war. The cover letter for this memo is on the stationery of the New York State Economic Council, 505 Fifth Avenue, and is addressed to Herbert Hoover.[7] The tone is foreboding. "The paradox," said Garrett's memo, "is that the conservative now becomes the radical."

A new publication would be difficult because paper was rationed. By mid-1943 Garrett was working on a deal to buy

The Pathfinder, a publication that had a government paper allotment. Edgar Queeny of Monsanto Chemical was ready to provide the capital, and Virgil Jordan of the National Industrial Conference Board had worked out a business plan, when publisher David Lawrence of *United States News* bought *The Pathfinder* for $100,000. Lawrence's intention, Garrett wrote, was "to strangle *The Pathfinder* to death and use its paper for his own magazine and charge it all off on his tax sheet."[8]

Garrett wanted to change the course of American politics, but the more he thought about fomenting a political movement the more he saw problems with it, and finally he gave it up. To a correspondent he wrote:

> Organized on a large scale, many supporting and many participating, there would adhere to us, as to the America First Committee, a lot of company not to our liking, going along for wrong reasons, and no way to get rid of it.
>
> What else? I don't know. I begin to think that such a thing, if done at all, had better be done by individual initiative with unlimited personal responsibility, probably in book form, especially as I agree with you that ideas must begin at the top and work down.[9]

Chapter 28 notes

1 SEP, "New Government," February 1, 1936.

2 SEP, "Out to Shake the World," May 17, 1941.

3 From "Idea," a memo attached to a letter from Garrett to Hoover, on stationery of the New York State Economic Council, August 19, 1942. Hoover papers.

4"Fortune Quarterly Management Poll," *Fortune*, Nov. 1941, pp. 200-205. The poll also asked what the business leaders thought was happening to the New Deal's more radical social and economic goals. Was the administration still pursuing them, using the war emergency as a pretext? Or had it put them aside for the duration, intending to pursue them after the war? Or were they done with radical social and economic goals? Of the presidents and directors, 76 percent said the first, 17 percent the second and 7 percent the third.

5 Frederick L. Allen, editor of *Harpers*, to Garrett, May 11, 1942; *Collier's* rejection letter, June 15, 1942; Harold Ober, Garrett's New York agent, to Garrett, undated. Garrett papers, Harvard.

6 From "Idea," a memo attached to a letter from Garrett to Hoover, August 19, 1942. Hoover papers. One of the authors practically blacklisted was John T. Flynn, who had been head of the New York chapter of the America First Committee. (John E. Moser, *Right Turn: John T. Flynn and the Transformation of American Liberalism*, New York University Press, 2005, p. 152.) Another was H.L. Mencken, who spent the war years writing the *Days* books and working on *The American Language*.

7 Garrett had just read the page proofs of the forthcoming book, *Problems of Lasting Peace,* by Herbert Hoover and Hugh Gibson, Doubleday Doran, 1942.

8 Garrett to Hoover, July 20, 1943. Hoover papers.

9 Letter to Lewis Harold Brown, undated. Garrett Papers, Harvard.

Chapter Twenty-nine
LIKE THE HAGFISH

Garrett had one incendiary pamphlet, "The Revolution Was," in his drawer. He had written it in 1938, the year after the Supreme Court had given up fighting the New Deal. The essay had not been printed in the *Saturday Evening Post*. Probably it was too radical. It began with a quote from Aristotle's *Politics*, about a country in which "the ancient laws remain while the power will be in the hands of those who have brought about a revolution within the state." That, he thought, had been the essence of Roosevelt's achievement.

Garrett had used the Aristotle quote in a *Post* editorial, but the work itself had not seen print. In the spring of 1944 he updated it, and showed a draft of it to Hoover, asking for suggestions.[1]

The greater problem was finding someone to publish it. The answer came from Isaac Don Levine, an anticommunist writer who played a role in the exposure of Alger Hiss, and 40 years later would have a cameo role in the movie *Reds*. Levine suggested that Garrett send his manuscript to the Caxton Printers in Caldwell, Idaho. Caxton's founder and longtime proprietor, J.H. Gipson, called himself a libertarian. He had reprinted Herbert Spencer's *The Man Versus the State* in 1940, and by printing Garrett and others would become the principal libertarian publisher in America.

Gipson had Garrett's pamphlet in his hands only 15 minutes before deciding to publish it. It was late in August 1944,
and he wanted to get it to the public before the November
election, when the Republican nominee, Thomas Dewey, had
a crack at unseating Roosevelt. To Rose Wilder Lane, Gipson
wrote: "I am supporting Dewey whole-heartedly. This must
not be taken to mean that I endorse and agree with everything
that Dewey says or does. Any change, however, must be for
the better..."[2]

Dewey lost, but Caxton did publish "The Revolution
Was," and it was a hit. Orders for 10 or 100 started coming in
from Roosevelt-weary businessmen. Leonard Read of the Los
Angeles Chamber of Commerce, which had published a
Garrett monograph on monetary policy the year before,
ordered 1,000 copies of "The Revolution Was," and then
another 1,000. Read was a libertarian—"probably the most
unusual chamber of commerce secretary in the United States,"
Gipson wrote.[3]

"The Revolution Was" pictured the New Deal as a revolutionary transformation of power. Many, including the New
Dealers themselves, had said that in a metaphorical way.
Garrett said it in a non-metaphorical way, using the language
of political seizure. Instead of saying that the New Deal's
strategy was to demonize business, he wrote that it was to
"mobilize by propaganda the forces of hatred." Instead of saying the New Deal created a coalition of union labor and farmers, Garrett wrote that it aimed "to attach to the revolution the
two great classes whose adherence is indispensable... called
in Europe workers and peasants."

The workers and peasants. It is a phrase redolent of the
hammer and sickle. The New Deal *had* attached those classes
to itself; it just hadn't used a hammer-and-sickle phrase to
describe its actions. Garrett used it. (And when Rexford
Tugwell, undersecretary of Agriculture under Wallace, spoke
of creating "a farmer-worker alliance in this country which

will carry all before it," Garrett compared his statement to rhetoric in *The Daily Worker.*)[4]

In "The Revolution Was," Garrett focused on the calculated way Roosevelt had called in the people's gold, then pronounced it confiscated, then took control of foreign exchange, then devalued the dollar and made all gold contracts payable in devalued dollars. The purposefulness of these moves belied the notion that Roosevelt and his brain trusters hadn't known what they were doing, and had made things up as they went along. That was the idea one got from reading John T. Flynn's pungently anti-New Deal book, *The Roosevelt Myth* (1948). When it came out, Garrett reviewed it, and liked the denunciatory tone of it, but he wrote:

> Many of us who lived through the early years of the New Deal… will feel that Mr. Flynn leaves something out… From the facts alone, as Mr. Flynn relates them, you might suppose that everything just happened; that when Mr. Roosevelt was elected he had no idea what he was going to do, never thought through any of the things he did do, and that the story of the New Deal made itself up as it went along. Events of revolutionary meaning took place, but they were happy and reckless inventions, launched in a spirit of experimental adventure, with no preconceived design and no thread of purpose at all.[5]

But seizing control of the monetary system, Garrett wrote in his review of Flynn's book, "requires certain definitive steps in a certain sequence." Flynn hadn't understood that. Garrett had—and he had outlined those steps in "The Revolution Was."

Garrett's essay was deeply pessimistic. To those who wanted to fight for the old American values, Garrett was saying: You have already lost. The revolution *was*. Through the debasement of money, the use of the taxing and borrowing power, propaganda and class warfare, nullification of the Commerce Clause and the exaltation of the president over Congress, the American political system had been fundamentally changed.

> Like the hagfish, the New Deal entered the old form and devoured its meaning from within. The revolutionaries were inside; the defenders were outside. [6]

Caxton was limited in its press run by the paper allocation of the War Production Board. This galled Gipson; by late November 1944 he was worrying that "The Revolution Was" would "take our entire ration of paper for 1945." It was a problem that could be surmounted by buying another publisher, as David Lawrence had done, or by finding help from another publisher. But there were always problems.

One of them was Garrett. He had no objection to having his pamphlet published by a small printer in Idaho. He offered it to Caxton for free, though Gipson insisted on paying him a 10 percent royalty. Garrett wrote, "My general position is that I don't care what happens to the pamphlet or who prints it, provided it gets circulation." But he did care. As he had done with his aborted multi-pamphlet venture, he worried about associations. One was with "Colonel" Robert McCormick, proprietor of the *Chicago Tribune*, the nation's most prominent anti-New Deal paper. In 1943 the *Tribune* had run Garrett's "The Mortification of History," in which he had argued that America had never been an isolationist nation, and that what was called "isolationism" was really just a healthy nationalism. In 1944 Caxton sent a review copy of "The Revolution Was" to the *Tribune's* Sunday editor, at Garrett's request. But Garrett was not interested in the *Tribune* printing it. He had written to Hoover after the first piece that there might be "some liability in going too far with McCormick."[7]

In 1945 came another interested party: Sewell Avery, the CEO of Montgomery Ward, the Chicago catalog retailer. Avery hated the New Deal. In 1935 had gotten the company fined for non-cooperation with the Blue Eagle. When war came, he was fighting a CIO union, which insisted on a contract for a closed shop. Avery refused to sign. The War Labor Board said he had to sign: it was a wartime requirement to keep up production. Avery said Montgomery Ward wasn't in a war industry and he wasn't going to do it. The matter went all the way to Franklin Roosevelt, who ordered the company to be seized. When Avery would not vacate his office, Roosevelt sent the U.S. attorney general, Francis Biddle. On April 27, 1944, Biddle barged into Avery's office with helmeted soldiers from a nearby Army base, and ordered Avery out. "To hell with the government!" Avery shouted. As two soldiers carried Avery out in a seated position, he turned to Biddle and said, "You... *New Dealer.*"

A photo of white-haired Avery in his dark suit being hustled out by two GIs ran in newspapers across America. The *Chicago Tribune* carried two cartoons of the Roosevelt atrocity, and the president responded by calling press conference. Four days later, the Army withdrew its troops.

It was understandable, then, that Sewell Avery wanted to bankroll a printing of Garrett's anti-Roosevelt essay, in the hundreds of thousands of copies with a national advertising campaign and a low price. Gipson was amenable. "Mr. Avery does not contemplate issuing this under Montgomery Ward's imprint, but as a private venture," he wrote Garrett.[8]

Garrett didn't like it. He wrote:

> Please will you treat this as a very personal letter. I have a strong intuition about keeping your imprint on the pamphlet, whoever else may reprint it. Sewell Avery had me on the telephone yesterday... I have nothing against Avery. I like him. All the same, my

feeling is that his name on the pamphlet would be a
liability...[9]

Probably he was right about that. There was some negoti-
ation about an edition without Avery's name on it, but it came
to nothing. There was also a report from Hoover that a man in
Chicago had boasted of mailing out 100,000 copies of "The
Revolution Was." It was not true; Caxton had not printed half
that many, nor had anyone else. But it had printed several tens
of thousands, and the Caxton Printers—which would become
the principal publisher of libertarian books in the 1950s—
would keep the booklet in print for 18 years.[10]

Garrett also published a book in 1944, *A Time Is Born,* an
update on the autarkic themes of *The Blue Wound.* War had
again attracted him to the theme of national self-sufficiency,
and given him such examples as synthetic rubber. The book is
beautifully written, but insofar as it was meant to be prophetic it is wrong.

By 1944 the war was approaching an end, and not the
grimly socialist end Garrett had foreseen. A socialist state was
about to be proclaimed in Britain, but in America the people
had had enough of social revolution. Postwar America was
not the hard country Garrett loved; the New Deal had saddled
it with a roll of middle-aged fat. But private investment
revived with a strength it had not shown since the 1920s, and
capitalism was back in business.

Chapter 29 notes

1 Hoover to Garrett, March 19, 1944. Hoover suggested that Garrett put more into it about power-lust as a motivation stronger than money, and about the practice of political smearing. A decade earlier, Hoover had had Garrett read his book, *The Challenge to Liberty*, while it was still in manuscript. (Garrett to Hoover, November 3, 1934. Hoover papers.) A word about the dates: Caxton placed the date "1938" below the title. The Western Islands paperback published in the 1960s replaced this with "1944." It is the same essay, written in 1938 but not published until 1944. Garrett's 1944 updating includes references to Vidkun Quisling, the wartime Nazi governor of Norway, and to *Wickard v. Filburn*, the 1942 case in which the Supreme Court declared that a farmer growing wheat for his own chickens could be regulated under the Commerce Clause. At the end, Garrett added a quotation from Abraham Lincoln on conspiracy, which was given to him by New York attorney Gilbert Montague in a letter dated November 18, 1942, held in the Garrett papers. The editorial that used the Aristotle quote was, "Within the Form," SEP, October 26, 1940.

2 Garrett to Gipson, August 21, 1944; Gipson to Garrett, August 25, 1944; Gipson to Rose Wilder Lane, October 16, 1944. Caxton Papers, Authors File, File 7 # 14, Box 62, Washington State University.

3 Gipson to Garrett, October 7, 1944. Caxton Papers, WSU.

4 SEP, "National Hill Notes," May 16, 1936.

5 "The Roosevelt Myth," book review in *American Affairs,* January 1949, pp. 44-45.

6 "The Revolution Was," *The People's Pottage*, 1953, p. 73.

7 Gipson to Garrett, July 8, 1954. From the files of the Caxton Press. Garrett to Gipson, January 1, 1945. Caxton Papers, WSU. Garrett to Hoover, December 31, 1943. Hoover papers.

8 Gipson to Garrett, January 31, 1945. Caxton Papers, WSU.

9 Garrett to Gipson, received February 15, 1945. Caxton Papers, WSU.

10 Hoover to Garrett, June 8, 1945. Caxton's records put the total press run of "The Revolution Was" at 37,695 through 1962. (Letter from Scott Gipson, March 8, 2006.)

Chapter Thirty
A CAPITALIST PEOPLE

Peace would end the concord with Stalin, an alliance that had given patriotic cover to American Reds and others on the Left. An early sign of the change came at the Democratic Party's 1944 convention, at which party insiders, acting with the tacit approval of the president, dropped from the ticket Roosevelt's pro-Soviet vice president, Henry Wallace, and replaced him with a safer man, Harry Truman. By the spring of 1945, Roosevelt was dead and Truman was in power. A man who interviewed Garrett in this period recalled, "He... could speak only with contempt of FDR, and could hardly bring himself to speak at all of Harry Truman."[1]

The defining thing about Truman was his decision to drop the two atomic bombs. Garrett found the whole project—which had been Roosevelt's—troubling:

On this Manhattan Project were thousands of wage earners and technicians who had not the faintest idea of what they were about... In the nature of the case, that had to be so. But when the bomb was ready, someone had to decide whether or not to release it for the purposes of destruction. That was a harrowing question, and one which if it had been presented to them would have divided people to the soul. It could not be presented to them, and that is precisely the

213

point; for what you have here is the definite case in which the freedom of people to make a momentous moral decision in a matter more terrible than war was suddenly nonexistent. Those whose labor did it unawares, whose money paid for it without their consent, whose children will have to live with it, had no more to say about it than the enemy on whom it fell.[2]

It was the decision of one man, Harry Truman. Garrett described the new president as "a sudden, brittle man" of "quick pugnacity, valor of prejudice, heroic mediocrity and an easy way with the words *yes* and *no*." He was a little man, Garrett said, "with no capacity for awe."[3]

The dropping of the bomb was a kind of science-fiction moment that seemed to change everything. At the time, Garrett wrote fancifully of "atom man," who "...steps off into space."[4] But the bomb changed only some things.

Meanwhile, Virgil Jordan of the National Industrial Conference Board had been working for almost three years to hire Garrett to edit a magazine of ideas. He had offered Garrett an editor's job in the fall of 1942, when Garrett was insistent on contributing to the war, and he had been involved in the abortive *Pathfinder* project.[5] In 1944 Jordan convinced Garrett to take charge of the Conference Board's quarterly publication, *The Economic Record*, and to make it a magazine to promote liberty and the free market. Such a magazine was out of character for the Conference Board, which had been started in 1916 by trade-association executives to collect economic data. But Jordan wanted the magazine, and he wanted Garrett to edit it.

Thus began a new time of Garrett's life. He and a secretary worked from Conference Board offices on Park Avenue. He made the 110-mile commute to Tuckahoe at the weekend, escaping from the suits on weeknights at the Salmagundi Club in Greenwich Village. The club was frequented by artists such as his friend Kenneth Hayes Miller, the American realist painter.[6]

Occasionally Garrett would have breakfast with Hoover at the Waldorf-Astoria, where Hoover lived.

Starting with the July 1944 issue, *The Economic Record* was a new magazine. Charts and data were out. Opinion was in. The first issue contained a review of John T. Flynn's *As We Go Marching*, a polemic that compared the New Deal with Nazism and Italian Fascism. A long article by Garrett suggested that American businessmen weren't confident of taking the full plunge into capitalism at war's end. "One gets the impression," Garrett wrote, "that in the great depression the mind of American business suffered a psychic injury from which it never recovered."[7]

In the January 1945 issue, which had 72 pages of heavy paper, all type and no ads, the magazine's name changed to *American Affairs*. Inside the cover it announced that it was "a publication that is not for sale" and that subscriptions were "not solicited." It was a statement of intention not to be influenced, and recalls Garrett's whimsical proposal for his home-made publication a decade before. *American Affairs'* no-subscriptions policy would change, but Garrett's determination to be independent would not.[8]

Much of the magazine was written by Garrett, some under his byline and some as "Washington Correspondent" or "Staff." Each issue had a column of editor's notes, an editorial article, and usually book reviews. Garrett published essays by business executives, usually those with academic backgrounds, though he had none. He published movie producer Cecil B. DeMille writing on the closed shop, political journalist Freda Utley writing on Russia, and *Herald-Tribune* book reviewer Isabel Paterson writing on the fallacy of the mature economy. He published Republican Robert Taft and Democrat James Byrnes and a dissent by Supreme Court Justice Robert Jackson, who had been a loyal New Dealer. He published the economists David McCord Wright, Jacob Viner, Walter Spahr, Wilhelm Roepke, John Jewkes, Friedrich Hayek and Ludwig von Mises. Of Mises, the Austrian advocate of laissez faire, Garrett wrote, "no writer has more powerfully or with fewer misgivings defended free private capitalism."[9]

Garrett's work in *American Affairs* noted the mileposts on the road of economic unfreedom. The April 1946 issue reported that wartime price controls had not been lifted, and that many feared lifting them would bring trouble. Garrett wrote, "It is better to meet the kind of trouble we know, and through trouble to arrive at a natural equilibrium, than to surrender the American economy to permanent government control..."[10]

Price controls were lifted. At the end of wage control, unions vowed to catch up with the postwar inflation. In 1946, when John L. Lewis's coal miners threatened to strike, Truman ordered the soft-coal mines seized by the government. To his business readers, Garrett argued that Lewis had broken no law and that it was Truman's action that was ominous. If the unions refused to mine coal for private owners, Garrett wrote, it could be said in a vague way that they were striking "against society." But if the mines were owned by the government, miners would be striking *against the government*. "That is a very different thing," Garrett wrote. "Thus, little by little we become accustomed first to the words and semantic tones and then the experimental acts of authoritarian government."[11]

Garrett wrote often about the implementation of socialism in Britain. Government there had taken over the coal mines, and Labour Party politicians, who had always been on the side of the workers, were now exhorting them to work longer hours for the good of the nation. Some Labourites were hinting of a policy to "direct" labor, which sounded a lot like conscripting it. That never happened, but that it was suggested,

Garrett wrote, bared the authoritarian essence of the system the socialists were trying to build.[12]

In America, Truman gave the coal mines back to the owners, though with a labor contract the owners hadn't wanted. Six years later, when Truman seized the steel mills, also to ward off a strike, the Supreme Court (and, famously, Justice Jackson) said the president didn't have the power to do it. That ended executive orders to seize private industry—but it came in the Truman administration's final year.

Another issue of executive power was war. Franklin Roosevelt had maneuvered America into World War II, and now Truman was committing America to a Cold War with the Soviet Union. In a 1947 review of a book about Pearl Harbor, Garrett wrote:

> The pattern is here... The conduct of foreign policy is in the hands of the President. In the field of foreign relations he may act without the advice and consent of the Senate and without telling it beforehand what he is going to do; and there is a kind of act that almost cannot be repudiated by either the Senate or the people because it involves the honor, the good faith, the 'face' of the nation. The announcement of the Truman Doctrine was such an act. Congress did not know beforehand that the President was going to declare cold war on Russia everywhere in the world. Yet when it was asked to appropriate $400 million to implement the doctrine in Greece and Turkey the feeling that carried it was that in the present state of the world the country could not afford to repudiate its President. The American people, who will pay for it and if need be fight for it, had nothing whatever to say about it.[13]

217

There were also issues of foreign economic relations. In 1946 came a Treasury loan to Labour-ruled Britain, which meant the American taxpayer was financing British socialism. Americans might want to put political conditions on a loan like that, but for the U.S. government to do it would cause offense. Capitalist financiers, Garrett wrote, would not have had that problem:

> It would not be necessary to say that among borrowers we should prefer free enterprise nations over those pursuing a socialist policy. That problem would take care of itself. The British steel people, for example, wanting an American loan, might be told that the rate of interest would be 15 percent. If they said, "But that is prohibitive," the American bankers would say: "The risk is high. After you have got your dollars the British Government may nationalize your industry and offer to pay back our money with blocked sterling." If to this the British steel people answered, "But we hear you are going to lend capital to the Belgian steel people at 4 percent," the American bankers would say, "That is true. It is a better risk. We think American dollars will be safer in Belgium." And if the British steel people said, "But this means that the British steel industry will be transferred to Belgium," the American bankers would need only to say, "That is something for the English people to think about."

That was not the Truman administration's way. And so, Garrett asked, "*Are* we a capitalist people?" He went on, "If you do not see the answer, then perhaps it got away; or, it may be that you are looking at it and do not see it, because it is endowed with so much protective coloring."[14]

The postwar 1940s was the birthing time of the United Nations, the International Monetary Fund and the

International Trade Organization. The supporters of these organizations tended to sell them as part of a planned world, which was a world Garrett didn't want. He denounced the ITO as a charter for state trading, and when governments failed to agree on it and settled for a looser organization, the General Agreement on Tariffs and Trade, Garrett denounced that as a gift of authority over American foreign trade to an international body.[15]

There was an aroma of a planned world in these organizations, but the dream was stronger than the reality. Half a century later, the GATT became the World Trade Organization, and governments did cede to it some authority over trade. But Garrett's fear that these agencies would cause trade to be dominated by politics and war mainly did not bear out. Trade expanded mightily in the last half of the 20th century, and was largely conducted by private parties for commercial reasons.

In hindsight, the *American Affairs* period was one in which Garrett was not on the losing side as much as it probably seemed at the time.

A few personal notes from this period: In April and May 1945, Garrett underwent a series of operations at the Ford Hospital in Detroit.[16] A friend from the late 1940s writes that Garrett had a secretary who "had kept him alive by making his bed over and over. When he had somewhat improved, she tore the necessary pages out of the yellow phone book and prayed for his survival in every church in Detroit. He told me, 'You have to marry a woman like that.' " The correspondent adds that Garrett thought she "had saved his life in Detroit and he felt a boundless obligation to her." [17]

The demonstrative secretary was Dorothy Goulet, a Catholic who had been married at a young age to a New York hotel man 19 years her senior. He had died in 1931, when their only child was an infant, leaving her to look for work at the time the economy was in free fall. She had had to put her baby in foster care and go out to find a job—and had found one at a New York newspaper. Though she would dive too heavily into drink, she had qualities of toughness, loyalty and a sassy personality that captivated Garrett, and on August 15, 1947, they were married at the Methodist church in Petersburg, N.J. He was 69; she, 37.

Garrett's best man was Frederick Simpich, his dinner companion the night he had been shot.

With Dorothy came her son James, then 16. Garrett, who had never had a child, became like a father to him. Says James's daughter, Sue Goulet: "They were very close. My dad was very much influenced by Garrett."[18]

Chapter 30 notes

1 John Tebbel to Carl Ryant, December 15, 1967. Ryant papers.

2 "Science—Before and After the Event of July 1945," *The Economic Record*, October 1945, p. 223.

3 *The American Story*, p. 363.

4 From Garrett's introduction to Virgil Jordan, *Manifesto for the Atomic Age*, Rutgers University Press, 1946, p. 8.

5 1942 offer: Jordan to Garrett, Oct. 22, Oct. 27 and Dec. 4, 1942. Garrett papers. Today Jordan is most often remembered for a speech he made to the Investment Bankers' Association of New York in December 1940. Jordan told his audience that their country was already in the war. America had become the defender of the British Empire, he said, and if Britain lost, America would become "the heir and residuary legatee or receiver for whatever economic and political assets of the Empire survive her defeat." In short, Jordan said, "Whatever the outcome of the war, America has embarked upon a career of imperialism, both in world affairs and in every other aspect of her life." Writers of the Left have seized upon this, because it sounds like the spokesman for corporate America advocating a policy of imperialism. See, for example, Peter Irons, *War Powers: How the Imperial Presidency Hijacked the Constitution*, Henry Holt, 2005, p. 161. But read in context, it is clear that Jordan was not advocating a policy but describing one.

6 Miller painted matronly and prosperous women shoppers of the 1920s and 1930s and taught several students who founded the "ashcan" school of social realism. Garrett's "The Painting of Hayes Miller," in *The New Republic,* July 27, 1921, was his only art review I know of. Miller wrote

Garrett on July 25, 1930, when Garrett was hospitalized. "I see you dimly, in a mist, and I feel a kind of grief," he wrote, "but I can't follow you and draw near." (Kenneth Hayes Miller papers, Archives of American Art)
7 "The Mind of American Business on Free Competitive Enterprise," *The Economic Record,* July 1944, p. 39.
8 Later issues have postcards soliciting subscriptions at $2.50 a year. Beginning with the issue of April 1946 the cover had the subscription rate and a single-copy price of 75 cents.
9 From a review of Mises' *Omnipotent Government* (1944) in *American Affairs,* January 1945. See also Mises, "The Myth of the Mixed Economy," *American Affairs,* July 1945, pp. 169-174; Richard Cornuelle's review of Mises' *Human Action* (1949), *American Affairs,* January 1950; and Mises, "The Idea of Liberty is Western," *American Affairs,* October 1950.
10 *American Affairs,* April 1946, p. 75.
11 *American Affairs,* July 1946, p. 146.
12 "Profile of a Labor Government," *American Affairs,* October 1947, pp. 207-213. Garrett was the probable writer of "The English Labor Crisis," an unsigned editorial in the *New York Times* of June 25, 1915, that commented on the Lloyd George government's threat to conscript labor. Then Garrett had taken it less seriously, saying, "You can compel a capitalist to operate his plant on Government orders at full capacity merely by threat of taking possession of it; but you cannot compel a skilled workman to work his best, to work full time, to work for certain wages or to work at all. If you threaten to shoot him—why, that is no compulsion. He is not in the Congo. He is in England. The threat will not be executed." The threat wasn't executed after World War II, either, but Garrett saw more meaning in the utterance of it.
13 "Pearl Harbor," *American Affairs,* October 1947, p. 242.
14 "Review and Comment," *American Affairs,* January 1948, p. 1.
15 "A World Trade Charter Anyhow," *American Affairs,* January 1948.
16 Garrett to Herbert Hoover, June 4, 1945.
17 Cornuelle, letters to the author, January 23, 2003, and March 24, 2006, and personal interview April 29, 2007. Cornuelle heard this story from Garrett a few years later.
18 Phone conversation with Sue Goulet, March 16, 2006; Sue Goulet, letter to the author, March 31, 2006.

GARET GARRETT

Chapter Thirty-one
WHERE I LEFT OFF

A t the end of 1950, *American Affairs* folded. It was losing $45,000 a year. And a magazine of opinion didn't fit with the data-gathering mission of the Conference Board, where most of the staff were academic types with leftish inclinations. Always the Conference Board had had a faction fervently opposed to the magazine, and in 1950 Garrett noted in a letter, "The Conference Board [must] either discontinue *American Affairs* or discontinue its editor."

Garrett was 72, and had some things he wanted to get done. "I have not retired from work," he wrote Hoover. "I intend to resume writing where I left off."[1]

He did it with the help of an $11,000 annual stipend from the William Volker Fund, the legacy of a Kansas City businessman. Garrett sometimes grumbled at the supporters of the profit system who thought they could save it with not-for-profit enterprises, but his own experience showed the value of it. (The Volker Fund also financed Ludwig von Mises' presence at New York University and Friedrich Hayek's at the University of Chicago.) [2]

Freed to write, Garrett once again addressed the American people. He had four years in which to reach them, and in that time he produced *The Wild Wheel* (1952), *The People's Pottage* (1953) and *The American Story* (1955). Most of this was a sharpening of what he had written before. But by 1950 he was not optimistic about his ability to influence his countrymen. To Hoover, he wrote, "There is an old proverb that says a people may be so stupid as to baffle their own gods."[3]

Garrett described *The Wild Wheel* as "Laissez Faire as a theme and Henry Ford as a subject," adding in postscript, "Henry Ford *was* Laissez Faire." A "wild wheel" was Garrett's image of the entrepreneur as ungoverned force, destroyer of equilibrium and constructor of the future. After years of the New Dealers accusing capitalism of instability, Garrett agreed with them. Great creators were not interested in stability. "Stability?" Ford had said in 1927. "What is it? It is a dead fish floating downstream."[4]

Ford's industrial radicalism was rooted in the way he looked at problems. He and his friend Thomas Edison called it "the value of ignorance." "What they meant," Garrett wrote, "was that in order to act upon a thing in an original manner you have to see it as it is, see it directly, with no labels on it to tell you what it is and no preconceived impressions about it." Instead, Ford let his mind run free. "He apparently never got anything out of books," Garrett wrote.[5]

Ford nonetheless wrote a book, published another and bankrolled a newspaper, some of which had to do with his campaign against the Jews. *The Wild Wheel* is not interested in this. It briefly covers the scurrilous campaign of Ford's paper, the *Dearborn Independent*. Ford's disavowal of it, under pressure, was "lame," Garrett wrote, and the paper "went to the ash can, to the great relief of Ford dealers."[6]

Garrett sent a copy of the book to Baruch, who responded after reading part of it. Baruch was Jewish, and didn't feel kindly toward Ford. He reminded Garrett that Ford had financed that crusade against the Jews. Baruch might have added, but did not, that Ford had crusaded against him personally. Ford's infamous book, *The International Jew*, called Baruch a "dictator" during World War I, the "ruling hand on productive America" and the principal agent of "Jewish money power." All of Chapter 14, "The High and Low of Jewish Money Power," was a diatribe against Baruch. And Ford's *Dearborn Independent* had falsely accused Baruch of profiting from the war.

What Baruch did tell Garrett was that Ford had been uncooperative with Wilson's War Industries Board. (Baruch had gone to Ford and asked him to stop producing cars and devote the company's entire output to munitions—and Ford had refused, saying he could produce both.[7]) Garrett responded that what Baruch had said was all true, and that he considered Ford not a hero but a genius.[8] An acquaintance of Garrett's said Garrett admired Ford not for his ideas but for his individualism.[9]

The Wild Wheel credits Ford with being distinctive as an industrialist in two ways. First, starting with $28,000 of investor money, he had financed Ford Motor entirely out of earnings, keeping it privately held and under his personal control. Second, he had refused to knuckle under to the Blue Eagle:

> When the New Deal came, he was the one who had the will and the courage to stand against it, and he stood alone. But for the Ford Motor Company, it would have to be written that the surrender of American business to government was unanimous, complete and unconditional.[10]

The one man. A hero still, in that respect.

The other thing honored in the book is laissez faire—not the idea in the abstract, but that place in American memory in which a man could do what he willed, "provided only he did not cross the right of another to do likewise." Wrote Garrett:

> It was a world many people grew not to want, or wanted so little they were unwilling to defend it. Only

225

GARET GARRETT

the strong could love it. Anyhow, it is gone. The number of those who knew it is rapidly declining. In a little while nobody who knew it will be able to remember it at all.[11]

1 Leftish inclinations: Cornuelle, letter to the author, March 6, 2006.
"Discontinue its editor": *Profit's Prophet*, p. 27. "Where I left off": Garrett to
Hoover, November 8, 1950. Hoover papers.
2 Cornuelle, letter to the author, November 8, 2005; Cornuelle, "The First
Libertarian Revival and the Next," *Critical Review Update*, Critical Review
Foundation, April 1993.
3 Garrett to Hoover, not dated, late 1950 or early 1951. Hoover papers.
4 Garrett to Gipson, received May 16, 1951. Caxton Papers, WSU. SEP,
"The Detroit Principle," January 3, 1937; "A World That Was," June 8, 1940;
"Review and Comment," *American Affairs*, April 1947, p. 66; *The Wild
Wheel*, p. 68.
5 *The Wild Wheel*, pp. 128, 140.
6 *The Wild Wheel*, p. 148.
7 Baruch, *My Own Story*, pp. 309-310.
8 The editor of FrontPageMagazine.Com, Ben Johnson, asserted (in
"Where Pat Buchanan Went Wrong," October 1, 2004), that Garrett was
anti-Semitic. In an e-mail I challenged Johnson to verify this, and he did not
respond. I suspect that he believes this because the Noontide Press, which
publishes Holocaust skeptic David Irving, published an unauthorized edition
of *The People's Pottage* entitled *Burden of Empire*, and at this writing is still
selling it. Scott Gipson of the Caxton Press writes: "This edition is especially
troubling to me as Noontide Press appears to be a group that questions the
veracity of the Holocaust and publishes and sells other such books that we
as a company would want to have no truck with. I wrote them in 2003 and
was able to persuade them to stop publishing the book although I granted
them the ability to sell the remainder of the 600 copies of *Burden of
Empire*." (Letter to the author, March 6, 2006). *Pottage* is deeply anti-
Roosevelt, but "That Man" was despised for many different reasons. There
is nothing pro-Nazi or anti-Semitic in *Pottage*, nor in Garrett.
As did many people in his time, Garrett occasionally made a generalization
about a race of people, but it was not a central thing with him. I know of two
about the Jews. One was in his journal, dated October 20, 1915, recalling
when *New York Times* publisher Adolph Ochs announced the death of the
city editor. "I was thinking of the Jewish character, generalizing about it,"
Garrett wrote. "I wondered again at its simple, reverent, mystic attitude
toward the three great enigmas—birth, marriage, and death. I have noticed
it often. I was trying to associate it with the wonderful family ego of Jewish
existence, when Mr. O spoke again..." The other occasion was in retelling

226

the story of his 1915 interview with Walter Rathenau, who he said, was "a man who possessed one of the very brilliant Jewish minds in the world. In him were combined one of the three high characteristics of his race, which are loyalty, intellectual realism, and dreaming imagination." (*Ouroboros*, p. 46; repeated verbatim in *A Time Is Born*, p. 161.) Garrett never lists any negative characteristics of Jews, nor does he speak against them in any of his novels, journalism, his personal journal or any letters I have found. On the contrary: Garrett admired people who were resourceful and successful, and many of them, such as Rathenau and Baruch, were Jewish.

9 Baruch to Garrett, June 25, 1952. Garrett to Baruch, July 3, 1952. Baruch papers. The acquaintance was federal mediator A.A. Desser. See Carl Ryant's notes of his interview with Desser, March 13, 1969. Ryant papers, University of Louisville.

10 *The Wild Wheel*, p. 153.

11 *The Wild Wheel*, p. 216.

Chapter Thirty-two
"THE PEOPLE'S POTTAGE"

Garrett's next book was *The People's Pottage* (1953). The title refers to Esau, a character in the Book of Genesis who exchanges his birthright for a bowl of lentil stew—traditionally recalled as "a mess of pottage." In Garrett's mind, the birthright of Americans was liberty, the right not to be taxed, regulated and managed—and the pottage is the welfare state. The title is distinctive, and better than his first suggestion, *These Twenty Sudden Years*—"sudden" being a favored word of his.[1]

The book has been in print almost continually for more than 55 years. It is the kind of book that provokes reactions. Its second printing had an outer dust jacket entirely of blurbs, printed on both sides, including Rep. Howard Buffett, R-Nebraska, the "isolationist" father of investor Warren Buffett. Another blurb was from historian Harry Elmer Barnes, who in one of his books had recalled the pre-World-War-I years as a time of minimal government, low taxes and "little or no witch hunting." Garrett's three essays, Barnes wrote in the blurb, "are indispensable to anyone who wishes to understand the strange death of liberal America."[2]

The first essay in *Pottage* was Garrett's anti-New Deal polemic, "The Revolution Was." There followed "Ex America," which extended his analysis backward, showing that crucial changes had come before Franklin Roosevelt, and also after.

"Ex America" is a story of the decline of a political idea. Caxton had published it in 1951 as a pamphlet and Garrett had sent a copy to Baruch, with the inscription: "To my dear B.M., who is an optimist." Wrote John Chamberlain, contrasting "Ex America" with *The Driver,* "The years have done something to Garet Garrett, making him a pessimist about the future."[3]

And about the present. Looking at the first half of the 20th century, Garrett wrote:

> Suppose a true image of the present world had been presented to [the American people] in 1900, the future as in a crystal ball, together with the question, "Do you want it?" No one can imagine that they would have said yes—that they could have been tempted by the comforts, the gadgets, the automobiles and all the fabulous satisfactions of mid-century existence, to accept the coils of octopean government, the dim-out of the individual, the atomic bomb, a life of sickening fear, the nightmare of extinction. Their answer would have been no, terrifically.[4]

The changes had come a step at a time, and the people were not asked whether they wanted them. "It is impossible, furthermore, at any moment of time to say what the people want or don't want," Garrett wrote. "They probably do not know." Their leaders led them, and afterward they consented.

The first crucial change in the American system, Garrett wrote, was the income-tax amendment. In 1913, he had not seen the meaning of it; in 1951 he wrote, "Only the intellectuals knew what it meant."[5]

One such was John W. Burgess, professor of political science and constitutional law at Columbia University, and one of the pioneers of political science. In *The Reconciliation of Government with Liberty* (1915), he had written that the income tax amendment had given the government the power "to take what it will and in any way it will from the Individual," in order to feed itself. Already voices were offering to create a welfare state, an empire or both—what Burgess called "a programme of Caesaristic paternalism."[6]

Garrett had read Burgess in the years since. In the same pre-New Deal tradition was Sterling E. Edmunds, professor of international law at St. Louis University, and author of *Struggle for Freedom* (1946). Garrett's copy of Edmunds' book has passages marked in slashes of red pencil and indexed in Garrett's nervous cursive on the end papers. Like Burgess, Edmunds pointed to the taking of the Philippines in 1898 as a turning point in the decline of the constitutionally limited American republic.[7]

The Philippine war would have been the one for Garrett to serve in—he would have been 20—but he did not. In 1951, during the Korean War, his wife's son James, who turned 20 that year, went into the Air Force. War had finally reached into Garrett's household.[8]

It was only after Caxton had published "Ex America" that Virgil Jordan suggested to J.H. Gipson that the two essays might be combined in a book. Gipson suggested to Garrett that he write a third essay, which he hoped would be less pessimistic than the first two, on "a theme of solution." But Garrett did not have an upbeat mind. In August 1951, he replied:

> I am extremely pessimistic about solutions if they have to be imposed. My feeling is that something else has to happen to the core first. I think anything I might write should be about alternatives, and I am positive it would not be optimistic. The fact is if we dare to face it that the days of the republic are gone

231

and the days of empire are beginning. However I am
going to think it over.[9]

In September, Garrett wrote that he was tearing his hair
over the third essay. By October, he had it. He had read the
histories of empire and placed the parallels on the page.
"When I begin to set down the analogies," he wrote, "they
startle even me."[10]

"Rise of Empire" is his most prophetic work. In it he pro-
claims that America had changed from republic to empire.
America had posted troops over the world and rigged a system of satellite nations. It had developed the domestic corol-
lary of empire: an imperial presidency, which had seized for
itself the power to make war.

"Rise of Empire" was not a voice of the Left. Here was no
argument that war was good for business, that it was necessary for "access" to resources, or that it was bad because it
crowded out programs for the poor. Garrett didn't believe any
of that. What he believed was that unending commitment to
war was incompatible with "constitutional, limited government in the republican form."

His skepticism about defending the whole world from
communists had not begun with the Cold War. It reflected the
experience of World War I and particularly the argument at the
outset of World War II.

The line crossed had been Lend-Lease. In a *Saturday
Evening Post* editorial in 1941, Garrett had written:

> We have broken with our past. We have thrown
> away our New World, our splendid isolation, our geo-
> graphical advantage of three to one against all aggres-
> sors, our separate political religion. There is no longer
> a New World, nor an Old World, but now one
> world... From now on for us there is no foreign war.
> Any war anywhere in the world is our war, provided

only there is an aggressor to be destroyed, a democracy to be saved or an area of freedom to be defended.[11]

When he wrote that, he was responding to Roosevelt's rhetoric about the "aggressors." The principle Roosevelt was asserting applied to "any war, anywhere," Garrett said; it wasn't just that Hitler had to be crushed, but that *every* Hitler had to be crushed. Garrett asked: "Every Stalin, too?" That also seemed to be implied in America's "fantasy to become moral emperor of the whole world." Before Pearl Harbor he had written, "Having saved the world from Nazism, should we not be morally obligated to go on and save it from Bolshevism?"[12]

America had little thought of an anticommunist crusade in 1941, but a decade later it was fighting reds in South Korea, a country Garrett discounted as "a waif satellite." The result was "an absurd war" in which America was both unwilling to win, because of the risk of a land war with China, and unwilling to lose, because of loss of prestige in Asia. Having committed itself to other people's fights, America had lost its freedom of action.[13]

Nowhere in "Rise of Empire" does Garrett say what, if anything, his government should have done in 1952 about the communist forces that had so recently rolled over Eastern Europe and China. In 1967, when I read "Rise of Empire," the Soviet Union had nuclear missiles pointed at my hometown. I filed away Garrett's essay as an anachronism. It was a response typical of conservatives. As Justin Raimondo wrote in *Reclaiming the American Right* (1993), there would be "no room on the political spectrum" for a man like Garrett "for as long as the Cold War lasted."[14]

Chapter 32 notes

1 Garrett to Gipson, December 15, 1951. Caxton Papers, WSU.

2 *Perpetual War for Perpetual Peace,* Caxton, 1953, p. 3. Regarding *The People's Pottage,* the original was published in hardback by the Caxton Press in 1953 and was kept in print for 30 years, for a total press run of 10,500. In 1961 Caxton sold the rights to *American Opinion,* the house organ of the John Birch Society, to print 25,000 paperbacks under the name of its publishing house, Western Islands. In 1992, a group called Truthseeker was authorized to print 2,000 copies. There was also an edition put out by Noontide Press under the title *Burden of Empire.* Caxton published *Ex America: The 50th Anniversary of The People's Pottage,* 2005, with an introduction, index and endnotes by Bruce Ramsey.

3 John Chamberlain, *The Turnabout Years: America's Cultural Life 1900-1950,* Jameson Books, 1991, p. 153. The inscription to Baruch is on a copy of "Ex America" in the Baruch papers.

4 *The People's Pottage,* 1953, p. 91.

5 *The People's Pottage,* 1953, p. pp. 91-92.

6 John W. Burgess, *The Reconciliation of Government with Liberty,* Charles Scribner's Sons, 1915, pp. 371, 380.

7Sterling E. Edmunds, *Struggle for Freedom: The History of Anglo-American Liberty from the Charter of Henry I to the Present Day,* Milwaukee: The Bruce Publishing Co., 1946, pp. 205-206. Garrett reviewed the book in *American Affairs,* April 1947. I was given Garrett's copy by Richard Cornuelle.

8 Phone conversation with Sue Goulet, March 16, 2006.

9 Garrett to Gipson, August 16, 1951. Caxton Papers, WSU.

10 Garrett to Gipson, September 14, and October 11, 1951. Caxton Papers, WSU.

11 SEP, "Toward the Unknown," March 29, 1941.

12 SEP, "Playing the Red," November 8, 1941; "Behold! The Brass Serpent," February 15, 1941.

13 *The People's Pottage,* 1953, p. 152; *The American Story,* p. 375.

14 Justin Raimondo, *Reclaiming the American Right: The Lost Legacy of the Conservative Movement,* Center for Libertarian Studies, 1993, p. 95.

Chapter Thirty-three
WHAT AWFUL MOMENTUM

By mid-century, when Garrett had passed 70, he was aligned with a political cause that had almost been wiped out. The political individualism of Herbert Spencer, which in its day had been called liberalism, had lost even the label. Yet the few who rallied around it in mid-century preserved an idea that was to have a comeback.

A handful of classical liberals, who would later be called libertarians, had published pointed and radical arguments for liberty or against socialism, each during 1943 or 1944: Garrett in "The Revolution Was," Ayn Rand in *The Fountainhead,* Isabel Paterson in *The God of the Machine,* Rose Wilder Lane in *The Discovery of Freedom,* Albert Jay Nock in *Memoirs of a Superfluous Man* and Friedrich Hayek in *The Road to Serfdom.* Each of these would inspire young adherents.

In 1949 Garrett met one of them, Richard Cornuelle. The son of a Presbyterian minister, Cornuelle never could accept his father's religion. He had been a teenaged believer in socialized medicine until he read *The Road to Serfdom.* Infected with classical liberalism, he ventured to New York at age 21 to study under Ludwig von Mises.

Years later, Cornuelle would become a vice-president of the National Association of Manufacturers, and write a book arguing for the private, nonprofit sector, *Reclaiming the American Dream* (1966). Starting out, he was hired by Garrett to help on *American Affairs*. "I was supposed to be his assistant," he said. "Mainly I functioned as his companion."[1] When *American Affairs* folded, Cornuelle kept in contact with Garrett on behalf of the Volker Fund.

Cornuelle recalls being "a kind of hanger-on and sometime batboy" to a group of Old Rightists that included Garrett, Lane, Frank Chodorov, Frank Meyer, George de Huszar, Murray Rothbard, John Chamberlain, Henry Hazlitt, Leonard Read, Hayek and sometimes Mises, who "was the great grey eminence" of the group but not much of an activist. Hayek had set the tone in *The Road to Serfdom*, which he had dedicated "To the socialists of all parties." Hayek's cell of individualists would meet at the mansion at Irvington-on-Hudson owned by the Foundation for Economic Education (FEE), which Read had founded in 1946. Cornuelle calls it "the safe house for this funny bunch of people." There they would talk and enjoy Lane's homemade pastries.[2]

This group had a quietly influential future. In 1950 Henry Hazlitt and John Chamberlain founded *The Freeman*, which would later become the house organ of FEE and survive into the next century. Hazlitt, who had written *Economics in One Lesson* (1946), was a columnist for *Newsweek* from 1946 to 1966. Chamberlain, a business journalist and historian, wrote *The Roots of Capitalism* (1959) and *The Enterprising Americans* (1963). George De Huszar, a foreign policy academic, wrote *Soviet Power and Policy* (1955). Frank Chodorov, a near-anarchist pamphleteer who was the literary heir of Nock, became *The Freeman's* editor. Frank Meyer went on to become a major figure at *National Review*, where he attempted to fuse libertarianism and conservatism. Murray Rothbard was a founding member of the Cato Institute, later broke with it and inspired radical libertarians who now congregate at the Ludwig von Mises Institute and LewRockwell.com ("Anti-state, anti-war, pro-market"). Friedrich Hayek, who had been a founder of the Mont Pelerin

Society (which still exists), would win a Nobel Prize in economics in 1974 and inspire Margaret Thatcher. Rose Wilder Lane's books, written with her mother, Laura Ingalls Wilder, would be made into a famous TV series. Called "Little House on the Prairie," it celebrated pioneer American values and ran on NBC from 1974 to 1983.[3]

All that came later. At mid-century, Cornuelle writes, the feeling was "of what an insignificant minority we had become, what awful momentum the opposition had achieved, and a haunting subliminal suspicion that we were fighting not a losing battle, but a battle already lost." Not all of them felt that way, but Garrett did.

Garrett also dabbled in politics through involvement with George Creel, an old progressive Democrat who had begun his career as a newspaperman. Creel had achieved fame, and also infamy, as Wilson's head of propaganda during World War I. In the early New Deal, Creel had been the Western director of Roosevelt's Works Progress Administration. In 1934 he had left that job to run for the Democratic nomination for governor of California. Upton Sinclair, the author of *The Jungle* (1906), ran on an openly socialist program called End Poverty in California, and beat Creel 52-to-34 percent, then went on to lose the general election to a Republican.

In that campaign, Creel had been put off by the radicalism of Sinclair and the competitive delusions of Dr. Francis Townsend, who had a scheme to give everyone $200 a month. Creel began noticing similar nonsense in the New Deal. By 1942, he wrote, "I had sickened of the crackpot demagoguery that passed for liberalism." He was moving rightward. By the late 1940s, he was complaining that the American Left had aligned itself with the Communists, and "now stands for the obliteration of individualism at the hands of a ruthless, all-powerful state."[4]

In 1952, at 75, Creel was organizing a cabal of 200 rightist "Constitutional Democrats" to oppose Harry Truman. They included novelist Louis Bromfield, who would argue in *A New Pattern for a Tired World* (1954) that America had adopted a "messiah complex" in foreign policy, and Arthur Bliss Lane, former ambassador to Poland, who had written *I Saw Poland Betrayed* (1948).

Garrett, then 74, wrote to Creel: "My very dim political affiliations are supposed to be Republican." But he was happy to support Creel, and supplied him with the addresses of several like-minded men, most of whom had appeared in *American Affairs.*

One was Joseph P. Kennedy, the Democratic banker, entrepreneur and speculator whose son would later become president. The elder Kennedy had been appointed in 1934 by Roosevelt as the first chairman of the Securities and Exchange Commission and in 1938 as ambassador to the United Kingdom. Kennedy, an Irish-American Catholic, had opposed Roosevelt's informal alliance with Britain. Smeared as an appeaser of Nazis, Kennedy was forced out of the post in 1940. He lost his first son in the war, and afterward was bitter against Roosevelt.[5]

The executives on the list of like-minded men were Virgil Jordan, who had retired from the Conference Board; B.E. Hutchinson, vice-president of Chrysler, and Edgar Queeny, chairman of Monsanto Chemical. From the press came Felix Morley, who had been editorial page editor of the *Washington Post* 1933-1940 and a founder of the conservative weekly newsletter *Human Events,* and Frank Hanighen, then editor of *Human Events.* Garrett also included old New Dealers Donald Richberg, who had briefly headed the National Recovery Administration, and Raymond Moley, an early defector from Roosevelt's "Brain Trust"—though of Moley, Garrett said, "I distrust him."[6]

On the Republican side, Garrett's choice for president in 1952 was a Cold War skeptic, Sen. Robert Taft of Ohio. But Taft was not strong enough in his opinions to suit Garrett.

"Hoover is trying to make believe that Taft's piccolo is a trumpet," Garrett wrote in one letter.[7] In another, he said:

> Here is Taft saying he can see no choice but to go through with our commitments, bad though they are. Recently I said to Charley White (Republic Steel), who found the money for the Ohio campaign, "Your Republican Party will find itself in a twilight zone again with Taft."
>
> White said, "He can't be a statesman until he gets elected."
>
> So they think they fool the people, and often I think they really do.[8]

Garrett offered his platform to Creel's Constitutional Democrats. It was four items: an immediate return to the gold standard, a nationalist foreign policy, withdrawal from the United Nations and an end to "federal intervention in the domestic affairs of the states," including federal subsidies to the states. That was enough, Garrett argued. "It will be hard enough to get any kind of working agreement on these four."

The loudest objections from Creel's correspondents were to an immediate return to gold. Creel wrote that Henry Hazlitt opposed it, "while no less than Bernie Baruch" supported it.[9] The group was unanimous in wanting to control federal spending, but Garrett argued that that would fail without a limit to money. "Nobody is able to say, 'That's all the money there is,' " Garrett wrote. "Nobody can say that about irredeemable currency." No other reform would do more to limit government, he argued, than to make the dollar redeemable in gold.

Many in the group wanted a constitutional amendment to limit federal income-tax rates to 25 percent, which the top rate had last been under Coolidge. Under Hoover, Roosevelt and

Truman it had risen to 91 percent. But Garrett reminded them that the Constitution could be changed:

> Who makes the law can unmake it. How did the federal income tax become legal? You are bound to come back to it: a redeemable dollar is the great answer.[10]

It was a lost cause. They had no candidate. In their support of states' rights, they undoubtedly attracted segregationists, a cause in which Garrett never expressed any interest—nor, in their correspondence, did Creel. In any case, the group was held together by dislike of Truman and fell apart when he withdrew. The Democratic Party went on to nominate Adlai Stevenson. The constitutionalists gravitated to Taft, who lost the Republican nomination to Dwight Eisenhower. By the end of the following year, Taft had died. So had Creel.

Garrett's political cabal had amounted to nothing. The influence of the circle around Hayek looked to be little better.

Chapter 33 notes

1 Cornuelle, interview with the author, New York, April 29, 2007.

2 Cornuelle, "The First Libertarian Revival and the Next," *Critical Review Update*, April 1993, Critical Review Foundation. "Safe house": Cornuelle interview, April 29, 2007.

3 De Huszar, a professor in European and Asian Studies at the University of Chicago, and author of *Practical Applications of Democracy* (1945), committed suicide. For an overview of the mid-century libertarians and how they influenced the revival of the Right, see George H. Nash, *The Conservative Intellectual Movement in America Since 1945*, Basic Books, 1976, chapter 1.

4 George Creel, *Rebel at Large: Recollections of Fifty Crowded Years,* G.P. Putnam's Sons, 1947, pp. 326, 370.

5 Thomas Fleming, *The New Dealers' War*, Basic Books, 2001, pp. 79-80, 457-458.

6 Edgar Monsanto Queeny, 1897-1968, had taken over his father's small company, Monsanto Chemical, in 1928, when he was only 30. At his retirement in 1962, it had $1 billion in sales. Bernard Hutchinson, 1888-1961, was hired by Walter Chrysler in 1921 and in 1935 convinced bankers to lend short-term money to pay off all of Chrysler's long-term debt. Felix Morley, 1894-1981, wrote a number of books, including *Freedom and Federalism* (1959). Donald Richberg, 1881-1960, went on to write *Labor Union Monopoly* (1957), published by Regnery. Raymond Moley, 1886-1975, attacked the New Deal in *After Seven Years* (1939), wrote *How to Keep Our Liberty: A Program for Political Action* (1952), and as an old man was awarded a Presidential Medal of Freedom by President Nixon.

7 Garrett to Lawrence Dennis, undated, Hoover Institution, Folder Ts US G 239.

8 Garrett to Creel, undated, typewritten. Ryant papers.

9 Garrett to Creel, undated, handwritten. Creel to Garrett, March 17, 1952; Creel to Garrett, April 22, 1952. Ryant papers. Garrett seemed to imply a return to gold at the 1879-1933 value, because he argued that the Treasury had enough gold to do it but that this would not be true for much longer.

10 Garrett to Creel, undated, handwritten. Ryant papers.

Chapter Thirty-four

IF HE WON

Garrett lived out his last years with Dorothy and their two Siamese cats, Copy and O'Malley, on the farm at Tuckahoe. Garrett wrote, worked in wrought iron and savored an extensive collection of country music. Dorothy was not his intellectual equal, but she was a spirited woman, and sometimes joined him in shooting pistols at coins and bottles. He also liked to cook; one of his favorite dishes was shad roe. For Dorothy he had a gas stove, but for himself had installed a hulking woodstove. Dorothy's granddaughter has a photo of him in the kitchen wearing a chef's hat.[1]

In response to a query from Gipson, Dorothy wrote about Garet:

> He is so very reticent about himself. For instance, would you guess he is a very fine cabinet maker and has made much of the furniture and book cases in our houses? He is a rabid gardener and has planted thousands of trees here. At his forge, he has made some of the most exquisite fireplace accessories I have ever seen. He has done some lovely etchings and paintings. And he ADORES plumbing... Just let trouble start in the cellar and he is happy as a lark with his wrenches and washers.[2]

One of Garrett's sisters lived in the farmhouse he had bought. Garrett and Dorothy had built a simple dwelling they called the studio house. It had a two-story living room with, at Garrett's insistence, a wooden floor, Navajo rugs and no television. (Dorothy quickly switched to wall-to-wall carpet and a TV after Garrett died.) The big room had a stone fireplace. On a shelf above was a bust of the 14th century B.C. Egyptian queen, Nefertiti—a long-necked woman in a black headdress. Garrett had seen the original at Berlin's Egyptian Museum, where it still is the star attraction. He had sent away for the copy. When the museum director asked whether he wanted the fully restored version, Garrett wired back: "Not as God made her but as the devil left her."[3]

Garrett sometimes invoked God, or "the gods," but on ultimate questions he inclined to an agnostic wonder. He would say, "It isn't arguable." In the 1920s he wrote that religious feeling "has not its source in the intellect and is probably, as a scientific fact, an instinct."[4] A few years later he had the same thought when he wrote to Lane, "Faith may be a quality of the liver."

Late in life he was attracted to holism, the philosophy of South African leader Jan Smuts. Garrett wrote of holism in one of his last letters to Lane:

> If it nourishes me it is because I find myself starving on a diet of bran. The mystic explains too much, but at least he tries; on the other hand, the rationalist explains nothing. He only describes; and that leaves me with a sense of incompleteness gnawing at my entrails...
>
> I am the measuring worm that comes to the top of the stalk, feels into space, then turns and goes down again—to its rational world.[5]

IF HE WON

After Garrett died, Lane wrote in a letter that he had had "a sickness in his mind, or temperament, or somewhere" that had made him "desperately, passionately, hellishly UNhappy—for no reason, so far as I could ever see, or guess—and he made his own picture of the world, of human life and history and the present situations, from that emotion." Garrett would not have seen it that way. When he asked why—Why am I born? Why is Life? Why is everything so messed up? –Lane's reaction was that it was really too bad that he never saw how *funny* people are.[6]

He complained to her of the philosophers:

> I have been having a bout with philosophy, and it does me a psychic damage. It must mean something. When Spinoza says that perfect substance would have no reality, or the greater the imperfection of the substance the more reality it has, he means something. He is trying to tell me. But because I cannot get it I feel like a very inferior substance.[7]

Regarding Plato, he wrote Lane:

> You cannot wave Plato at me. The supreme chestnut peddler of all time. He believed in angels, private spirits and a Utopia of the elite. One rainy evening in New York I went to bed with Socrates' Defense, thinking I should have a wonderful experience. At the end I asked myself this question: "As an Athenian, how should I have voted?" The answer was: "Kill him." Then I read the second part, and asked the same question. The answer was: "Kill him twice."

Only a few descriptions survive of Garrett himself. His academic biographer, Ryant, who published *Profit's Prophet*

in 1989, had not known Garrett but in the late 1960s had interviewed several who had. He summed up their descriptions:

> Partially bald, he seldom went to the barber or
> worried about his appearance in general. He wore
> bow ties that matched the color and material of his
> shirts, often in vivid, solid tones. At times, he forgot
> to wear a tie. He wore baggy pants and tweed coats
> that were old and ragged at the elbows. Yet his hand-
> made shoes were shined daily— sometimes two or
> three times a day for special occasions. He was stout
> and red in the face... Somewhat profane, he was a
> slow and meticulous writer. He chain-smoked
> cigarettes and loved good bourbon, particularly
> Virginia Gentleman. At home, he was a do-it-your-
> selfer, the type who fell out of an apple tree while
> pruning it.[8]

Cornuelle remembers Garrett as "a small, impish, elegant
man with a Gilded-age mane of flowing white hair. He
dressed in tailored tweeds, wore a black Borsolino and carried
a cherry-wood walking stick."[9] He adds:

> Garrett was careful about his official appearance,
> but on the farm he usually wore old clothes. He some-
> times pretended he was the gardener so he could
> screen the strangers who came hoping to see him.
> Ryant's suggestion that he was a clumsy do-it-your-
> selfer contradicts my experience. He had good tools
> and used them expertly. He got a little unsteady as he
> got older, and drove a car longer than he should have.
> I was terrified to ride with him as he talked waving
> his hands and swung from one lane to another, but I
> was too shy to say anything.[10]

At the Park Avenue offices of the Conference Board, Garrett would sometimes stamp his stick at Cornuelle's desk to get the young man's attention. He was also salty in his speech, which was the reason he cited for avoiding interviews. It was too much trouble not to swear. Cornuelle writes:

> I remember a scene at a Conference Board staff meeting. After some fatuous declaration by one of those present, G.G. muttered "bullshit." The chairman, probably hoping for a denial or a retraction, asked, "What's that, Mr. Garrett?" and G.G. said, "BULLSHIT."[11]

Garrett was not one to be intimidated. In one case, an editor at Caxton questioned Garrett's statement in "Ex America" that in *The Communist Manifesto* Karl Marx had championed the income tax. The editor suggested that an error "could be grounds for some reviewers to misinterpret this sentence entirely, out of malice."

Garrett cited his source, and replied: "Malice to those who malice think."[12]

He also liked strong drink, though Cornuelle says, "I never saw him drunk." The Brighton Hotel in Atlantic City had named a concoction of rum and rye the Garrett Punch, but on the screen porch he sipped his favorite 90-proof bourbon, Virginia Gentleman. "Once, having resolved to drink less, I asked for sherry," Cornuelle recalls. "G.G.'s eyes widened as he announced, 'Sherry is the masturbation of a drunkard.'"[13]

By then, Garrett was considered an elder of free-market conservatism. "That characterization fit him badly," Cornuelle writes, "and he was more often than not embarrassed by his following. When one or another of his hot-eyed adherents came looking for him in the office, he would hide between the stacks in the library, smoking restlessly." Garrett saw his job as writing, not creating a movement, and approvingly quoted industrialist William Mullendore, who had once said about libertarian evangelist Leonard Read, "What would he do if he won?"

Cornuelle recalls his time, age 22 to 27, when Garrett taught him the ways of the journalistic mind:

> [It was] a vulnerable, impressionable time. I think maybe fate sent me to him at a time when he needed a young, eager listener, and I needed someone to introduce me to reality when I was in a dream world of libertarian abstractions. When I submitted a critique of John L. Lewis's three-day week, saying that as other fuels reduced the demand for coal, the marginal firms would "disappear," G.G. (actually I was never able to call him anything but Mr. Garrett) exploded, and sent me off to interview Lewis and visit some of the allegedly disappearing miners.[14]

When Garrett worked on an essay, he would read voluminously—in later life, the *New York Times*, the *Congressional Record* and the proceedings of the British Parliament. Then, writes Cornuelle,

> He would sit for days in his little office, muttering and fuming and cursing quietly. Then, suddenly, he would seize an old-fashioned pen holder, jam a new point into it, and scrawl on white foolscap, often for hours, panting and sweating, jabbing the pen in the ink now and then, until he had it all down. Then he'd howl impatiently for Kelly, his secretary, and dictate what he'd written while he could still read it.

Cornuelle recalls two rules Garrett had about his writing style. The first was, "If you like it, leave it out." The second was to use familiar words in unfamiliar senses. And to Lane, in defense of his use of the collective *we*, he said, "More and more I write by ear...and let the purists go hang themselves."

And the cave? Garrett did not like to write about himself, and when pressed by J.H. Gipson for some dust jacket copy for *The People's Pottage*, Garrett wrote:

> Since retiring last year from the editorship of *American Affairs* I have been looking at the world from a cave on the edge of the Tuckahoe River, and that is all about me.

The "cave" was a building. Cornuelle writes that Dorothy was an alcoholic, and sometimes Garrett had to put some distance between them to get any writing done.

> He built a cement-block study near the river about fifty yards from the house. It had insulation and heat and water, but no toilet. When I asked him why, he said, "I want to go home that often." He called it "the cave."
>
> I remember Dorothy telling me that when youngsters were brought to the farm, G.G. hid in the cave.[15]

Cornuelle recalls sitting with Garrett "mornings on the screen porch of his house on the Tuckahoe River during his last year, scratching and yawning and talking." He'd talk about his retreats with Ford and Edison, his breakfasts with Hoover at the Waldorf-Astoria (which Cornuelle had to promise not to discuss), being a pallbearer at Lorimer's funeral, or about America. Writes Cornuelle, "He was mourning a society that had first showed so much promise and now seemed so surely doomed."

Chapter 34 notes

1 Cornuelle, letter to the author, March 24, 2006; Sue Goulet, letter to the author, March 31, 2006.

2 Dorothy Garrett to Gipson, May 20, 1951. Caxton Papers, WSU.

3 Cornuelle, letters to the author, November 11, 2005, and March 24, 2006.

4 *The American Omen,* p. 231.

5 Lane papers. Written about June 1953.

6 Lane to Jasper Crane, August 25, 1955, *The Lady and the Tycoon,* p. 127.

7 From his last letter to Rose Lane, Lane Papers.

8 *Profit's Prophet,* p. 28, citing letters to the author from Bernard Herberick and John Tebbel, and an interview with S. Avery Raube. Ryant had interviewed them for "Garet Garrett's America," Ph.D. thesis, University of Wisconsin, 1968.

9 Cornuelle, introduction to GG Journal.

10 Cornuelle, letter to the author, March 6, 2006.

11 Cornuelle, letter to the author, November 8, 2005.

12 D.M. O'Neil to Garrett, July 11, 1951; Garrett to O'Neil, July 14, 1951. Caxton Papers, WSU.

13 Garrett punch: *George Horace Lorimer and the Saturday Evening Post,* p. 274. "Never saw him drunk": Cornuelle interview, April 29, 2007. Sherry: Cornuelle, letter to the author, November 8, 2005.

14 Cornuelle, letter to the author, March 6, 2006. He also tells this story in *Reclaiming the American Dream,* Random House, 1965, p. xiii.

15 Cornuelle, letters to the author, January 23, 2003 and March 24, 2006. In a letter of March 28, 2006, Cornuelle wrote: "Dorothy died about a year after G.G., but I don't know what killed her. I would bet alcohol was involved. I remember the sounds of her vomiting in the kitchen every morning and her great sigh of satisfaction when, after several failures, she kept the first bourbon and milk of the day down."

Chapter Thirty-five
IN DIMNESS I LEAVE IT

In a letter to Rose Lane, Garrett wrote of his last literary effort:

> I've finished the terrible book. I shudder to think what your two-edged mind will make of it, when and if it is printed—and you happen to read it. You will find it full of things your puristic soul abhors, editorial pronouns and such, and fore and after the gods. If you tell me they are non-existent, so much the better; for then they are what I say they are and nobody can disprove it.
>
> One thing I hold for the book. In the end it blows up with prejudice. I have been walking through the graveyard where all my life I had been putting away my murdered prejudices, and, praise be, I got some of them back...
>
> I doubt if anybody will print it.

In June 1954, Garrett wrote to Baruch, "I have just sold another book, and that means I am still going."

There never was any doubt that somebody would buy his last book. The idea for it had been J.H. Gipson's. He had conceived it as a history text for the public schools, which he regarded as the country's most influential institution. Gipson called his imagined book the Libertarian History, and had tried to persuade Albert Jay Nock to write it. But Nock had declined, and in 1945 had died. As soon as he read "The Revolution Was," Gipson began working on Garrett, who begged off: he was busy with *American Affairs.* When that ended, Garrett was busy with *The Wild Wheel,* and then "Ex America" and then "Rise of Empire." For seven years Gipson was after him. "Don't let's put it off too long," he wrote. "Time is running out as far as our side is concerned."[1]

To Gipson's mind he had commissioned the work. Furthermore, he wrote, publishing it "offered a possible chance for us to regain some of the very staggering losses that we have sustained in publishing the books that make up our Libertarian library."[2]

Caxton would remain the publisher loyal to Garrett, keeping *The People's Pottage* in print long after he died and bringing it back in 2004 as *Ex America: The 50th Anniversary of the People's Pottage.* But in 1954 Garrett was under no contract, and he sold his last book to Henry Regnery, who had founded a publishing house in 1947 and had affronted academia with young William F. Buckley's *God and Man at Yale* (1951). Garrett apologized to Gipson for choosing Regnery:

> I am sad about it. The facts are these. It took two and a half years to do it. Toward the later end I found myself in a jam and was obliged to accept sponsorship. After that I was no longer quite a free agent. The sponsors preferred Regnery. I trust this will not injure our happy relationship.[3]

That is not what he said to Regnery, who he had met in 1952. Garrett wrote that two of his previous publishers (meaning Caxton and Pantheon) had been expecting to see the book, one of whom "I am sure is going to feel hurt." But, he wrote, "I like the way you merchandise books." Garrett objected to

Regnery's royalty terms as "terrible" and negotiated a better deal. He also refused to give Regnery an option on his next book. He had done that with Pantheon in his contract for *A Time Is Born*, and he wasn't going to do it again. "I like to keep free," he wrote.

Regnery's only objection to Garrett's manuscript was the prologue, which he thought was "so pessimistic... that the average reader could hardly feel there is enough hope left for America to justify reading a book about it." Garrett wrote back that he could add a few lines to it "which I hope will save it in your esteem." Regnery also didn't like Garrett's title. Regnery and his sales manager Howard Clark preferred *The American Story;* Garrett had wanted to call the book *So Far America,*[4] which better fit the essence of it.

Garrett's book was a biography of America, and not with a happy ending. To Rose Lane he wrote of his country:

> I found it in darkness and in dimness I leave it, only that the first dimness was luminous, convictions were hot-blooded and reckless and danger was sweet; where this last dimness is opaque, convictions are economic and people demand of government two things, comfort and security... First a Constitutional, representative, limited government in the republican form; then democracy; now Empire, with soldiers in 49 countries and unlimited military commitments to defend half the human race. In the name of what? In the name of a free world. And nowhere a friendly nation. Only boughten allies and satellites. What a sequel!

In *A Life With the Printed Word* (1982) John Chamberlain remembered Garrett vowing to hang on until he finished his last book. Garrett said, "You can't die while you are still mad."

Garrett died November 6, 1954, of a stroke. He was 76, and surely still angry. They found him in the "cave" among the galley proofs of *The American Story*.

On the day the book came out, John Chamberlain reviewed it lovingly for the *Wall Street Journal*. He said it was "probably the most brilliant long historical essay on America that has ever been written; it is also, when it comes to 'Apostrophe' at the close, the most forlorn and bitter." [5] It was there that Garrett had grumbled that America had let in too many immigrants, who had come with alien ideas, and who had changed the Founders' political culture. It was a very unfashionable view, even then.

The book was not a big seller, and is long out of print. Garrett was no longer a name in American journalism, though the newspapers marked his passing. His former colleagues from the Conference Board sent Dorothy a statement of remembrance. In part, it said:

> Garet Garrett was one of the keenest minds of our time... He had a rare faculty for getting directly to the heart of a problem, and his provocative thinking was a constant challenge to all of us... He was a great editor, with an intuitive feeling for style... An individualist himself, Garet had a genuine and profound respect for the individuality of other people. He hated sham in all its forms... but with rare intellectual discrimination he never allowed his antagonism to an idea degenerate into a personal animosity to the one who held it... Beneath a rugged exterior Garet had a wonderfully kind heart.[6]

After ceremony at the local Masonic lodge, Garrett was buried in the Head of River Cemetery, which is next to a small Methodist church built near Tuckahoe by two sawmill owners in the early 1800s. It is not recorded what was said at the obsequies, but he would not have wanted anything florid. As a younger man, he had grumbled in his journal that the funeral of *New York Times* city editor Arthur Greaves had made him squirm. "Somebody asked what anybody thought of it. I said the possibility of having to lie helpless under all that banality was enough to take the zest out of dying."[7]

Garrett left everything to Dorothy, including "several thousand silver dollars buried in buckets under the porch, a remarkable collection of books and a tangled jumble of papers. You could tell from the way these were arranged that they belonged to a man who looked at the world in his own way—file folders labeled, 'Size,' 'Wheels,' 'Numbers,' and the like."[8]

Dorothy Garrett died a year later, at 45. Cornuelle writes that she was "still grieving... She believed that Mr. Garrett was a man for the ages and that everyone knew it." Her will had left his papers to Harvard. The Houghton Library sent "an apprentice in library science," Cornuelle writes, who "carried away a few first editions and a handful of letters signed by such celebrities as Hoover and Baruch, and left the rest behind." After Dorothy died, her executor allowed Cornuelle to take the journal and a few papers. But most of Garrett's books—a working library of 2,000 to 3,000 volumes—were "sold off in bundles...at a roadside auction, and most of his papers were destroyed." [9] Passed down into Dorothy's family were an engraved silver wedding ring, a few photos, some cast-iron pans and a set of dishes.[10]

Chapter 35 notes
1 Gipson to Garrett, May 17, 1951. Caxton Papers, WSU.
2 Gipson to Garrett, June 28, 1954. Files of the Caxton Press. Caxton's libertarian books included Herbert Spencer's *The Man Versus the State* and Harry Elmer Barnes's *Perpetual War for Perpetual Peace.*
3 Garrett to Gipson, June 23, 1954. Files of Caxton Press. Gipson *was* disappointed, but he took it graciously.
4 Garrett to Regnery, May 14, 1954; Regnery to Garrett, May 18, 1954; Garrett to Regnery, May 18, 1954, and June 17, 1954; Regnery to Garrett, June 22, 1954; Garrett to Regnery, undated; Regnery to Garrett, July 1, 1954. Henry Regnery Papers, Hoover Institution Archives, Box 24, Folder 7.
5 John Chamberlain, "The Bookshelf: How the 'Machine People' Misuse a Unique Wisdom." *Wall Street Journal* editorial page, February 1, 1955. John Chamberlain, *A Life With the Printed Word*, Regnery Gateway, 1982, p. 140.
6 Property of Sue Goulet. It is dated November 17, 1954, and signed by the president, vice president and secretary of The Conference Board and by 10 division directors.
7 GG journal, October 20, 1915.
8 Cornuelle, letter to author, January 23, 2003.
9 Cornuelle, letters to author, January 23, 2003 and March 6, 2006.
10 Phone interview with Sue Goulet, March 16, 2006.

Chapter Thirty-six
THE UNSANCTIONED VOICE

S tephen Cox, the biographer of Isabel Paterson, wrote, "If people alter their opinions, it is not so much because they're attracted by good arguments as because they're attracted by good arguers." Mainstream opinion doesn't have to be made memorable. Minority opinions do, because they assert themselves under threat of extinction. Wrote Cox, "The unsanctioned, non-endowed minority needs to express itself vividly if it wants to remain alive."[1]

Garrett did that. His style is why I bought *The People's Pottage* in 1967, read it, remembered it and undertook to research Garrett more than 30 years later. It was *what* he said, of course—but also *how* he said it. Garrett could etch his thought images into the reader's skull—and a writer that good needs to be saved. That he was on the losing side makes him all the more worth saving.

In today's terms, Garrett is a radical, though in his youth such views would have been ordinary. A century ago it was assumed that each man was responsible for himself and his family, that government was limited and that its role in the world was to look out for America's interests. The assumptions changed. In his last book, Garrett wrote:

> In one generation three events worked a metamorphosis.

The first was World War I, which shattered the tradition of non-entanglement in the quarrels of foreign countries. It was a precious vase and could never be restored.

The second event was the Great Depression [during which]... the imperious tradition of limited government was sacrificed, and the ground principles of free, competitive enterprise were compromised beyond redemption...

The third was World War II. We are not yet far enough away to comprehend that this was the incomparable disaster since the Fall of Man, and a penalty perhaps for the same sin, namely vanity of knowledge. The temptation was power, and the last form assumed by the illusion of power was the atomic bomb.[2]

With these events came two tides of thought. One was socialist. Garrett fought it in the 1920s in the battle over farm supports and in the 1930s over the New Deal. The other was internationalist. Garrett fought it in the 1920s over the European loans and in the early 1940s over entry into the war. Each undermined the old limited-government republic.

If, by the mid-1940s, Garrett was a gloomy man, there was reason for it. His cause had lost large pieces of ideological territory, and looked likely to lose more. The doctrine of capitalism as a self-regulating system had been refuted by events, or so it seemed, leaving open the question of a replacement. The socialists had one answer. John Maynard Keynes had another. Something like a planned economy was coming—indeed, with World War II it was already there. All this was happening when Garrett finalized "The Revolution Was," and is why that essay is filled with such foreboding and alarm, and is so beloved by aficionados of conspiracy and pessimism.

Half a century after Garrett's death, liberty has got some of its territory back—more, indeed, than its champions often like to admit. Internationally, the socialist ideal is dead. Capitalist economics, under the banner of Chicago, has retaken the academy. In America large industries have been freed to make their own price and product decisions—railroads, airlines, trucking, gas pipelines, wholesale electricity, telephones and cable TV. Finance has been taken back by the private sector, and it creates new forms faster than government can control them. The growers of wheat, corn and a handful of other crops are still sheltered with subsidies, but farmers may grow what they will and avoid the federal dole if they like.

The adventurers of capitalism, dismissed in Garrett's later years as "rugged individualists" out of place in a social age, have come back. So have the great fortunes. In the 1940s, the towering figures of the American economy were labor leaders. No more, and in the private sector the percentage of workers in unions is back where it was before the New Deal. The new industries are non-union and world-competitive.

America has not become just like Europe, and it remains defiant over the differences, which run far deeper than the death penalty and guns. American capitalism is more effervescent, more freewheeling, than the species native to the European Union. Tax rates here are lower, and social padding less. America has refused to embrace the European idea of a worker's right to his job, and it is the Europeans who are under pressure to change their system. Capitalism is no longer on the defensive.

Its victory, however, is not complete. Political victories rarely are. Capitalism carries on its back a welfare state that wants to grow, and the people's appetite for guaranteed medicine threatens to enlarge it. But overall, the change since Garrett's time in economic thinking and economic rules has been in his direction.

Not so in foreign affairs. Before Garrett died, he warned that Americans had become imperialists, and that it had not brought them peace of mind:

> With a navy equal to the next largest two and the paramount air force and the atomic bomb in stockpiles—now suddenly they were afraid to stand alone in their own hemisphere... They had won two world wars and they were committed to defend the whole free world, whatever that was, but alone they could not be sure of saving themselves...
> What of peace?
> It was not there. The thought of imposing peace on the world by force is from the Book of Empire. Pursuing it for more than 40 years the Americans had arrived at a permanent war economy.[3]

And now, what? Fifty years on, America has a military that costs as much as all the other militaries in the world combined and the people still do not feel secure. Having beaten Communism they have transferred their fears to Islam, and launch a War on Terror. How long it will last no one knows; the enemy, "terror," is not a thing that negotiates, or surrenders.

Why, then, remember Garet Garrett? Because he stood against state dominance at home and state intervention abroad, and showed that the two are connected. Capitalism has able advocates on the American Right, but in the years of fighting communism the Right became far too comfortable with war. It scorns government programs, forgetting that war is also a government program, and that, as Randolph Bourne said, "War is the health of the State."

Garrett's view, however, is not extinct. As I write, Rep. Ron Paul, Republican of Texas, is running a presidential campaign on the themes of a restrained state, a restored

Constitution, sound money, national sovereignty and an end to foreign wars. It is a remarkably Garrett-like platform. Rep. Paul is not going to win, but he creates a stir. He attracts fervent supporters, many of them young.

There is a market for these ideas. That being so, there is a reason to remember one of the writers who most brilliantly expressed them. Garet Garrett was against empire, but was never one to "blame America first." He celebrated America first. To him, his country was a place of self-reliance and liberty that needed always to keep itself "safe and free and dangerous."[4]

Chapter 36 notes

1 Stephen Cox, "Fruitless Controversies," *Liberty*, October 2005, p. 29.
2 *The American Story*, pp. 385-388.
3 *The American Story*, p. 381.
4 "Safe and free and dangerous," is from SEP, "While Yet There Is Time to Think," September 7, 1940.

Bibliography:
A List of Garrett's Work

BOOKS
1911 *Where the Money Grows* (Harper & Bros.)
1921 *The Blue Wound* (G.P. Putnam)
1922 *The Driver* (Dutton)
1923 *The Cinder Buggy* (Dutton)
1924 *Satan's Bushel* (Dutton)
1926 *Ouroboros, or the Mechanical Extension of Mankind* (Dutton)
1927 *Harangue* (Dutton)
1928 *The American Omen* (Dutton)
1932 *A Bubble That Broke the World* (Little, Brown)
1944 *A Time Is Born* (Pantheon)
1952 *The Wild Wheel* (Pantheon)
1953 *The People's Pottage* (Caxton), consisting of:
    1944 "The Revolution Was"
    1951 "Ex America"
    1952 "Rise of Empire"
1955 *The American Story* (Regnery)

REPRINTS
1965 *The People's Pottage* (Western Islands)
1992 *The People's Pottage* (Truth Seeker)
1990 *Burden of Empire (The People's Pottage)* (Noontide)
1997 *Where the Money Grows* and *Anatomy of the Bubble* (Wiley)
2002 *Salvos Against the New Deal* (Caxton)
2003 *Defend America First* (Caxton)
2004 *Ex America: The 50th Anniversary of The People's Pottage* (Caxton)
2005 *Insatiable Government* (Liberty Cap)
2008 *Insatiable Government*-revised (Caxton)

CONTRIBUTIONS TO OTHER BOOKS

1922. "Business," a chapter in Stearns, Harold E., *Civilization in the United States:An Inquiry by Thirty Americans*, Harcourt.

1939. "Federal Theater for the Masses," reprinted from SEP in Simpson, Claude; Brown, Stuart; Stegner, Wallace, *An Exposition Workshop: Readings in Modern Controversy,* Little, Brown.

1946. Introduction to Jordan, Virgil, *Manifesto for the Atomic Age*, Rutgers University Press.

1952. "Nullification by Treaty," reprinted from *The Freeman*, in Holman, Frank E., *Story of the Bricker Amendment (First Phase)*, New York Committee for Constitutional Government.

1976, "Undergoing a Caesarian," excerpt from *The Cinder Buggy* in Demarest, David Jr., ed., *From These Hills, From These Valleys*, University of Pennsylvania Press.

1960. Review of Keynes' *General Theory,* reprinted from *American Affairs,* in Hazlitt, Henry, ed., *The Critics of Keynesian Economics*, Van Nostrand.

1980. Rothbard, Murray; Garrett, Garet, *The Great Depression and New Deal Monetary Policy: Two Essays*, Cato Institute, reprint from *A Bubble That Broke the World*.

1988. Torey, Wharton & Garrett, Garet, *Just Another Kid, Roman Fever & the Wild Wheel,* Reader's Digest large print condensed book.

1992. Hendrickson, Mark; Poirot, Paul, *The Morality of Capitalism*, Foundation for Economic Education, reprint of "Laissez Faire."

PAMPHLETS:

1931 "Other People's Money" (The Chemical Foundation)

1943, Dec. 15. "On the Wings of Debt" (Los Angeles Chamber of Commerce)

AMERICAN MAGAZINE

1910, Jan. "Interesting People: Robert Scott Lovett"

1910, Mar. "Interesting People: J. P. Morgan, Jr."

1910, June. "Interesting People: Henry Pomeroy Davison"

COLLIER'S MAGAZINE

1911, Dec. 23: "Finance—The Division of Wealth: Our Daily Meat"

1911, Dec. 30: "Finance—The Division of Wealth: How Failure Pays"

1912, Jan. 6. "Finance—The Division of Wealth: Guggenheim Finance"

1912, Jan. 13. "Finance—The Division of Wealth: The Money Stewards"

1912, Jan. 27. "Finance—The Division of Wealth: The Wall Street Boys"

EVERYBODY'S MAGAZINE

As JOHN PARR:

1909, Mar. "The Stock Yards of New York"

1909, Apr. "The Game Gets You"

1913, Nov. "Everybody's Money: Parables of Wealth I"

1913, Dec. "Everybody's Money: Parables of Wealth II"

1914, Jan. "Everybody's Money: The Great Diversion"

1914, Feb. "Everybody's Money: A Dying Merry-Go-Round"

1914, Mar. "Everybody's Money: Fables of Finance III"

1914, Apr. "Everybody's Money: Your Money at Work."

1914, May. "Everybody's Money: Money Itself"

1914, June. "Everybody's Money: The Plight of the Little Capitalists"

1914, July. "The Unfinancial Farmer"

1914, Aug. "Everybody's Money: The Use and Misuse of Savings Banks"

1914, Sept. "Everybody's Money: A Work for Wall Street"

1914, Oct. "Everybody's Money: A Work for Wall Street" "Three Economic Miracles"

1914, Nov. "No Market"

As GARET GARRETT:

1914, April. "Henry Ford's Experiment in Good-Will"

1914, May. "The High Price of Speculation"

1914, July. "Things That Were Mellen's and Things That Were Caesar's"

1914 Aug. "Three Ways with the Railways"

1914, Oct. "Economics of the Sword"

1914, Dec. "When Christians Fight, Are They Christians?"
1915, Jan. "A Tin-Plated Millionaire"
1915, May. "The Snarl of Waking Asia"
1920, Sept. "The Shyest Man" (story)
1923, Feb. "Once Chance Nodded." (story)

NEW YORK EVENING POST
Probable Garrett pieces, unsigned
1910, Mar. 26. "Looking Ahead"
1910, Apr. 23. "What Next?"
1910, May 7. "Conjectural History"
1910, May 21. "In the Slack of the Market"
1910, June 18. "Diary of a Manipulator"
1910, July 2. "A Customer's Diary"
1910, July 16. "A Trader's Diary"
1910, Aug. 6. "A Banker's Diary"
1910, Aug 27. "On a Lower Level"
1910, Sept. 3. "Imagination"
1910, Sept. 17. "The Trader" (verified GG)
1910, Sept. 24. "The Insider"
1910, Oct. 1. "The Tipster"
1910, Oct. 8. "The Hoodoo" (verified GG)
1910, Oct. 15. "The Manipulator" (verified GG)
1910, Oct. 22. "The Stock Broker"
1910, Nov. 12. "Inferences"
1910, Nov. 19. "Conducting a Market"
1910, Nov. 26. "From the Gallery"
1910, Dec. 3. "A New Street Tragedy"
1910, Dec. 10. "A Real 'Inside View'" (verified GG)
1910, Dec. 24. "Receiving a 'Bank Statement'"
1911, Jan. 7. "Amateur Analytics"
1911, Jan. 14. "How Investments Wear"
1911, Jan. 21. "'Sizing Up' a Bond Issue"
1911, Jan. 28. "The Market for Tips"
1911, Feb. 4. "Wall Street and Its Habits" (verified GG)
1911, Feb. 11. "With a Bank President" (verified GG)
1911, Feb. 18. "The Customer's Man"
1911, Feb. 25. "The Financial Reporter"
1911, Mar. 4. "Taking Trouble Home" (verified GG)

1911, Mar. 11. "Stocks Coming and Going"
1911, Mar. 18. "When Wall Street Was Young"
1911, Mar. 25. "The 'Wire Business'"
1911, April 1. "The Way of a Client" (verified GG)
1911, April 8. "The Wall Street Wolf" (verified GG)
1911, April 15. "The Hall of Delusions" (verified GG)
1911, April 22. "News-Getting in Wall Street"
1911, April 29. "The Chart Follower"
1911, May 6. "The Infallible Man"
1911, May 15. "The Invisibles" (verified GG)
1911, May 20. "The Exiles"
1911, May 27. "A Short Sale"
1911, June 3. "The Specialist"
1911, June 10. "The Farmer's Side of It"
1911, June 17. "The Philosophy of It"
1911, July 1. "The Crop Expert"
1911, July 8. "The Board Boy"
1911, July 15. "An Obligation Discharged"
1911, July 22. "No. 38 Broad Street"
1911, July 29. "At a Ticker"
1911, Aug. 5. "Morocco by the Tape"
1911, Aug. 12. "Mr. Gates"
1911, Aug. 19. "Women of Wall Street"
1911, Aug. 26. "A Wall Street Philosopher"
1911, Sept. 2. "In the New Street Lobby"
1911, Sept. 9. "The Pier Interview"
1911, Sept. 23. "The Country Merchant"
1911, Oct. 7. "The Bear Plunger"
1911, Oct. 14. "A Joint Account"
1911, Oct. 21. "When One Has Positive Ideas"
1911, Oct. 28. "Discussing the Fundamentals"
1911, Nov. 4. "The Public"
1911, Nov. 11. "At the Fireside"
1911, Nov. 18. "When a House Fails"
1911, Nov. 25. "A Great Thought"
1911, Dec. 2. "A Lost Idea"
1911, Dec. 9. "A Business in Jeopardy"
1911, Dec. 16. "Wall Street Venders"
1911, Dec. 23. "An Arab in New Street"

1912, Jan. 6. "Every Speculator's Secret"
1912, Jan. 13. "A Day with a Money King"
1912, Jan. 20. "An Annual Excursion"
1912, Jan. 27. "A Directors' Meeting"
1912, Feb. 3. "The Rush to Fill a Vacuum"
1912, Feb. 10. "New Street's Restraint"
1912, Feb. 17. "Passing the Tip Along"
1912, Feb. 24. "The Promoter"
1912, Mar. 2. "A Flurry in Stocks"
1912, Mar. 9. "Another Alarum"
1912, Mar. 16. "A Trick in Psychology"
1912, Mar. 23. "An Office Incident"
1912, Mar. 30. "A Freak of Luck"
1912, April 6. "The 'Money Trust' Again"
1912, April 13. "Humoring A Client"
1912, April 20. "Psychology"
1912, April 27. "A Bull Leader"
1912, May 4. "A New Client"
1912, May 11. "A Ticker Moth"
1912, May 18. "Nothing Bid"
1912, May 25. "Ticker Statesmanship"
1912, June 1. "Nobody's Customer"
1912, June 8. "A Railroad President"
1912, June 15. "Building a Speech"
1912, June 22. "The Hay Letter"
1912, June 29. "An Error in Bonds"
1912, July 6. "A Flurry in Steel"
1912, July 13. "The Tale of a Desk"
1912, July 20. "Any Specific Thing"
1912, July 27. "'The Call' of Old"
1912, Aug. 3. "Shake-Up in the Street"
1912, Aug. 10. "How It Happens"
1912, Aug. 17. "An Office in Wall Street"
1912, Aug. 24. "Contrasts"
1912, Aug. 31. "The 'Telephone Boy'"
1912, Sept 21. "A Western Sketch"
1912, Sept. 28. "Some Delusions in Finance"

NEW YORK TIMES ANNALIST

Probable Garrett pieces, but unsigned:
1913, Jan. 20, through 1914. Weekly editorial column
1913, Jan. 27. "What If There Should Be a Gold Deluge?"
1913, Feb. 3. "The Washington Experiment"
    "James J. Hill as a Farmer"
1913, Feb. 10. "The Steel Rail"
1913, April 28. "May Organized Labor Restrain Trade?"
1913, Nov. 17. "What Hinders a Tower of Babel"
1913, Dec. 29. "The Riddle of Unemployment"

THE DELINEATOR
As JOHN PARR
1914, May. "The Best Ways to Save"
1914, June. "Women and Their Money"
1914, Oct. "Women and Their Money"
1914, Nov. "Life Insurance for Women"

THE NEW YORK TIMES
Probable Garrett editorials, based on the subject and treatment
1915, May 9. "Plenty of Bread"
1915, May 14. "The Press and the People"
1915, May 27. "The Nation's Turning Point"
1915, May 30. "A Credit Limit on War"
1915, June 7. "The Meekness of Big Business"
1915, June 9. "Mental Capital"
1915, June 10. "The Tragedy of Innocence" (verified GG)
1915, June 13, "The War Account"
1915, June 16. "The Imperious Customer"
1915, June 25. "The English Labor Crisis"
1915, July 2. "Capital Is Pacific"
1915, July 7. "Germany's Impotent Gold"
1915, July 10. "The Prodigal Country"
1915, July 16. "The American Dollar"
1915, July 18. "Class Ego"
1915, July 22. "War's Lesson in Thrift"
1915, July 23. "Reason Unstrung"
1915, July 26. "Should Directors Speculate?"
1915, Aug. 8. "Waking a Giant"
1915, Aug. 9. "The New Business of Lending"

270

1916, June 30. "Varieties of Martyrdom"
Bylined German correspondence:
1915, Dec. 20. "Germany, Pacific Toward Us, Hesitates to Speak in the Hearing of the World, Lest It Be Interpreted as Weakness"
1916, Jan. 2. "War Dolls Express Spirit of Berlin"
1916, Jan. 18. "No Starvation in Germany"
1916, Jan. 19. "Modern War on a Tribal Plan"
1916, Jan 20. "How Germany Pays for War"
1916. Jan. 21. "Germany as a Unit in War"
1916, Jan. 22. "Yearnings of Young Germany"
1916, Jan. 23. "Delusions of German Logic"
1916, Jan. 24. "Self-Seeing in Germany"
1916, Jan 25. "Germany on a Blind Errand"
1916, Jan 26. "How Germans React to War"
1916, Jan. 28. "Peace Feeling in Germany"
Other bylined pieces:
1916, Mar. 5. "The Week's War Operations and Their Meaning"
1916, Mar. 12. "The Week's Operations on the Various War Fronts"
1922, July 16. "Edison's Idea for a New Kind of Money," and "Discussion of the Edison Money Plan"
1922, Nov. 26. "Shall Europe Pay Back Our Millions?" (Reprint of "Notes on the War Debts," *SEP*)

CURRENT HISTORY
1916, March. "Inner Germany" (reprint from *New York Times)*

THE NEW YORK TRIBUNE
1916, Aug. 1-Dec. 4. Daily "Finance-Economics" column
1916. Aug. 1-8. "West of East"
1916, Oct. 8. "This World's Emotional Reaction to the Economic Curse of War"
1916, Oct. 29. "The Eternal Problem of a City's Stomach"
1917, Jan. 1. "Finance-Economics" column
1918, Jan. 23-26. "This Stumbling Giant"

THE NEW REPUBLIC
1914, Dec. 26. "Baiting the Commerce Commission"
1920, Nov. 3. "The Whirling Pyramid"
1920. Nov. 24. "Anarchic Business"

1920, Dec. 29. "Alice Economics"
1921, May 18. "The God of Supply and Demand"
1921, Jun. 22. "The Wage Curve"
1921, July 27. "The Painting of Hayes Miller"
1921, Aug. 10. "Mumbling the Railroads"
1921, Oct. 19. "Ghosts in the Trade Door"
1921, Nov. 19. "Tinsel and Tonnage"
1928, June 6. "War Debts and Wartime Purchases"

McCLURE'S MAGAZINE
1921, Feb. "The Tolerant Tax Payer"
1921, Sept. "Look in Uncle Sam's Boot"
1922, June. "The House a Wop Built" (story)

CENTURY MAGAZINE
1922, Sept. "The Goose-Man" (story)

ANNALS OF THE AMERICAN ACADEMY
OF POLITICAL AND SOCIAL SCIENCE
1923, July. "Dangers of Inflation"

COUNTRY GENTLEMAN
1923, Oct. 27-Dec. 22. *Satan's Bushel*

SATURDAY EVENING POST
With GARET GARRETT byline:
1917, Jan. 6. "The Gold Token," (story)
1920, Apr. 3. "Red Night," (story)
1920, Aug. 14. "A Gilded Telegrapher," (story)
1921, Jan. 15. "A Wall Street Baptism" (story)
1921, Mar. 26. "A Luck Leper's Tale," (story)
1921, Dec. 24 & 31; 1922, Jan. 7, 14, 21 & 28. *The Driver*
1922, Nov. 25. "Notes on the War Debts"
1923, Jan. 13. "The Public Debt Mania"
1923, Feb. 17 & 24, Mar. 3, 10, 17 & 24. *The Cinder Buggy*
1923, Feb. 24. "On Saving Europe"
1923, Apr. 21. "Thus Germany Wept"
1923, Apr. 28. "Why Germany Drowned Her Credit"
1923, May 5. "The Black Grail of Europe"

1923, May 19. "To Speak of England"
1924, Feb. 2. "Our $3,500,000,000 Nucleus"
1924, Feb. 9. "A Rudderless Merchant Marine"
1924, Feb. 16. "U.S. Ships: U.S. Mud"
1924, Feb. 23. "The Great Meaning of Ships"
1924, Mar. 1. "U.S.S.B.S.S. Suspicion"
1924, Apr. 12. "That Pain in Our Northwest"
1924, Apr. 19. "Fifty-year Crisis in Agriculture"
1924, July 19. "As Citizens Thereof"
1924, Aug. 9. "Lo, the Native American"
1924, Oct. 11. "Bringing up the Northwest"
1924, Nov. 8. "Exposing the Farm Problem"
1924, Nov. 22. "How in the West?"
1925, Jan. 17. "The Tale of Uncle Sam's Voyage in an Irrigating Ditch"
1925, Feb. 7. "What a Demagogue Knows"
1925, Mar. 28. "France Mends Her Stocking With Magic Thread"
1925, Apr. 25. "From Caesar to Mussolini"
1925, May 16. "Signs in England"
1925, May 23. "Telling Europe's Fortune"
1925, Oct. 3. "The Natural History of Railroads"
1925, Oct. 10. "Taming the Railroads"
1925, Oct. 24. "The Railroad Apple"
1925, Dec. 12, Dec. 26. "This Is Well-Being"
1926, Aug. 21. "Public Debts and Private Loans"
1926, Aug. 28. "The French Crisis"
1926, Sept. 4. "Then to Let Germany Off"
1926, Sept. 11. "The Pound Sterling"
1926, Sept. 18. "The Apologetic American"
1926, Oct. 2, 9 & 23. *The Trees Said to the Bramble,*
"Come Reign Over Us"(Harangue)
1926, Nov. 20. "American Notes on the League of Nations"
1927, Jan. 15. "A Primer of Propaganda"
1927, Feb. 12. "The League of Debtors"
1927, Apr. 2. "McNary-Haugenism"
1927, Apr. 16. "Industry, Agriculture and Co."
1927, Apr. 30. "The Fourth Age of Agriculture"
1927, May 14. "The Land Belonging"
1927, May 28. "Iowa's Debits and Credits"

1927, Dec. 10, 17 & 24; 1928, Jan. 7, 14 & 28.
The American Book of Wonder, (The American Omen)
1928, Mar. 10. "A Tale of Thirteen Billions"
1928, Apr. 28. "Machine People"
1928, June 2. "Hoover of Iowa and California"
1928, July 28. "Peace Building"
1928, Aug. 11. "What Has Happened to War"
1928, Sept. 29. "Revolution in Agriculture"
1928, Oct 6. "The Corn Belt"
1928, Oct. 13. "Farming with Security and Independence"
1929, Mar. 2. "New and Unfinished Business"
1929, Mar. 16. "Government by Tumult"
1929, Apr. 13. "The Seven Sound Years"
1929, May 4. "Speculation"
1929, May 11. "The New Picture of Agriculture"
1929, May 25. "Faith in Bonanza"
1929, Sept. 28 and Oct. 12. "Travel Notes"
1929, Nov. 2. "West Coast, East Coast"
1929, Dec. 28. "Wall Street and Washington"
1930, Jan. 18. The "Wild Wheel in the Business Machine"
1930, Feb 15. "Energy, Wild or Tame"
1930, Mar. 1. "The First Hoover Year"
1930, June 21. "Farm Relief So Far"
1930, Aug. 2, Aug 9. "Points South"
1930, Oct. 18. "Los Angeles in Fact and Dream"
1931, Jan. 24. "Our Asiatic Attribute"
1931, Feb 7. "The American Raising of the Filipino"
1931, Feb. 21. "Void of the Philippines"
1931, Mar. 14. "Looking in the Ditch"
1931, July 4. "Uncle Sam Learning the Lender's Lesson"
1931, July 18. "The Curse of Plenty"
1931, Aug. 8. "A Story of Banking"
1931, Sept. 26. "The Rescue of Germany"
1931, Oct. 17. "As Noble Lenders"
1931, Dec. 12. "Opening the Golden Goose"
1932, Jan 23. " 'America Can't Come Back' "
1932, Mar. 12, Mar 19. "Book of the Debts"
1932, May 21. "News of Delusion"
1932, June 25. "Insatiable Government"

274

1932, Aug. 6, Oct. 8. "Notes of These Times"
1932, Nov. 12, Nov. 19. "Notes of These Times: The Farmer"
1933, Jan. 21. "Unemployment—What Is It?"
1933, Feb. 18. "Unemployment—In the Light of Happening"
1933, Mar. 11. "Unemployment—What We Do About It"
1933, Apr 15. "The Economic Drive Against America"
1933, May 20. "Why Some Banks Fail and Others Don't"
1933, July 1. "This Thing of Trade"
1933, Aug. 12. "The Hundred Days"
1933, Oct. 14. "Since the Tower of Babel"
1933, Nov. 4. "Concerning Inflation"
1933, Dec. 9 and Dec. 16. "Washington Miscellany"
1934, Feb. 3. "Concerning Money"
1934, Mar. 3. "Two Chapters in the Story of Gold"
1934, May 19. "The Balance Sheet of Capitalism"
1934, June 16. "Socialism in the Red"
1934, July 28. "The Articles of Progress"
1934, Aug. 18. "The Great Moral Disaster"
1934, Sept. 29. "The Forgotten Road"
1934, Oct. 27. "Section Seven A at Sheboygan"
1934, Dec. 29. "The Boll Evil"
1935, Feb. 23. "When Wishes Think"
1935, Mar 9. "Economic Fascinations"
1935, Apr. 20, May 4. "Pieces of Money"
1935, June 22 and July 6. "Surrender of the Purse"
1935, Aug. 3. "The House We Live In"
1935, Aug. 31. "The Wealth Question"
1935, Oct. 19. "Saving Agriculture"
1935, Nov. 2. "Managed Agriculture"
1935, Nov. 16. "Plowing Up Freedom"
1936, Jan. 18. "Your Government"
1936, Feb. 1. "New Government-a Catechism"
1936, Feb. 29. "National Hill Notes"
1936, Mar. 28. "The Lost American"
1936, May 16. "National Hill Notes"
1936, June 20. "Federal Theater for the Masses"
1936, July 25. "The AAA Experiment in Birth Control of Wealth"
1936, Aug. 8. "Agricultural Excursions"
1936, Aug. 22. "The Political Curse on the Farm Problem"

1936, Sept. 19. "Security"
1936, Oct. 3. "Credit"
1936, Oct. 24. "We Overtake Europe"
1936, Nov. 7. "The Youth Document"
1937, Jan. 2 "The Detroit Principle"
1937, Mar. 13 & 20. "This Is Florida"
1937, June 26. "Putting the Law on the Boss"
1937, July 17. "The Labor Weapon"
1937, Sept. 4. "Labor and Napoleonism"
1937, Oct. 9. "The Labor Mask"
1937, Dec. 4. "The Crime of Economic Royalism"
1938, Jan. 22, & 29. "A Washington Errand"
1938, Mar. 5. "Fifth Anniversary N.D."
1938, May 7. "Over the Dam with TVA"
1938, May 28. "Explorations of Our First Federal Province"
1938, Sept. 3 & 10. "Roads Going South"
1938, Oct. 8. "The Problem South"
1938, Nov. 12. "Machine Crisis"
1938, Mar. 18. "Labor at the Golden Gate"
1939, Mar. 25. "Whose Law and Order?"
1939, Apr. 8. "Great Works"
1939, June 24. "Give Us This Day"
1939, Sept. 9. "Peace on the Rails"
1939, Sept. 23. "One to Make a Bargain"
1940, Jan. 13. "War Has Lost Its Pocket"
1940, Mar. 2. "The AAA in Its Own Dust Bowl"
1940, June 8. "A World That Was"
1941, May 17. "Out to Shake the World"
1941, May 31. "Tanks from a Cornfield"
1941, June 14. "Salute American Air Power"
1941, Oct. 4. "How Are We Doing? A Report on the State of Defense"

Principal unsigned editorials:
1927, Dec. 24. "Borrowers"
1939, Apr. 8. "Who Cultivate War"
1939, Aug. 12. "The Crisis Is Moral"
1939, Nov. 4. "What War Is Not"
1939, Nov. 11. "Design for Freedom"

1940, Mar. 23. "That of our Own"
1940, June 22. "And They Were Unprepared"
1940, July 6. "Will We Do It?"
1940, July 13. "Quo Vadis?"
1940, July 20. "There Is a Star"
1940, July 27. "Also Defense"
     "Who Is Friend?"
1940, Aug. 3. "Marvelous Rescue of the Mosquito Fleet"
1940, Aug. 10. "Work"
1940, Aug. 17. "Foreign Policy Ad Lib"
1940, Aug. 24. "This Was Foretold"
1940, Sept. 7. "While Yet There Is Time to Think"
1940, Sept. 14. "The Mental Bottleneck"
1940, Sept. 21. "The Spirit Would"
1940, Sept. 28. "Conscription"
1940, Oct. 3. "A Law Happens"
     "The Betrayed Tool Secret"
1940, Oct. 12. "Your Government"
1940, Oct. 19. "On Going to War"
1940, Oct. 26. "Within the Form"
1940, Nov. 2. "Not on the Ballot"
1940, Nov. 9. "Burma Road"
1940, Nov. 16. "Gold Marbles"
1940, Nov. 23. "As If"
     "In the Great Tradition"
1940, Nov. 30. "Priorities"
     "Status by Law"
1940, Dec. 7. "Billions Wild"
1940, Dec. 14. "Strategy"
     "The German Word"
1940, Dec. 21. "Labor"
     "The Law Backstage"
1941, Jan. 4. "And America"
1941, Jan. 11. "The Escape Phantasy"
1941, Jan. 18. "Man of Britain"
1941, Jan. 25. "If England Should Yield"
     "Sequel Postponed"
1941, Feb. 1. "Definition"
     "The And-Americans"

"Our Forgotten Neutrality"
1941, Aug. 2. "The Foreign Malady"
1941, Aug. 9. "This Hitler Myth"
1941, Aug. 16. "Historical Fragment"
1941, Aug. 23. "In the Spiral"
1941, Aug. 30. "Inter Vivos"
1941, Sept. 6. "The False Fear Theme"
"At the Spearhead"
1941, Sept. 13. "Fifty Billions Wild"
"The Mind of Hitler"
"In Parenthesis"
1941, Sept. 20. "Government by Consent"
1941, Sept. 27. "Declaration of the Atlantic"
"A Year Ago"
1941, Oct. 4. "The Saving of England"
1941, Oct. 11. "The Drift"
1941, Oct. 18. "The More We Pay Now"
1941, Oct. 25. "Whose America?"
"Delicate News"
1941, Nov. 1. "Down to the Lean"
"A Text for Loyalty"
1941, Nov. 8. "Playing the Red"
1941, Nov. 15. "What Will We Do With It?"
"Iceland"
1941, Nov. 22. "The American Guilt Theme"
1941, Nov. 29. "The Soil of Unity"
1941, Dec. 6. "The Meaning of Total"
1941, Dec. 13. "Omens in Germany"
"Total Taxation"
1941, Dec. 20. "Review"
1941, Dec. 27. "What Goeth Before a Fall"
1942, Jan. 3. "Fate and War"
1942, Jan. 24. "Censorship"
1942, Feb. 28. "Our Own New Order"

THE ATLANTIC MONTHLY
1943, Jan. "Age of Alchemy"

THE AMERICAN MERCURY
1943, June. "The Press and Congress"
1943, Oct. "Change-Over to Peace"

THE CHICAGO TRIBUNE
1943, Sept. 19. "The Mortification of History"

THE ECONOMIC RECORD
1944, July: "Review and Comment"
"The Mind of American Business on Free Competitive
Enterprise"
Reviews: Flynn, *As We Go Marching*
Nathan, *Mobilizing for Abundance*
1944, October: "Review and Comment"
"The Outline of a Planned Economy in Great Britain"
"The Fiscal Realism of Beardsley Ruml"
"The Spectacular Entry of Cooperatives into Production"
Reviews: Hayek, *The Road to Serfdom*
Laski, *Realism and Civilization*

AMERICAN AFFAIRS
1945, January: "Review and Comment"
"Mythologies of Reconversion"
"Resolve by Congress to Overtake Government"
Reviews: Mises, *Omnipotent Government*
Warburg, *Foreign Policy Begins at Home*
1945, April: "Review and Comment"
"High Finance for the People"
"The Rising Form of a Planned Economy"
Reviews: Beveridge, *Full Employment in a Free Society*
Croce, *Politics and Morals*
Berge, *Cartels: Challenge to a Free World*
1945, July: "Review and Comment"
"The American Menace"
Reviews: White, *Report on the Russians*
League of Nations, *Economic Stability in the Postwar
World*
Hansen, *America's Role in the World Economy*
1945, October: "Review and Comment"

280

"Notes on the Yankee Dollar"
"Science—Before and After the Event of July 1945"
"Albert Jay Nock"
Reviews: Terborgh, *The Bogey of Economic Maturity*
      Wallace, *Sixty Million Jobs*
1946, January: "Review and Comment"
"The Loan to Great Britain"
Reviews: Johnson, *The Secret of Soviet Strength*
      Snow, *The Pattern of Soviet Power*
      Illin, *New Russia's Primer*
      Dallin, *Russia and Postwar Europe*
      Barmine, *One Who Survived*
Review: 20th Century Fund, *Financing American Prosperity*
1946, April: "Review and Comment"
"Compulsion"
"Instrumental Money"
Reviews: Finer, *Road to Reaction*
      Wootton, *Freedom under Planning*
      Baker, *Science and the Planned State*
1946, July: "Review and Comment"
"The News"
"A Law to Save the Constitutional Life of Congress"
"A Tool on the Shelf: Digest of the Full Employment Act"
"Our Kept Corporations"
"Trying to Audit the RFC"
"The House of Labor"
"Directive 103"
Reviews: Keynes, *The General Theory*
      Bowles, *Tomorrow Without Fear*
1946, October: "Review and Comment"
"Since Bikini"
"A World Food Board"
"New Global Law of the Air"
Reviews: Hazlitt, *Economics in One Lesson*
1947, January: "Review and Comment"
"The American Proposals for a Collectivist World System"
Reviews: Belloc, *The Servile State*
1947, April: "Review and Comment"

Cortney, *The Economic Munich*
Barnett, "The Supreme Court and the Capacity to Govern"
Moulton, "Economic Systems"
1949, July: "Comment"
"Monster Government"
"How It Happened to the Farmer"
Reviews: Harris, ed., *Saving American Capitalism*
Bonn, *Wandering Scholar*
1949, October: "Comment"
"At the Toll Gate"
"At the World's Bedside"
Reviews: Morley, *The Power in the People*
1950, January: "Comment"
"The Debacle of Planning"
"Whose Point Four Will It Be?"
Reviews: Terborgh, *Dynamic Equipment Policy*
1950, April: "Comment"
"The March"
"Story of Subsidized Agriculture"
"Horoscopics"
"The Soviet Worm in School Libraries"
Reviews: Fellers, *Thought War Against the Kremlin*
1950, July: "Comment"
"Jobs and the Man"
"Joy of Public Money"
Reviews: de Jouvenel, *On Power*
Lasky and Toledano, *Seeds of Treason*
1950, October: "Comment"
"What Do You Read?"
"The Dichroic ITO"
Reviews: Budenz, *Men Without Faces*

CONGRESSIONAL DIGEST
1948, Nov. "Charter for a Planned World" (from *American Affairs*)

THE FREEMAN
1952, Feb. 25. "Decline of the American Republic" (from "Rise of Empire")
1952, Apr. 21. "Once There Was Henry Ford" and "Marks of

Empire"
1953, May 4. "Nullification by Treaty"

U.S.A., THE MAGAZINE OF AMERICAN BUSINESS
1952, March. "Mr. Churchill's World"

LOOK
1952, Mar. 25, Apr. 8, Apr. 22. "The World that Henry Ford Made"

READER'S DIGEST
1935, Sept. "Surrender of the Purse" (from *Saturday Evening Post)*
1952, May. "The Man Who Thought With His Hands" (from *The Wild Wheel)*

FAITH AND FREEDOM
1954, April. "The Suicidal Impulse"

LEFT AND RIGHT
1966, Winter. "The American Empire"

THE AMERICAN SCHOLAR
1967, Summer. "Remembrance of the *Times*," excerpts from Garet Garrett's journal edited by Richard Cornuelle

LIBERTY
2004, Dec. "Crisis of the Soft-Money Plague" from *The Driver*
2005, Aug. "The Paper-Money Crusade of 1894" from *The Driver*

UNPUBLISHED MANUSCRIPTS
1915-1916, *Garet Garrett Journal,* property of Richard Cornuelle
1920, approx. *That Satan Said.* A play, property of Houghton Library
1952. "Our Leaning Schoolhouse." An essay, property of the Caxton Press

286

Index of People

Mises, Ludwig von 3, 216, 223, 235, 236
Moley, Raymond 238
Morgan, J.P. 21
Morley, Felix 238
Mullendore, William 248
Mussonlini, Benito 92, 153

N

Nasaw, David xii, 78-79
Neall, Adelaide 181, 196
Nelson, Donald 196
Nestos, H.A. 106-107
Newcomb, Simon xiii, 120, 122, 156
Nock, Albert Jay 235, 252
Noyes, Pierrepont 94

O

Ochs, Adolph x, 43-45, 48-53, 55, 57, 58, 64-65
Oney, Steve 48

P

Palmer, A. Mitchell 79
Parr, John (pseudonym) 27,36
Paterson, Isabel 195, 215, 235, 257
Paul, Ron 260-261
Phagan, Mary 47, 49
Plato 245
Pullman, George 16

Q

Queeny, Edgar 202, 238

R

Raimondo, Justin 233
Rand, Ayn 115-116, 121, 123, 238
Rathenau, Walter x, 61-62, 93
Read, Leonard 206, 236, 248
Regnery, Henry xii, 252-253
Reid, Daniel Gray 36

Richberg, Donald 238
Rockefeller, John D. 137, 139
Rockwell, Lew 236
Roepke, Wilhelm 216
Roosevelt, Franklin 1, 25, 56, 109, 150, 153, 155, 156, 158, 163, 165, 168, 175, 176, 178, 191-195, 200, 201, 205-207, 209, 213, 217, 230, 233, 237-239
Roosevelt, Theodore 109
Root, Elihu 101
Rothbard, Murray 236
Ryant, Carl ix, xi, xii, 193, 245-246

S

Simpich, Frederick 139, 140, 141, 220
Sinclair, Upton 237
Slaton, John 49, 51
Smith, Adam 120
Smith, Al 179
Smuts, Jan 244
Snyder, Carl 192
Socrates 245
Spahr, Walter 216
Spencer, Herbert 119, 205, 235
Spinoza 145
Spengler, Oswald 183
Stalin, Josef 169, 191, 213, 233
Steffens, Lincoln xii, 127-128
Stevenson, Adlai 240
Stout, Wesley Winans 186, 196

T

Taft, Robert 215, 238-240
Talese, Gay xii, 2, 3, 44
Thatcher, Margaret 237
Thompson, Charles 50
Thompson, Dorothy 155
Townsend, Dr. Francis 179-180, 237
Truman, Harry 213-214, 216-218, 237, 240

289

Tugwell, Rexford 183, 199, 206

U

Utley, Freda 215

V

Van Anda, Carr 43, 44
Viner, Jacob 216
Volker, William 223

W

Walker, Francis Amasa xiii, 120
Wallace, Henry 199, 200, 206, 213
White, Charley 239
Wilder, Laura Ingalls 182, 237
Willkie, Wendell 193
Wilson, Woodrow 25, 31, 56, 57,
63, 70, 77-79, 91, 225, 237
Wright, David McCord 216

Other thought-provoking
titles from
CAXTON PRESS:

INSATIABLE GOVERNMENT
by Garet Garrett
ISBN 978-087004-463-2
$17.95

DEFEND AMERICA FIRST
by Garet Garrett
ISBN 0-87004-433-8
$13.95

SALVOS AGAINST THE NEW DEAL
by Garet Garrett
ISBN 0-87004-425-7
$12.95

EX AMERICA
by Garet Garrett
ISBN 0-87004-442-7
$16.95

CAXTON PRESS

312 Main Street
Caldwell, Idaho 83605

www.caxtonpress.com